ANTIOCH AND ROME

P9-DDS-733

A NEW TESTAMENT study of the beginning of two major Christian communities where both Peter and Paul bore witness, and where conflicting Christian strains were reconciled in a way that would contribute to the formation of the church catholic.

REV. TIMOTHY G. DALSTROM
First Presbyterian Church
144 Conduit Street
Annapolis, Maryland 21401

The art motif for the cover was inspired by early fifth-century mosaics in the church of St. Sabina in Rome. The two women represent "The Church from the Circumcision" and "The Church from the Gentiles" and were associated respectively with Peter and with Paul.

ANTIOCH AND ROME

NEW TESTAMENT CRADLES
OF CATHOLIC CHRISTIANITY

Raymond E. Brown, S.S.

John P. Meier

PAULIST PRESS
New York/Ramsey

Cover by Ragna Tischler Goddard.

Nihil Obstat:
Edward J. Ciuba
Censor librorum

Imprimatur:
Peter L. Gerety, D.D.
Archbishop of Newark

Date:
December 14, 1982

The Nihil Obstat and Imprimatur are official declarations that a book or pamphlet is free of doctrinal or moral error. No implication is contained therein that those who have granted the Nihil Obstat and Imprimatur agree with the contents, opinions or statements expressed.

Copyright © 1983 by
Raymond E. Brown, S.S. and Rev. John P. Meier

All rights reserved. No part of this book may be reproduced or transmitted in any form or by any means, electronic or mechanical, including photocopying, recording or by any information storage and retrieval system without permission in writing from the Publisher.

Library of Congress
Catalog Card Number: 82-063171

ISBN: 0-8091-0339-7 (cloth)
     0-8091-2532-3 (paper)

Published by Paulist Press
545 Island Road, Ramsey, N.J. 07446

Printed and bound in the
United States of America

With admiration, affection, and gratitude

to
Monsignor Myles M. Bourke

Scholar, Professor, Pastor, Ecumenist, Liturgist
on the occasion of his
sixty-fifth birthday
and
fortieth anniversary in the priesthood

PREFACE

THE NEW TESTAMENT (NT) gives indications of very diverse views *within* Christianity, as well as references to Christian groups regarded as radically deviant by NT writers. Sometimes the views are espoused by different groups coexisting within the same city as, for instance, the four affiliations described in I Cor 1:12 or the dispute at Antioch (Gal 2:11–14). Sometimes one form of Christian outlook may have been prominent in one area and another in a different area, as we can deduce from comparing very different NT works that show no knowledge of each other. Nevertheless, the image of a totally homogeneous Christianity in the first Christian century is hard to erase.

Within some modern reconstructions of a nuanced character simple homogeneity is dismissed, but the thought of Paul is still assumed to be the dominant factor in the Christian mainstream, especially as regards freedom over against the Mosaic Law. It is recognized, of course, that within the first Christian century faith in Jesus spread *east* from Palestine as well as to the west; and that this eastern thrust (about which the NT is totally silent) would have had little or no contact with Paul's thought. Acts 18:24–25 seems to imply that Christianity of a distinctively non-Pauline hue had reached Alexandria by the mid-50s (when Paul came to Ephesus). Nevertheless, it is often assumed that in the areas of NT Mediterranean Christianity which really came to matter in subsequent western church history (Syria, Asia Minor, Greece, and Italy) Paul's thought "won

out." That assumption will be severely tested by the independent
work of the two authors of this volume.

Coincidentally each of us was studying the origins of Christianity in NT times at an influential center in the Mediterranean area,
Meier working on Antioch in Syria, and Brown on Rome. In conver-
sation, we discovered that our analyses of the origins of such
churches were somewhat alike in both method and results. These
were two cities where Paul featured alongside another very prominent early Christian, Peter; and we were convinced that in both cases
it was not the Pauline view about the Law and Judaism that prevailed but a moderate view that could be associated with Peter—
even though ultimately some of the Pauline strains were domesticated and incorporated into that Petrine strain. Ignatius of Antioch
wrote *ca.* A.D. 110 about the church catholic (*hē katholikē ekklēsia*),
a church more widespread geographically than the churches in any
one city or area, but also a church that had managed to blend together diverse strains of thought so that the resultant *koinōnia,* "communion," among Christians involved common views on important
issues. We are convinced that the somewhat-right-of-Paul strains of
Christianity that emerged at Antioch and Rome in association with
Peter were a key factor in the emerging church catholic. Such an
analysis does not detract from the enormous power and challenge of
Paul's letters and thought; but it warns that a purely Pauline Christianity was not dominant in NT times or afterwards. To some, the
failure of Paul to dominate represents the loss of Christian vitality.
Others of us believe that the only Christianity that can do justice to a
NT containing diversity is one that resists sectarian purism in favor
of constructively holding together tensions. Blending Paul into a
wider mix, therefore, is what made the Pauline Epistles biblical, i.e.,
part of a Bible meant to guide, serve, and challenge the church catholic.

In joining the two studies on Antioch and Rome that constitute
the two main parts of this volume, we have made an effort to take
into account each other's work so that a unified book would result.
Nevertheless, we must issue some cautions about how to read our
joint book. *First,* each author is responsible for only what he wrote
(which is clearly indicated). Reviewers who applaud or disagree
should be precise whether they are referring to one author or both.

Second, there is an element of speculation in this work, and so constructive disagreement is expected and hoped for. We invite scholars to add to and modify our historical pictures of the two churches. We are aware that, in a way, we are breaking new ground; and our goal is to attract interest so that the investigation will be carried on by many others. *Third,* in mentioning the speculative, we know that because of the very nature of the material discussed, some parts of our hypotheses are less verifiable than others. For instance, Meier must depend on the Gospel of Matthew for reconstructing the middle period ("second generation") of his survey of Antioch. Most scholars would agree that Matthew was written at Antioch but may disagree as to what percentage of the Matthean Gospel reflects the situation existing at Antioch when the author wrote and what percentage represents an earlier period of tradition—perhaps tradition preserved elsewhere and representing the conditions of that other time and place. Certainly the evidence in Matthew is more speculative in reconstructing Antiochene history than Paul's description of what happened at Antioch in the Letter to the Galatians. Brown must depend not only on letters to Rome (which reflect on the Roman situation) but also on letters from Rome to other Christian communities. Descriptions in the latter may reflect either the customs and thoughts of the Roman senders or problems that exist among the recipients or both; and one must read such documents with caution. We are willing to be evaluated on whether we have shown good judgment in observing the methodological cautions we have emphasized, but we cannot agree with those who would rather say nothing about Antioch and Rome than proceed with the likelihood of making some mistakes. To study the NT as if it could tell us no major historical facts about Jesus or about the early Christians and their emerging churches is, in our judgment, an overreaction to an earlier scholarship that took everything in the NT as history. Exegetes and church historians must and do operate on the basis of reconstructions that fill in gaps left by evidence. If our reconstructions are found wanting, we shall be happy if at least we have prodded others to replace them with more adequate reconstructions. That would be a more satisfactory reaction than insisting on certitude and thus being content with silence.

   If coincidence brought our independent studies together, an

even more fortunate set of coincidences is involved in the dedication of this volume. John Meier was a student at St. Joseph's Seminary (New York Archdiocese) during the twenty-year period when Myles Bourke served there as a distinguished Professor of Sacred Scripture and later sat in his class at the Pontifical Biblical Institute in Rome where Msgr. Bourke taught as visiting professor. Interest aroused by the teacher and encouragement received from him contributed to Meier's doctoral studies and subsequent scholarly career. Raymond Brown knew and respected Myles Bourke as a fellow scholar for years before Brown became Auburn Professor of Biblical Studies at Union Theological Seminary in New York City in 1971. But, as fate would have it, Msgr. Bourke had been serving since 1966 as pastor of Corpus Christi Church, the parish across the street from Union, so that now for a decade he has been Brown's host for daily celebration of the Eucharist. Thus we two authors can join enthusiastically in dedicating our combined volume to a dear and appreciated friend who has helped us differently as professor and pastor, as scholarly and priestly advisor. His two anniversaries in 1982 prompt us to wish him *ad multos annos* in a life and priesthood that has served so many so well.

September 30, 1982
Feast of St. Jerome

Raymond E. Brown, s.s.
Auburn Distinguished Professor
of Biblical Studies

Union Theological Seminary
3041 Broadway
New York City 10027

John P. Meier
Professor of New Testament
and Chairman of the
Scripture Department
St. Joseph's Seminary
(Dunwoodie)
Yonkers, NY 10704

TABLE OF CONTENTS

INTRODUCTION*

Antioch and rome were among the largest cities in the Roman
Empire,[1] dominantly Gentile in population but with major Jewish settlements. It is not surprising, then, that the story of the rise of
Christianity in these two cities involves both Jews and Gentiles. As a
preliminary the reader must have an idea of the complexity of the
relations between Jews and Gentiles in the early Christian missionary activity. An older generation of scholars spoke of the Jew and the
Gentile (or of Jewish culture and Hellenistic culture) as if they existed in different or separate worlds. However, since the time of Alexander of Macedon in the late fourth century B.C. the main Jewish
populations known to us had been living under kings descended from
the Macedonians and under Roman puppet kings and prefects, and
thus in a world where the dominant culture was Hellenistic. Obviously pockets of Jews resisted acculturation while others embraced it
willingly, but that diversity makes it all the more difficult to speak of
Jewish and Hellenistic cultures as two distinct entities. The interrela-
tion becomes even more complicated when we consider the spread of
Christianity.

Since Jesus lived in Galilee and Judea, most of the people to

---

*This introduction was written by Raymond E. Brown.
    1. Grant, *Augustus,* 10: "A significant feature of life in the Roman Empire was
the important role played by the big cities." Strabo (*Geography* 16.2.5), writing about
the time of Jesus' birth, listed the three largest cities in the East as Alexandria, Antioch, and Seleucia.

whom he spoke were Jews; and inevitably the earliest preaching by his Jewish followers was to fellow Jews, first in Jerusalem and then in the cities of the diaspora. Later (in steps that will be discussed in this book) preachers began also to convert Gentiles to belief in Jesus. Paul thinks of himself as an "apostle to the Gentiles" or uncircumcised (Gal 2:8; Rom 1:13; 15:16). However, despite the attention given in the NT to Paul's role among the Gentiles, we must adamantly resist the notion that there was only one theological approach (Paul's) adopted in preaching to the Gentiles, and that therefore all Gentile converts shared in the same outlook (Paul's). In terms of what faith in Jesus implied by way of Jewish observances, there were differences among the Jews who came to believe in Jesus; and every different type of Jewish-Christian outlook won adherence among Gentile converts to Christianity. Therefore, one should not speak of Jewish Christianity and Gentile Christianity but of varying types of "Jewish/Gentile Christianity." The NT shows *at least* the following diversities:[2]

Group One, consisting of Jewish Christians and their Gentile converts, who insisted on *full observance of the Mosaic Law, including circumcision,* for those who believed in Jesus. In short, these ultraconservatives insisted that Gentiles had to become Jews to receive the messianic blessings brought by Jesus. Such a demand was advocated by the Jewish Christians at Jerusalem whom Acts calls "of the circumcision" (11:2) and describes as "of the sect [*hairesis*] of the Pharisees" (15:5), and whom Paul, less diplomatic than Luke, speaks of as "false brothers who slipped in to spy out our freedom" (Gal 2:4). Since these people were at Jerusalem and presumably were not

---

2. In what follows I am presenting only the simplest form of diversities based on the relations of Christians to Judaism. Surely the situation was more complex with further subdivisions based on christology and other factors. Furthermore, within the "Groups" spoken of, inevitably there would have been a spectrum, so that, for instance, the more conservative of Group Two (James) might at times be close to Group One, and the more liberal (Peter) close to Group Three. Also, some who associated themselves with James may have been more conservative than James (see pp. 42–43 below). At different moments in their career various NT personalities may have moved from one Group to another (or within a Group, from one end of the spectrum to another). A halting step in recognizing this diversity was made by Michaelis, "Judaistische," who distinguished at least two classes of Gentile Christians (in addition to Jewish Christians): those who allowed themselves to be circumcised and those who did not. See R. E. Brown, "Not Jewish Christianity."

enthusiastic about Gentile converts, many scholars have ignored their views in speaking about the (single) Christian mission to the Gentiles. However, the whole of Paul's letter to the Galatians shows that Jewish Christians of similar persuasion had made inroads among his Gentile converts in Galatia in distant Asia Minor. (Professor J. Louis Martyn of Union Theological Seminary in his commentary on Galatians in the *Anchor Bible* most plausibly reconstructs the argumentation used by such Jewish Christian missionaries of the strict observance and explains why such teaching would be attractive.) Chapter 3 of Philippians shows a fear of similar Jewish Christian propaganda among Gentile converts in Greece, while 1:15–17 hints at such preaching where Paul is imprisoned (Rome? Ephesus?). Therefore, we must speak of a *mission* to the Gentiles that was quite antagonistic to Paul and resulted in the existence of a Jewish/Gentile Christianity of the strictest Law observance, not only in Palestine but in some of the cities of Asia Minor and Greece, at least.

Group Two, consisting of Jewish Christians and their Gentile converts, who did *not* insist on circumcision but did require converted Gentiles to keep *some Jewish observances.* One may speak of this as a moderately conservative Jewish/Gentile Christianity. According to Acts 15 and Galatians 2, James (brother of the Lord and head of the Jerusalem church) and Peter (Cephas, the first among the Twelve), whom Paul deprecates as "so-called pillars" (Gal 2:9), agreed with Paul that circumcision was not to be imposed on Gentile converts. But according to Acts 15:20 James insisted on certain Jewish observances, particularly food laws;[3] and according to Gal 2:12 "men from James" created embarrassment at Antioch over the question of Jewish Christians eating with Gentiles and thus presumably

---

3. Scholars dispute what is imposed by the demands on the Gentiles in Acts 15:20, 29. Probably there are four prohibitions: from food dedicated to idols, from sexual relations and marriages within the forbidden degrees of kindred (*porneia,* sometimes vaguely translated as "unchastity, impurity"), from meat of an animal that was strangled with its blood still inside, and from animal blood. The prohibitions echo in part Lev 17 – 18 where certain actions were forbidden even to non-Israelite strangers, e.g., a non-Yahwistic and hence idolatrous sacrifice (17:8–9), eating blood (17:12), eating the flesh of an animal that was strangled with its blood inside (17:14–15), and sexual relations with near of kin (18:16–18), something that I Cor 5:1 described as *porneia.*

not keeping the food laws. Acts 15 (14–15, 19–21, 22–29) suggests that, while such a demand associated with James was not originally Peter's idea, he went along with it peaceably as did other Jerusalem notables; but Gal 2:11–14 makes it clear that Peter's acquiescence was only under pressure. The facts that "men of James" came to Antioch with demands about certain law observances (Gal 2:11–12), that a letter embodying James' position was sent to Gentile Christians (brothers) in "Antioch, Syria, and Cilicia" (Acts 15:23), and that Paul has to debate against the *imposition* of Jewish food sensibilities at Corinth (I Cor 8) suggest once again that we are dealing with a *missionary* thrust that produced another style of Jewish/Gentile Christianity, less rigid than that described in Group One above, but less liberal toward the Law than that in Group Three to be described below. One can speak of this as a mediating view, inclined to see a value in openness (no demand of circumcision) but preserving some of the wealth of the Jewish Law as part of the Christian heritage. This Jewish/Gentile Christianity would have been particularly associated with the Jerusalem apostles. The Gospel of Matthew, which speaks of a church founded on Peter, gives the Eleven Apostles a mission to all nations (28:16–20). (See also Acts 1:2,8.) *Didache*, written in part ca. A.D. 100 and close in many ways to Matthew, is entitled: "The teaching of the Lord to the Gentiles *through the Twelve Apostles*."

Group Three, consisting of Jewish Christians and their Gentile converts, who did *not* insist on circumcision and did *not* require observance of the Jewish ("kosher") food laws. Despite the evidence in Acts 15:22 implying Paul's and Barnabas' acceptance of James' position, Gal 2:11–14 makes it clear that, while Barnabas yielded, Paul vigorously resisted the views advocated by the men from James in reference to the Gentiles. Paul did not *require* Christians to abstain from food dedicated to idols (I Cor 8), a requirement imposed by James according to Acts 15:20,29. While Paul is the main NT spokesman for this liberal attitude, we can be sure that the Jewish Christians with whom he associated in missionary activities, especially after 50 (the approximate date of the dispute with the men from James), would have shared his views. Having opposed Cephas/Peter face to face (Gal 2:11) and having ceased to work with Barnabas (Gal 2:13; Acts 15:39) over this issue, Paul would scarcely have tolerated diversity about it among his missionary companions. Thus, we may speak of a Pauline (and perhaps more widespread) type of Jewish/Gentile Christianity, more liberal than that of James and of Peter in regard to certain obligations of the Law.

Paul states that Christ delivered us from the Law's curse against those who do not observe all things written in the Law (Gal 3:10–13) and that now because of faith in Christ we are no longer under the custodianship of the Law (3:24–25). This rhetoric has caused many to classify him at the liberal extreme of the early Christian spectrum of possible relationship to the Law. I shall argue in Part Two below that Paul was not systematic theologically and that his view in Romans is more nuanced and modified than that in Galatians. But even if we leave that observation aside, there are ambiguities in Paul's attitude. His admonitions or imperatives in the second parts of many of his letters show that clearly he expected all Christians to live by the Ten Commandments and by the high morality of Judaism. Acts 20:6,16 suggests that he kept Jewish feasts, such as Unleavened Bread and Weeks (Pentecost), mandated in the Law; and Acts 21:26 has Paul worshiping in the Jerusalem Temple even as did the Jewish Christian leaders who lived in Jerusalem.[4] The evidence in Acts 16:1–3 that Paul had Timothy (an uncircumcised Christian born of a Jewish mother and hence Jewish) circumcised[5] raises the issue that I facetiously call "the problem of Paul's son." Paul is clear that cir-

---

4. Interpreters, skeptical of the historicity of Acts, have called into doubt Paul's observance of Jewish cultic practices because it is not attested in the Pauline correspondence (even though such correspondence might have little reason to mention such practices). However, few doubt that there was a division between Hebrew Christian and Hellenist Christian as described in Acts 6:1–6 or that Hellenists were anti-Temple (7:47–51—see Bruce, *Peter* 49–85). Acts 9:29 portrays Paul as anti-Hellenist, and his own correspondence has him on two occasions (II Cor 11:22; Philip 3:5) clearly identifying himself as a Hebrew (of the Hebrews), when he is emphasizing his pure Jewish status. Thus the thesis that Paul might not be anti-Temple has some Pauline confirmation. Moreover, Paul's desire that his collection of money be acceptable in Jerusalem is surely historical. Could Paul have hoped for acceptance by such a Temple-observer as James if he had totally abandoned Jewish ritual? Finally, the observance of feasts is so logically worked into the travel narrative of Acts 20 that it is difficult to dispense with one and not with the other—and there is no reason to doubt the substantial historicity of the return to Jerusalem described there.

5. While this cannot be verified in Paul's letters, it is not contradicted by his statement in Gal 2:3 that Titus was not compelled to be circumcised, for Titus was a Gentile.

cumcision was not necessary for justification and that Gentiles did not have to be circumcised, but what would he have done if he were married (to a Jewess, of course) and had a son? Would he have had this Jewish son circumcised? Such a question dramatizes that we cannot be sure that Paul's insistence on the non-necessity of circumcision would have led him to suggest that *Jewish* Christians should not be circumcised. A memory is preserved in Acts 21:20–21 that Paul's *opponents* among the Jewish Christians at Jerusalem charged him on this score: "You teach all the Jews who are among the Gentiles to forsake Moses, telling them not to circumcise their children or observe the customs." Possibly in reaction to such a charge (which could find some substantiation in the heated rhetoric of Galatians), Paul's oratory about Jewish privileges in Rom 9:4–5 suggests that circumcision and faith in Christ together would have made Paul's hypothetical son a child of Abraham on both accounts (Rom 4:11–12), benefiting from the faithfulness of God manifested both to Israel and in Jesus, so long as the boy understood that the two gifts were not at all equal in value and only one was truly necessary.

Group Four, consisting of Jewish Christians and their Gentile converts, who did not insist on circumcision or observance of the Jewish food laws and who *saw no abiding significance in Jewish cult and feasts.* The reason I discussed Paul in the last paragraph is because I believe that one can detect in the NT a considerable body of Jewish Christians more radical in their attitudes toward Judaism than he (a group with whom his opponents in Acts 21:20–21 would associate him). In Part One, Chapter II below, there will be a discussion of the "Hellenists" of Acts 6:1–6 who made Gentile converts (11:19–20). The best explanation of the name is that they were Jews (in this instance Jews who believed in Jesus) who had been raised with heavy Greek acculturation,[6] perhaps often to the point of being able to speak only Greek, not a Semitic language. We can only sur-

---

6. That the Hellenists were Christian Jews and not Gentiles is shown by the fact that one of them is described as a proselyte or convert to Judaism with the implication that the others were born Jews. Their acculturation is shown by the pure Greco-Roman names they bore (Acts 6:5), quite unlike the names borne by most of Jesus' Twelve (whom Acts counts among the Hebrews, i.e., among the group it has distinguished from the Hellenists).

mise about their attitude toward circumcision and the food laws,[7] but Stephen's speech indicates a disdain for the Temple where God does *not* dwell—an attitude quite unlike that attributed by Acts to Paul who is kept distinct from them. (See Acts 9:29; yet Luke is not clear about Christian and non-Christian Hellenists, so that scholars are in disagreement about the relationship of the early Paul and of Barnabas to the Hellenists, as stressed in footnote 79 below.) A later and more radical expression of Hellenist thought may be found in the Gospel of John[8] where the law pertains only to the Jews and not to the followers of Jesus (10:34; 15:25: "your Law"; "their Law"), and where the Sabbath, Passover, and Tabernacles are alien feasts "of the Jews" (5:1,9b; 6:4; 7:2).[9] The Temple is to be destroyed and replaced by the temple of Jesus' body (2:19–21); and the hour is coming when God will not be worshiped in Jerusalem (4:21).[10] Similarly the Epistle to the Hebrews would see Jesus as replacing the Jewish high priesthood and sacrifices, and would place the Christian altar in heaven.[11] There is every reason to think that John and Hebrews were written by Jewish Christians, and clearly John envisions Gentile converts (12:20–24). Neither work could conceivably think of Gentiles as a wild olive branch grafted on the tree of Israel, as does Paul in Rom 11:24. And granted Luke's admiration of the Hellenist Stephen, it is not surprising to find that the Lucan Paul's last words in Acts 28:25–28 despair of the conversion of Jews[12]—unlike what may have been

---

7. Michaelis, "Judaische" 87, argues that the Hellenist mission to the Gentiles insisted on circumcision. That can scarcely have been a lasting policy if we judge from later works that scholars have associated with the Hellenists (e.g., Hebrews, John).

8. For similarities between the Johannine Community and the Hellenists, see R. E. Brown, *Community* 38–39, 48–49.

9. See R. E. Brown, *Gospel* 1.201–4 for the theme of replacement of the feasts.

10. An even more radical attitude would be displayed in the post-NT period by Marcion, a Christian who rejected the Jewish Scriptures and demoted the Jewish God to a demiurge.

11. Stephen seems favorable to the Tabernacle, the sacred meeting place of Israel in the desert (Acts 7:44), but Hebrews would regard the earthly Tabernacle as having been replaced through Christ. After the NT period, such works as the *Epistle of Barnabas,* the *Epistle to Diognetus,* and the apologist Aristides represent a further hardening in the rejection of Jewish cult.

12. Because the earlier part of Acts is not overly hostile towards Judaism, some scholars (e.g., J. Jervell) doubt that the ending of the book can be so definitively negative about the likelihood of Jewish conversion. But Luke is describing a progressive

the genuine last words that Paul himself wrote on the subject in Rom 11:11–12 where the full inclusion of Israel is envisioned once the conversion of the Gentiles has made the Jews envious. Thus there is sufficient evidence in the NT of a Jewish/Gentile Christianity that had broken with Judaism in a radical way and so, in a sense, had become a new religion, fulfilling Jesus' saying in Mark 2:22 that new wine cannot be put into old wineskins since it causes them to burst.[13]

*   *   *

In the spectrum of Jewish/Gentile Christianity in the NT period there may have been more varieties in regard to the Law than the four detected above, but at least those are solidly verifiable. In describing each group I have insisted that the respective Jewish Christians were carrying on an active mission to convert Gentiles. That means that the four groups would have been disseminated through the Mediterranean area which past scholarship has sometimes painted monochromatically as Pauline in its Christianity. True, where Paul preached, since he disliked building on anyone else's Christianity (Rom 15:20; II Cor 10:15–16), his form of Jewish/Gentile Christianity would have been exclusive for a while, but often others (particularly from Groups One and Two) arrived on the scene to challenge it. The Ephesus region was evangelized by Priscilla and Aquila (friends of Paul) and then for about three years by Paul himself in the mid-50s (Acts 18–19:41). Yet drawing on the Book of Revelation (Apocalypse), on the locale usually assigned to the Johannine Gospel and Epistles, and on an analysis of the opponents in Ignatius' *Ephesians,* we have good reason for thinking that by the end of the century the four groups described above (and perhaps more) would have had house churches in the capital of the province of Asia. The

---

hardening of Christian attitudes, so that the final situation as he knows it is not what it was in the earlier days of the mission. For instance, there is a kindly attitude toward Temple worship in Luke 1–2 and Luke 24:53. But in the 80s Luke may well have judged that after all Stephen's Hellenist outlook had been proved correct in rejecting the central feature of the Jewish cult, for the future of the Christian movement lay with the Gentiles.

13. For the possibility that Mark was more radical than Paul, see p. 199 below.

situation would have been even more complicated where Paul did not begin the Christian mission; and the two cities discussed in this book, Antioch and Rome, are precisely in that situation. Inevitably the first missionaries in Antioch and Rome would have been Jews who believed in Jesus. In both cities there was eventually a large number of Gentile converts, so that probably by the last third of the first century the majority among the Christians was ethnically Gentile. But it is meaningless to speak of *the* Jewish Christianity or *the* Gentile Christianity at either city without specifying which type or types of Jewish/Gentile Christianity and without challenging the supposition that, because Paul visited each city, Pauline Christianity was dominant.

PART ONE

<u>ANTIOCH</u>

by
John P. Meier

"IT WAS at Antioch that the disciples were first called Christians" (Acts 11:26). What may thus be called the cradle of Christianity was, according to Josephus, the third greatest city in the Roman Empire.[14] Situated on the Orontes River and capital of the Roman province of Syria, Antioch was the first important urban center of the Christian movement outside Jerusalem. From Ignatius, the bishop of Antioch in the early second century, to John Chrysostom, priest of that church in the late fourth century, Antioch was the home of great theologians and strong bishops (recognized later as patriarchs), the seat of a celebrated school of exegesis, and a hotbed of heretical tendencies as well. Anyone interested in the development of Christianity from NT communities of the first century to the church catholic (Ignatius' *hē katholikē ekklēsia*) of the second and third centuries[15] must pay special attention to Antioch. Founded before A.D. 40, the church at Antioch quickly became the battleground of the most important apostles known to us: Paul, Peter, and James. At the beginning of the second century, Antioch is the first church known

---

14. *War* 3.2.4; #29; he means third, after Rome and Alexandria. Meeks, *Jews* 1, prefers the more general statement that Antioch was "one of the three or four most important cities in the Roman Empire."

15. Modern scholars call this "the Great Church" or even "the ancient church." For the methodological problems involved in distinguishing "primitive Christianity" from this church, see Paulsen, "Zur Wissenschaft"; see also Lohse, "Entstehung"; and the various essays in Sanders, *Jewish and Christian Self-Definition*, vol. 1.

to have articulated a rationale for authoritative church structure centered on a single bishop surrounded by a group of presbyters and deacons (the so-called "monarchical" episcopate, or more accurately monepiscopate). Such a trend-setting center is of vital importance for understanding the transition from the NT to the patristic period.

The NT supplies some clear information about the beginnings of the church at Antioch. From the first Christian generation we have the eyewitness account of Paul in his letter to the Galatians (2:11–21), written in the middle or late 50s, only a few years after the Antiochene incident he narrates. (This can be supplemented with information gleaned from the Acts of the Apostles written some 20 or 30 years later, provided Acts is used with caution.) More than a half-century after Paul wrote about Antioch to the Galatians we have letters written by Ignatius of Antioch between A.D. 108 and 117, also giving us first-hand information. What seems to be lacking in the eyes of many scholars is reliable information about the period in-between. Part One of this book will contend that Matthew wrote his Gospel at Antioch around A.D. 80–90 and that this Gospel may be used to fill in our knowledge of Christianity in that city. Thus, if we use the language of generations,[16] we may speak of literature about the first generation of Christians at Antioch in the years 40–70 (Galatians supplemented by Acts; Chapter II below), literature about the second generation in the years 70–100 (Matthew; Chapter III), and literature about the third generation in the years after 100 (Ignatius; Chapter IV).

A pressing question pursued throughout the investigation of this literature will be: Can one give a reasonable explanation of how such apparently different churches as the church of Paul and Peter, the church of Matthew, and the church of Ignatius could all be progressive developments of one and the same local church? Would it not be

---

16. In this volume the first generation covers the Christian lifespan of the better known apostles or companions of Jesus. Since Peter, Paul, and James (the brother of the Lord) all died in the 60s, the first generation covers the 30s through the 60s. The second generation covers the estimated period of influence of the immediate disciples of the apostles, and thus roughly the last third of the first century. The third generation covers the ministry of those who knew those disciples and reaches from the end of the first century into the second century. Sometimes this third generation is described as immediately post-NT or subapostolic, although the latter term is more correctly applied to the second generation.

easier to assume that different churches existed side by side at Antioch? Appealing as that suggestion may at first seem, we shall see that there is no reason to assume that different churches grew alongside each other at Antioch in the first three generations. Rather, the concatenation of Paul/Peter–Matthew–Ignatius does make eminent sense, once the internal dynamics of the Antiochene church are understood. And we may find that understanding the internal dynamics of the Antiochene church may help us to understand better the dynamics of church life today, at a time when the church seems threatened again by "the disappearance of the middle." Moreover, while no formal sociological analysis is attempted in this study, the results may prove of use for those pursuing a sociological analysis of NT churches.[17] Such analysis, while risky, may aid us in grasping the sociological problems of the present-day church.

---

17. Such as can be found, e.g., in Holmberg's *Paul.* Holmberg's book is one of the few satisfying sociological studies of the NT yet to appear. The problem with sociological analyses of NT data is twofold. (1) The data are often insufficient to serve as a basis for sociological analysis. In particular, statistics, so important for sociological study, are almost entirely lacking. (2) The analyses have at times been attempted by exegetes without adequate knowledge of the diversity of sociological schools. To present a full-blown sociological analysis of the NT is to adopt, at least implicitly, one specific school of sociological thought. The option, however, is sometimes neither expressly stated nor explained.

CHAPTER I

Locating Matthew's Church in Time and Space

As I have just indicated, it is vital from the beginning to show that the Gospel of Matthew was written *ca.* A.D. 80–90, most probably in Antioch of Syria.

THE TIME OF THE COMPOSITION OF MATTHEW'S GOSPEL

With regard to the time of composition, a wide variety of critics place the gospel after A.D. 70.[18] This view is almost axiomatic for those who hold that Matthew depends on Mark,[19] since most critics would place Mark's gospel *ca.* A.D. 70.[20] Further considerations make it likely that Matthew wrote at a relatively late period in NT formation. Matthew's gospel represents the end-term of a complicated literary process. Before Matthew began to write, a number of

---

18. Scholars who hold this view (with various nuances) include Bonnard, Brandon, R. E. Brown, Davies, Fenton, Filson, Goulder, Grundmann, Kingsbury, Kümmel, Perrin, Rigaux, Schmid, Schniewind, Schweizer, and Strecker.

19. Marcan priority has again come under attack in recent years, most notably from W. Farmer, *Synoptic Problem; idem,* "Modern Developments of Griesbach's Hypothesis," NTS 23 (1976–77) 275–95. See Also H.-H. Stoldt, *Geschichte.* By way of contrast, see Meier, *Law* 2–6, and the explanatory note in Meier, "John the Baptist in Matthew's Gospel," JBL 99 (1980) 386, n. 13. A solid statistical basis for Marcan priority has been offered by R. Morgenthaler, *Statistische Synopse* (Zurich: Gotthelf, 1971). A good summary of the arguments for the two-source hypothesis is given by Fitzmyer, "The Priority of Mark and the 'Q' Source in Luke" in *To Advance the Gospel* (N.Y.: Crossroad, 1981) 3–40. It should be noted that the position on dating defended in the text appeals primarily to Marcan priority, not necessarily to the two-source hypothesis in its full form.

20. So, e.g., Gnilka, Grundmann, Kümmel, Perrin, and Pesch.

sources—Mark, Q (a collection of Jesus' sayings), and the special Matthean source(s) [M], each with its own tradition history—were woven together, both in oral and written stages. Similarly, Matthew's gospel also reflects a complicated historical process whereby a stringently Jewish-Christian community opened itself up to a Gentile mission (see Matt 10:5–6; 15:24; 28:16–20).[21] This Gentile mission is apparently free from disputes about circumcision (28:16–20, with "trinitarian" baptism as the initiation rite) and food laws (15:11), i.e., free from disputes that marked Paul's lifetime in the first generation.[22] The gospel displays mature theological reflection on the questions of history and eschatology. A view of salvation history has been developed that looks back on the life of Jesus as a sacred past event, not to be repeated.[23] The first Christian generation agonized over the imminent second coming or parousia, but Matthew has come to terms with the so-called "delay of the parousia" by a type of realized eschatology that stresses the presence of the risen Lord in his church for the foreseeable, and indefinite future (28:20: "And behold, I am with you all days until the end of the age").

Matthew's version of the parable of the great supper (22:1–14, contrast Luke 14:15–24) does seem to contain an allusion to the destruction of Jerusalem in A.D. 70.[24] Yet Matthew's gospel does not strike one as obsessed with the problem of the Jewish War and the destruction of Jerusalem. Hence, composition immediately after A.D. 70 is unlikely. If we grant that Matthew's church has already broken with the synagogue—a hypothesis which D. Hare's work has made quite probable[25]—then a date around or after A.D. 85 should be fa-

---

21. Meier, "Salvation-History."

22. Barth, "Matthew's Understanding" 90, and Carlston, "Things" 88, try to avoid seeing a revocation of the food laws in Matt 15:11. For a refutation of this view, see Broer, *Freiheit* 114–22; and Meier, *Vision* 100–4.

23. See Strecker, *Weg* 86–118, for this tendency, which he calls "historicizing."

24. To the contrary, Rengstorf, "Stadt," argues that the destruction of the city in the parable is simply a fixed motif used in the OT to portray punitive expeditions. One must still ask, however, why Matthew went to the trouble of inserting this separate narrative into a parable in which it does not fit (see the delay of the prepared supper while the city is destroyed, and also the absence of the theme in the Lucan parallel). The simplest explanation for this awkward intrusion is a reference to the destruction of Jerusalem.

25. Hare, *Theme;* it is only around or after A.D. 85 that we get clear references in Jewish and Christian literature to a break with the synagogue.

vored. On the other hand, the fact that the letters of Ignatius of Antioch use material from Matthew's gospel prevents a date far into the second century, for Ignatius died no later than A.D. 117.[26] Consequently, the period between A.D. 80–90 is the best choice.

Most critics would accordingly agree with a dating after 70, though there have always been those who favored an earlier date. Notable in recent years is J.A.T. Robinson, who tries to fix the writing of all the books of the NT canon before 70.[27] Robinson's work does offer a healthy reaction to a dogmatism which takes for granted that almost all the NT writings beyond the undisputed epistles of Paul are to be dated after 70. His treatment of Matthew, however, suffers from vagueness and logical leaps. Robinson expresses grave doubts about the two-source hypothesis—a hypothesis which certainly makes a pre-70 date for Matthew very dubious—yet his counter-suggestion remains nebulous. Robinson posits a proto-Matthew, whose extent is never clearly delineated. Robinson is aware of the lengthy history lying behind our Matthew,[28] but he fails to draw the proper methodological conclusion: namely, given so many different strata of traditions, one must attend to the material stemming from the *final* redaction to determine the date of final composition. Robinson, instead, stresses the material of primitive, Jewish-Christian coloration, while ignoring some salient additions by the final redactor.

For example, Robinson appeals to chapter 24 of the apocalyptic discourse, which, he claims, shows no indication of an interval between the fall of Jerusalem and the parousia.[29] He fails to notice that most of Matthew 24 takes over Mark 13 with few editorial changes, while Matthew chooses to express his own outlook on eschatology at the end of Matthew 24 and through the whole of Matthew 25. Thus, Robinson neglects the important Matthean theme-song of delay. In 24:48, the wicked servant thinks his master *is delaying* (*chronizei*). In

---

26. The use of Matthew by Ignatius will be discussed below, under the question of the place of composition.

27. Robinson, *Redating.* On pp. 86–117 he mentions other authors who prefer a pre-70 dating for Matthew.

28. *Idem* 102: "But it is *Matthew* that gives evidence of the longest formation history."

29. *Idem* 103.

25:5, the bridegroom is delaying (*chronizontos*). And in 25:19, the master comes *after a long time* (*meta de polyn chronon*). Moreover, Robinson never comes to grips with the redactional elements, pointed out by Hare, which suggest that Matthew's church has already separated from the synagogue. In short, for all their insight and wit, Robinson's arguments fail.[30] Consequently, we may safely continue to uphold the scholarly consensus which places Matthew after 70.

THE PLACE OF THE COMPOSITION OF MATTHEW'S GOSPEL

If the post-70 dating of Matthew's gospel has met with relatively little disagreement, the same cannot be said of any one theory concerning the place of composition. A number of sites have been proposed.

(1) *Jerusalem.* M. Albertz, appealing to the gospel's conservative tone and the stress on praxis, suggested the church of Jerusalem as the place of origin.[31] But if we have already decided on a date after 70 for the composition of the gospel, Jerusalem (or any other Jewish settlement in Palestine) is extremely unlikely. As Brandon has pointed out, the Jewish War caused major disruptions in both Jewish and Jewish-Christian communities throughout Palestine.[32] That, in the wake of such a disaster, a Palestinian Christian community would have the time, energy, and financial resources to undertake a major work like Matthew's gospel is highly improbable.[33]

Added to this consideration is the problem of the language in which the gospel is written. All agree that Matthew is the ecclesiastical gospel *par excellence,* both in its treatment of church topics and in its intention to serve the church in all its activities (liturgy, catechesis, advanced instruction for church leaders, apologetics, polem-

---

30. For a critique of Robinson's whole project, see the review by Grant, who emphasizes Robinson's inconsistent use of the patristic evidence. See also Fitzmyer's review.

31. Albertz, *Botschaft* I/1, 223; others who have proposed Palestine as the place of origin have usually been older, conservative authors.

32. Brandon, *Fall,* passim.

33. The precise fate of the church at Jerusalem after A.D. 70 is shrouded in uncertainty. Whether we can trust stories recounted by Fathers like Hegesippus and Eusebius is still debated among scholars. See von Campenhausen, *Jerusalem* 3–19; and Lüdemann, "Successors."

ics).[34] Consequently, it is only reasonable to suppose that Matthew wrote his gospel in the language which was the ordinary, common language of the members of his church. Clearly, then, the ordinary, common language of Matthew's church is Greek. This seems to exclude an origin in Jerusalem or Palestine, where the commonly used language of the ordinary people was Aramaic.[35] This is not to deny what Hengel, following many other scholars, has shown abundantly, namely that Greek was used widely in certain areas of Palestine during the Hellenistic period.[36] Indeed, as Acts 6:1 tells us, the early church in Jerusalem included Greek-speaking Jews, the Hellenists.[37] But, unless we wish to restrict Matthew's audience to some intellectual elite in Jerusalem—an elite whose "liberal" theology seems quite different from the "conservative" tone of much of the M tradition—we must look to the diaspora.[38]

(2) *Alexandria.* Brandon tried to make a case for the Egyptian capital, but a major problem inherent in such a position is our almost total ignorance of the origin and growth of Christianity in Alexandria during the first century A.D. The rapid diffusion and acceptance of Matthew's gospel would rather argue for a church which had already achieved a good deal of prestige and influence by the end of the first century.[39]

(3) *Caesarea Maritima.* This seat of the prefect or procurator of

---

34. Trilling, *Israel* 220–21, is especially good on the varied functions of Matthew's gospel within Matthew's church.

35. See Fitzmyer, "Languages" 38, where he reaffirms the view that Aramaic was the most commonly used language in Palestine in the first century A.D., though both Greek and Hebrew were used as well.

36. Hengel, *Judaism,* especially 1.58–65. Likewise, Freyne, *Galilee* 139–45, relying on Sevenster, *Greek,* who perhaps pushes a good case too far. For all his emphasis on Greek, however, Freyne does accept Fitzmyer's view that Aramaic remained the most commonly spoken language of the vast majority.

37. Fitzmyer, "Languages" 37, thinks that the Hellenists were those Jews or Jewish Christians who habitually spoke only Greek. See above p. 6, and below p. 34.

38. Hengel, *Judaism,* 1.105, asks whether the gospel of Matthew might not come from Greek-speaking Jewish-Christian circles *in Palestine.* In light of what has been said above, the answer is no. Freyne, *Galilee* 104, notes that Mark seems better acquainted with Palestinian geography than either Matthew or Luke (although some find mistakes in Mark's geography as well). On p. 364, he explicitly rejects Galilee as the place of composition of Matthew's gospel and leans toward Syria.

39. See Brandon, *Fall* 221, 226, 232, 242–43. The attempt of van Tilborg, *Leaders* 172, to revive Brandon's choice of Alexandria has not met with wide acceptance.

Judea has been suggested recently by B. Viviano. The difficulties facing his theory are formidable. Josephus records a massacre of Jews in Caesarea Maritima in A.D. 66; surviving Jews fled from Caesarea. Viviano cannot prove any large resettlement by Jews in the following decade. Hence, the composition at Caesarea Maritima of a gospel which displays some narrow Jewish-Christian roots, and which presupposes lengthy growth out of a Jewish-Christian matrix, is difficult to maintain.[40] Moreover, if one holds that some sort of historical event lies behind the narrative of the conversion of Cornelius in Acts 10, then the church at Caesarea Maritima arose partly through the conversion of a pagan centurion and his household. This early state of Caesarean Christianity is difficult to reconcile with some of the early strata of the Matthean tradition, which are stringently and narrowly Jewish. One should also recall the activity and extended presence of one of the "liberal" or "Hellenist" Seven at Caesarea, namely Philip (8:40; 21:8). Finally, Viviano's positive arguments are drawn almost entirely from patristic citations of the second and subsequent centuries. They prove little about the composition of Matthew's gospel in the first century.

(4) *Syrian countryside or Edessa.* Another area which has proven more popular among Matthean scholars is what is called, with distressing vagueness, the "North Syrian hinterland"[41] or, farther south, "the border area between Syria and Palestine."[42] Goulder suggests that Matthew was a "humble provincial copyist-schoolmaster" in some town in Syria.[43] These suggestions run up against the same problem which the suggestion of Jerusalem had to face: the most commonly used language of the ordinary people. While the city of

---

40. Viviano, "Where." The relevant texts are found in Josephus' *War* 2.13.7; #266–270; and 2.14.4–5; #284–292; and *Antiquities* 20.8.7,9; #173–178; 182–184. Foerster, "Caesarea," states on p. 14 that at the outbreak of the Jewish War, "nearly the entire Jewry of Caesarea, some 20,000 in number, comprising a considerable portion of its population, was butchered." On p. 17 he says: ". . . following the First Revolt . . . the city [Caesarea] contained very few, if any Jews at all." Viviano does supply a useful history of the whole question of the place of composition of Matthew's gospel; the opinions of many other authors are listed there and need not be repeated here. Another good summary of opinions can be found in Hill, *Matthew* 50–52.

41. Kennard, "Place" 245.

42. So, as one possibility among others, Grundmann, *Matthäus* 43; so also Käsemann, "Anfänge" 83, 91.

43. Goulder, *Midrash* 13, 11, 9.

Antioch was, for Syria, the center of Hellenistic learning and the Greek language, Greek did not triumph among the common people of the countryside.[44] Moreover, it must be explained how a gospel composed in the hinterlands of Syria became so quickly and widely known.[45] Even if one chose the hinterlands of Syria as the place of composition, one would almost have to posit dissemination from Antioch, as indeed Kennard does.

It is likewise surprising to see cities to the east or northeast like Edessa mentioned as candidates for the place of composition.[46] As far as we can ascertain, the Christianity of Edessa always used Aramaic or Syriac. Almost all inscriptions in Edessa from the first three centuries A.D. are in Syriac. The earliest full literary texts preserved from Edessa are in Christian Syriac, and references and fragments indicate that pre-Christian literature was also written in Syriac.[47] As for Damascus, it was important to Jews as a center of commerce, not as a center of rabbinic learning and Scriptural study. It is therefore ill-suited as a matrix for the learned Jewish-Christian debate behind Matthew's gospel. Moreover, except for the early history of Paul, Damascus remains for us an unknown quantity during the NT period. And Greek does not seem to have been widely used in Damascus.[48]

(5) *Phoenicia.* Kilpatrick suggested a commercial coastal city such as Berytus, Tyre, or Sidon.[49] While one cannot positively exclude such a possibility, one must remember that the gospel of Matthew mirrors the various stages in the lengthy history of some

---

44. In his *Early Versions* 5, Metzger states flatly: "Outside the gates of Antioch, Syriac was the language of the people." See also Prümm, *Handbuch* 653–54; Pfeiffer, *History* 96; and Bietenhard, "Die syrische Dekapolis" 251.

45. The observation of Streeter, *Gospels* 486, remains true: The church from which Matthew's gospel came "must have been one of great influence, or the gospel would not have secured universal acceptance so soon."

46. For cities of eastern Syria and/or Edessa, see Kennard, "Place" 245; and Green, *Matthew* 21, depending on Bacon, *Matthew* 15–16, 35–36. In a similar vein, McNeile, *Matthew* xxviii.

47. For references to Old Syriac inscriptions of the first three centuries A.D.— inscriptions antedating Christian Syriac—see Fitzmyer, "Phases" 83, n. 108; Drijvers, "Hatra" 799–906.

48. See W. McCullough, *A Short History of Syriac Christianity to the Rise of Islam* (Chico, Ca.: Scholars Press, 1982) 9.

49. Kilpatrick, *Origins* 133–34. Blair, *Matthew* 43, speaks of either Syria or Phoenicia.

Christian church, a church important and lively enough to produce a gospel that was successful in being accepted by the Christian church at large in the second century (see below, p. 86).[50] We know next to nothing about the Christian communities on the Phoenician coast in the NT period, and there is no indication that they exercised great influence on other early Christian churches. Of Berytus the NT speaks not a word. One passage in Acts indicates that Christians lived in Tyre (Acts 21:3–7); the same is true of Sidon (Acts 27:3). We hear nothing further of these Christian communities in the NT period, and very little about them in the early patristic period.

(6) *Antioch.* In contrast to such silence is the abundant information about the most likely candidate for the place of composition of Matthew's gospel, Antioch, the capital of Syria.[51] To demonstrate this point, we must anticipate material to be examined at greater length later on. Antioch was a predominantly Greek-speaking metropolis, a natural site for a gospel written in Greek. It had a large Jewish population, probably the largest in Syria.[52] It also had one of the earliest Christian communities outside Palestine. The church there was founded probably in the late 30s[53] by Jewish Christians from the Hellenist group who began a circumcision-free mission at Antioch. This mission was hobbled for a while by the strict policies imposed by the James party from Jerusalem (see footnote 2 above). However, well before the time of Ignatius of Antioch (*ca.* 100), the circumcision-free mission won out and proceeded unabated.

These facts would explain satisfactorily the tensions among the

---

50. As Massaux has shown in his book *Influence,* Matthew is the gospel that the second-century Fathers most often quote or allude to.

51. The magisterial work on Antioch, a work to which this essay is greatly indebted, is Downey's *History;* for a short summary of his views on the biblical period, see his article on Antioch in IDB 1.145–48. More specialized studies on Jewish and Christian aspects of Antiochene history include Krauss, "Antioche"; Kraeling, "Antioch"; and Meeks, *Jews;* for a recent archaeological report, see Lassus, "La ville." In the twentieth century, the great champion of Antioch as the place of the final redaction of Matthew is Streeter, *Gospels* 500–7; Streeter's views will be discussed below. It should be clear from the start that espousing Antioch as the place of composition of Matthew does not necessarily mean embracing all of Streeter's theories. Kümmel, *Introduction* 119, considers Antioch to be the common view today; likewise, R. E. Brown, *Birth* 47. Kingsbury, *Matthew* 93, states: "Scholars generally associate Matthew's Gospel with the city of Antioch in Syria."

52. See Stern, "Diaspora" 138.

53. See Downey, *History* 187, 275.

various strata of tradition that we find in Matthew's gospel. The earlier strata would reflect the period of domination by the James party, with a very strong tie to Judaism. The large Jewish population at Antioch would explain the Jewish tone of the gospel, with its echoes of Semitic usage, its interest in Jewish customs and rites, its Jewish mode of argumentation, its great concern over the Mosaic Law, its heavy emphasis on the fulfillment of prophecy, and its disputes with Pharisaic Judaism. At the same time, one gets a sense of a gospel written on the borderline between Jewish and Gentile areas. Matthew's gospel is written in better Greek than Mark's, with some familiar Greek plays on words inserted. More importantly, Matthew ends his gospel with a resounding legitimation of a mission to all nations, a mission foreshadowed in the stories about the Magi (2:1–12), the centurion with the sick slave (8:5–13), the Canaanite woman (15:21–28), and the centurion and his companions at the cross (27:54). As a whole, therefore, Matthew's gospel reflects a meeting place and melting pot of Jewish and Gentile influences. Antioch is a perfect location for this encounter and clash.

Since the church at Antioch had arisen in the late 30s, it enjoyed the lengthy, continued existence of a Jewish-Christian church necessary to explain the composition of Matthew's gospel. The gospel has behind it a developed scribal tradition and even perhaps a scribal school in which the various forms of the OT texts—including the Septuagint or Old Greek version (see 1:23; 12:21)—were studied and appropriated for proof texts.[54] In such a scholarly milieu, the adaptation and combination of Mark and Q (a collection of Jesus' sayings) may have begun before Matthew set to work. The composition of this lengthy gospel would demand great financial resources as well as great learning. Indeed, some have claimed that internal evidence indicates that Matthew's church was a relatively affluent urban church.[55] The well-established church of Antioch could easily fulfill this description by the 80s of the first century. A particular point in favor of Antioch is the special Petrine traditions preserved in the gospel and the special place Matthew gives Peter in his redaction.

---

54. In this context of learning and scholarship, it might be recalled that Antioch was noted for its library; see Downey, *History* 94, 132.

55. So, e.g., Kingsbury, *Matthew* 97–98.

That Peter was active at Antioch, indeed, was at the center of a *cause célèbre,* is clear from Gal 2:11–14, where Paul describes his confrontation with Peter. So strong was Peter's influence that even Barnabas sided with him against Paul. Paul soon found it expedient to leave Antioch on mission to Asia Minor—without Barnabas. Paul rarely returned to Antioch (see Acts 18:22–23), not mentioning Antioch again in his letters after Gal 2:11–14. Paul went on to imprint his vision of Christianity on Asia Minor and Greece, while James stayed in Jerusalem. But Peter, having won out over Paul at Antioch, may have remained the dominant figure there for some time. This may be the historical basis of the later, anachronistic tradition that Peter was the first bishop of Antioch. It is hardly surprising, therefore, that such an authority on Antioch as Downey thinks that Matt 16:18 represents the tradition of Antioch concerning the foundation of the church there.[56]

The Antiochene origin of the gospel is confirmed by the fact that Ignatius of Antioch is the first father of the church to use Matthew. At least three times he alludes to material found only in Matthew. (1) In Matt 3:15, Jesus says to the Baptist: "It is fitting for us to fulfill all justice." Ignatius echoes this in *Smyrneans* 1:1: "The Lord Jesus Christ . . . [was] baptized by John, in order that all justice might be fulfilled by him." The words of Matt 3:15, "to fulfill all justice" (*plerōsai pasan dikaiosynēn*), are peculiar to Matthew's account of the baptism and are probably his redactional creation. "To fulfill" (*plēroō*) and "justice" (*dikaiosynē*) are key Matthean words, and the colloquy between the Baptist and Jesus in Matt 3:14–15 seems to be the result of the theological reflection of the evangelist, inserted into what is basically a Marcan pericope.[57] We may therefore conclude

---

56. Downey, *History* 283.

57. See Meier, *Law 73–80;* idem, *Matthew* (Glazier commentary series) 26–27. Köster, *Überlieferung* 24–61, attempts to deny all direct dependence of Ignatius on Matthew's gospel. Yet he admits that the frequent similarities between Ignatius and Matthew are striking and even that *Smyrneans* 1:1 does show that Matthew's gospel had already been written, since Matt 3:15, alluded to there, is redactional. Not being able to deny the Matthean origin of the passage, Köster is reduced to making Ignatius' dependence on Matthew indirect. *Smyrneans* 1:1 is declared to contain a kerygmatic formula which had already incorporated Matt 3:15; but no proof for this assertion is given. Köster thus avoids the simple and natural explanation: Ignatius knew Matt 3:15 from Matthew's gospel. Once this point is granted, the other Matthean allusions

that Ignatius is alluding not to stray oral tradition but to the written gospel of Matthew. (2) Matt 10:16b ("Be therefore as prudent as the serpents and as innocent as the doves") is alluded to in *Polycarp* 2:2: "In all things be as prudent as the serpent and always as innocent as the dove." Now, although most of the missionary discourse in Matt 10 comes from the sermons in Mark and Q, 10:16b is found only in the Matthean version and is likely a redactional insertion. (3) Matthew's story of the Magi and the star is developed by Ignatius in a lyrical passage, *Ephesians* 19:2–3. This poetic expansion may indicate that Ignatius had meditated on, preached upon, and reworked Matt 1–2 for some time.[58] Ignatius contains no corresponding abundance of allusions to Mark or Luke, though some traces of Lucan tradition may be discernible. The written gospel known to Ignatius is the gospel of Matthew, to which at times he may be referring when he uses the word "gospel" (*euaggelion*).[59] Even if one were to hold that Matthew's gospel was not written at Antioch, certainly it soon became known there and thence was diffused to the churches at large. Consequently, it seems a useless complication of theories to posit composition in some unknowable and uncontrollable locale, only to shift adoption, use, and diffusion of the gospel to Antioch.

One final objection that might be raised against the Antiochene provenance of Matthew's gospel is the Matthean form of the eucharistic words at the Last Supper (Matt 26:26–29) as opposed to the form found in Paul (I Cor 11:23–26) and echoed in Luke (22:17–20). If Paul's form represents the form used in Antioch in the 40s, as J. Jeremias claims, why is it that in the 80s Matthew copies, with modi-

---

are most easily explained as coming directly from Matthew's gospel. Also in favor of Ignatius' knowledge of Matthew's gospel is Corwin, *Ignatius* 66–68.

58. Some would see in Ignatius' *Ephesians* 19:2–3 a reference to the gnostic theme of the secret descent and the public ascent of the Redeemer; so Schlier, *Untersuchungen* 29; Köster, *Überlieferung* 31–32. Opposed to this opinion is Bartsch, *Gut* 140–54. The Matthean context seems to be Ignatius' starting point, even though he may be widening the reference.

59. So Streeter, *Gospels* 506–7, referring to *Philadelphians* 8:2 and 5:1–2. Needless to say, Köster, *Überlieferung* 8–9, 25, disagrees. In his view, *euaggelion* ("gospel") in Ignatius always means the oral kerygma. Nevertheless, in the view of the present writer, the *euaggeliō* in *Philadelphians* 8:2, opposed as it is to the *archeiois* ("archives") of the Jews (probably the written OT), may indeed mean a written gospel. If it does, that written gospel is Matthew's.

fications, the form found in Mark?[60] In answer, one should first note
that Jeremias himself makes a distinction in his theory: Paul received
the eucharistic tradition at his conversion, but the precise formulation quoted in I Corinthians 11 was learned by Paul later, at Antioch.[61] Still, even granted this distinction, one might ask whether
things were this simple. Paul was converted at Damascus; he traveled to Jerusalem to meet Peter; he spent some years in Tarsus; and
then ministered in the church at Antioch. The possibility must be allowed that both the Damascus and the Jerusalem Christian communities—of Tarsus we cannot speak—had their effect on the
formulation preserved by Paul in I Corinthians 11. Indeed, Paul's insistence that he received this tradition "from the Lord" (I Cor 11:23)
might argue better for either the place of his conversion or the mother church in Jerusalem than for the church at Antioch, which Paul
joined only at a later date. Moreover, it is questionable whether we
should suppose that in the second decade of Christianity (the 40s)
the Antiochene church or any other Christian group knew and used
one and only one formulation of the words of institution. A number
of forms might well have circulated in the missionary church at Antioch during the first generation. It may have been precisely the reception of Mark's gospel in the Antiochene community which led to
the predominance of the Marcan formulation enshrined with modifications in Matthew's gospel. But even in Matthew's church we probably should not suppose that the prophets and teachers—still
charismatic figures!—always used exactly the same formulation of
the words of institution. Hence, the difference between the Pauline
and Matthean formulations is no obstacle to placing Matthew's gospel at Antioch.[62]

---

60. See Jeremias, *Words* 188.

61. *Ibid.*

62. If Fitzmyer (*Luke* 1.41–47) is correct in suggesting that Luke comes from
Syrian Antioch, one might also ask why Luke's formulation of the eucharistic words
differs from Matthew's. In answer I should first note that I do not find Fitzmyer's
arguments for Luke's origins in Syrian Antioch convincing. I would not be as confi-
dent as he is of the value of the patristic evidence. It should be noted, however, that
Fitzmyer does not claim that Luke wrote *for* the church at Syrian Antioch. Indeed,
Fitzmyer's description of Luke's readers (p. 59: "Gentile Christians in a predominantly Gentile setting") would seem to argue against Antioch. This leads me to my second
point: Luke is probably writing for a church which stands in the Pauline tradition, be

In sum, the most viable hypothesis is that Matthew's gospel was written at Antioch *ca.* 80–90. But this conclusion immediately gives rise to a further question, the question this study seeks to address. Antioch is well-known to us as a Christian center both in the 30s and 40s of the first century (from NT documents) and again in the early decades of the second century (from the letters of Ignatius)—a span of almost 100 years. At one end of this span stand Barnabas, Paul, Peter, and (at a distance) James; close to the other end stands Ignatius. Needless to say, towards the end of the span the Antiochene church looks very different from the way it appeared at the beginning. And somewhere in between, we have concluded, stand Matthew, his gospel, and his church, serving in some way as a link between the Antioch of Paul and Peter and the Antioch of Ignatius.[63] We spoke above of a three-stage history: the first generation, the church of Barnabas, Paul, Peter, and James (roughly A.D. 40–70); the second generation, the church of Matthew (roughly 70–100); and the third generation, the church of Ignatius (after 100). How are we to explain the development from one stage to the next? This is the problem we must wrestle with in the next three chapters.

---

it located in Asia Minor or in Greece. It is hardly surprising, then, that Luke uses a modified Pauline formulation, even though he has the text of Mark in front of him. All this says nothing against the origin of Matthew's gospel at Antioch.

63. Perhaps the greatest weakness of Downey's treatment of the church at Antioch is the gaping hole he allows to stand during the Antiochene church's second generation (A.D. 70–100). The period is filled in only with vague statements about the development of the "Nicolaitan heresy" and gnosticism, without a critical eye being cast on the patristic sources of our knowledge; see Downey, *History* 288–92.

CHAPTER II

The Antiochene Church
of the
First Christian Generation

(A.D. 40–70—Galatians 2; Acts 11–15)

R ELIABLE sources for the history of the Antiochene church in the first Christian generation are limited principally to two sections of two documents: Paul's Epistle to the Galatians (2:11–21, or perhaps only 2:11–14) and the Acts of the Apostles (notably chapters 11–15). While the account in Galatians must be preferred to that in Acts because the former represents a first-hand witness, Paul's testimony is not without its problems. Galatians 2:11–21 treats of only one incident at Antioch; indeed, it is the only time Antioch in Syria is mentioned in the whole body of Paul's writings. Moreover, Gal 2:11–21 is a highly apologetic and polemical passage, and so Paul's personal bias must be taken into account when evaluating his information.[64] Nevertheless, Gal 2:11–21 is the single most important piece of information we have about the first Christian generation at Antioch. It is the only literary source which is autobiographical, coming as it does from a Christian who took part in the incident nar-

---

64. The limited space of this study does not permit a complete exegesis of Gal 2. Fortunately, our problematic is concerned primarily with ascertaining the objective course of historical events, not with Paul's theological positions. For exegesis and bibliography for Gal 2, see the standard commentaries, especially Lightfoot, *Galatians* 102–32; Burton, *Galatians* 66–142; Lagrange, *Galates* 22–55; Schlier, *Galater* 64–117; Beyer-Althaus, "Galater" 14–22; Mussner, *Galaterbrief* 90–204; Betz, *Galatians* 57–127.

rated and who writes the letter to the Galatians only a few years after the event.[65]

The author of Acts writes at a later date; also, he has a noted tendency to smooth over fierce battles in the early church. To what extent his peaceful vision molded his narrative and, indeed, to what extent he enjoyed reliable sources for early Christianity, is still disputed among Lucan scholars. The history of the debate can be found in Gasque's *A History of the Criticism of the Acts of the Apostles.*[66] A problem surfaces even in Gasque's survey: one could easily receive the impression that the believing British are to be preferred to the skeptical Germans. While Gasque himself shows that the front is not so clearly drawn along national lines, it can be said with a certain amount of truth that the majority of Germans (e.g., Haenchen, Conzelmann, Vielhauer, and, to a certain degree, Dibelius) have proven more reserved towards the historical reliability of Acts than the British and Americans, especially those from the evangelical tradition (e.g., Bruce, Mattill, and Gasque himself). Hengel and Munck on the more trusting side, and C. Talbert on the more cautious side, serve to remind us that these geographical or national distinctions can be taken only as vague generalities. Faced with this disagreement, not to say disarray, among Acts-scholars, we would do well to pursue a middle course in which Acts is neither dismissed lightly as pure theologizing nor accepted naively as pure history. Each text must be judged on its own merits and on available information from other sources (notably Gal 2). Here at least we can agree with Gasque: speculative hypotheses must give way to and be based upon careful exegesis.[67]

Fortunately, most scholars accept Luke's narrative of the early

---

65. Jewett, in his *Chronology*, places the conflict at Antioch in early 52 and the writing of Galatians *ca.* 53–54 (see the chart at the end of his volume). Other writers would allow a somewhat longer interval: e.g., Hengel, *Acts* 136, places the conflict *ca.* 48; Fitzmyer, "Life" 2, 219, places it in 49. The standard dating of Galatians is the mid 50s (e.g., Kümmel, *Introduction* 304, says *ca.* 54–55).

66. Full bibliography on the authors mentioned in this paragraph can be found in Gasque's work. For the more precise question of the reliability of Acts as a source of our knowledge of Paul, see the various positions outlined in Mattill's "Value" 76–98; also Richard, *Acts* 1–31; Müller, "Paulinismus" 157–201; Löning, "Paulinismus" 202–34.

67. Gasque, *History* 308.

days of the Antiochene church as reliable at least in its basic outline. Such is the case especially with recent works on Antioch like those of Downey and Meeks-Wilken.[68] Even the more skeptical authors like Haenchen and Conzelmann are willing to accept some elements from the basic narrative of the origins of the Antiochene church.[69] Starting from this consensus, we shall try to assemble the data necessary to reconstruct the early history of Christians at Antioch.

Besides the major sources of Galatians and Acts, various other ancient sources offer a few rays of light, at least indirectly.[70] While archaeology offers no direct information on first-century Christians, the ancient historians offer a few glimmers. I and II Maccabees, Philo, Josephus, and rabbinic material give some passing information on Jewish life at Antioch—as do John Chrysostom and John Malalas at a later date (fourth and sixth centuries respectively). It is to this information we must turn, with due caution, for the immediate background of the Christian community at Antioch.

THE JEWISH COMMUNITY AT ANTIOCH[71]

Jews inhabited Antioch from the time of its foundation by Seleucus Nicator (300 B.C.). At least by the middle of the second century B.C., the Jews enjoyed the right to observe their own customs as a distinct group within Antioch, though it is doubtful that they all enjoyed full citizenship. No doubt the anti-Jewish measures of Antiochus Epiphanes (175 B.C.) meant hardship for the Jews living on his

---

68. While acknowledging Luke's own point of view, Meeks, *Jews* 13, says that there is "no reason to doubt the accuracy" of the singling out of Antioch in Acts 11:19–26 as the scene of the first mission to the Gentiles.

69. The limitation implied in the phrase "some elements from the basic narrative" should be noted. Haenchen, for instance, warns against accepting Luke's succession of events at this point. Haenchen also suggests that Barnabas was not sent at a later date by the Jerusalem authorities to Antioch, but was rather one of the Hellenists who had to flee from Jerusalem. According to Haenchen, Barnabas may have been the first to make the decisive step of converting Gentiles without circumcision (see his *Acts* 370–72); similarly, Conzelmann, *History* 59, 66.

70. All the available sources for our knowledge of ancient Antioch are listed by Downey, *History* 24–45. See the notes to the opening essay in Meeks, *Jews* 37–52.

71. The sources for the following statements can be found in the works cited above in footnote 51. References to the ancient sources relating the events treated in this section can be found in the notes of the opening essay of Meeks, *Jews* 37–52.

very doorstep. Antiochus Epiphanes' successors, however, seem to have given back what the Antiochene Jews had lost during the "reform" of the persecutor. With the exception of Antiochus Epiphanes' persecution, the Antiochene Jews lived peaceably and prosperously under the Seleucid monarchs. Indeed, they probably constituted the largest single Jewish community in Syria. Kraeling conjectures that they numbered about 45,000 during the reign of Augustus, though Meeks-Wilken prefer a modest 22,000.[72] The Jews were no doubt spread among all classes: wealthy leaders, shopkeepers and artisans, many poor, and some slaves. The Jewish community at Antioch seems to have been presided over by some chief officer, whom Josephus calls the "ruler" (*archōn*) of the Antiochene Jews.[73] Meeks-Wilken suggest that he was the head of the council of elders (*gerousiarchos*). The elders, in turn, were the representatives of the various synagogues in the city and in the suburb of Daphne. The council of elders (*gerousia*) would thus be the governing body for all Antiochene Jews.[74] One wonders whether the structure of one ruler presiding over a body of elders might have provided a remote model for the one bishop (*episkopos*) presiding over a council of elders (*presbyterion*) in Christian Antioch at the time of Ignatius.

Josephus claims that the religious ceremonies of the Jews constantly attracted multitudes of Greeks[75]—an intriguing precedent for the first outreach to the Gentiles by Christian Jews at Antioch. The Roman conquest of Syria in 64–63 B.C. meant no great change for the Jewish community. Now incorporated into the Roman province of Syria, they were allowed to enjoy their traditional privileges, including the use of the Mosaic Law for internal questions of the Jewish community, the maintenance of close relations with the Holy Land, and the contribution of money to Jerusalem—again an intriguing model for the close connections between the Christians in Antioch and the Christians in Jerusalem in the first generation.

Prior to the first Jewish War, Jews enjoyed relative peace at Antioch, the one exception being the uproar over Caligula's order that a statue of himself be placed in the Jerusalem Temple, in the winter of

---

72. Kraeling, "Antioch" 136; Meeks, *Jews* 8.
73. Josephus, *War* 7.3.3; #47.
74. Meeks, *Jews* 6–7.
75. Josephus, *War* 7.3.3; #45.

A.D. 39–40. Perhaps connected with this is the attack on Jews in A.D. 40, recorded in a highly embellished narrative of Malalas; the kernel of truth in the story is difficult to extract. Downey suspects the Christian outreach to the Gentiles played a part in the disturbance.[76]

The first Jewish War (A.D. 66–73) occasioned massacres of Jews in many places in Syria, but in the beginning the Jews at Antioch were spared. After Vespasian's arrival in Syria, however, a Jewish apostate called Antiochus stirred up the pagan populace with rumors of Jewish plots. Riots and murders followed (A.D. 66–67), only to be repeated four years later. When Vespasian's son Titus arrived at Antioch, the Gentiles asked him to expel the Jews or at least to revoke their rights and privileges. Titus refused both requests, though he did set up on the city gate leading to Daphne (a heavily Jewish suburb) some of the spoils from Jerusalem as a memorial of the Jews' humiliation. Since there was no major dislocation of Jews at Antioch, the Christian church at Antioch had a constant and largely unperturbed matrix out of which to grow and against which to define itself.

THE BEGINNINGS OF THE CHRISTIAN CHURCH AT ANTIOCH

The origin of the Antiochene church is narrated in Acts 11:19–20:

> Now those scattered on account of the persecution which broke out because of Stephen journeyed as far as Phoenicia, Cyprus, and Antioch, speaking the [Christian] message to no one except Jews. But there were some of them, men from Cyprus and Cyrene, who, when they came to Antioch, spoke [the Christian message] to Gentiles as well, proclaiming [to them] the good news of the Lord Jesus.

The words "those scattered" in Acts 11:19 refer back to the statement that "all were scattered" in 8:1 (which ends the narrative of Stephen's martyrdom with a general reference to a "great persecution") and to 8:4, which is picked up almost word-for-word in 11:19–20. Despite the "all" in 8:1, the larger context of Acts suggests that

---

76. Downey, *History* 190–95.

only the Stephen party, the "Hellenists," were actually scattered. They included men from Cyprus and Cyrene, who at Antioch began to convert Gentiles (the *Hellēnas* of 11:20).[77] Perhaps in their number were Lucius of Cyrene and Symeon Niger (13:1). Since one of the Jerusalem Seven was Nicolaus, an Antiochene Gentile who had converted to Judaism (6:5), it was natural enough for some of the dispersed Hellenists to go to Antioch and seek Gentile converts there. As we have already noted, Josephus claims that many Antiochene Gentiles were attracted to Jewish rites. The Lucan narrative is, therefore, quite plausible; and most critics agree that the first determined mission to Gentiles with no requirement of circumcision did take place at Antioch.[78]

More problematic is the exact role of Barnabas in all of this. Acts 11:22–23 claims that the church at Jerusalem, hearing of the success of the Antiochene mission, sent Barnabas to Antioch to encourage and guide the endeavor—and no doubt bring it under the supervision of the Jerusalem community. Haenchen is skeptical about this order of events. He sees here Luke's tendency to bring various missionary endeavors under the aegis of Jerusalem. According to Haenchen, since Luke knew that Barnabas was originally a well-known member of the Jerusalem church (4:36) and later was a leader of the Antiochene church (13:1), Luke deduced that Jerusalem sent Barnabas to Antioch. But, claims Haenchen, Barnabas, being himself a Cypriot (4:36), could have been among the scattered Cypriot and Cyrenean Hellenists who began the Gentile mission at Antioch. Thus, Barnabas would have gone there as an independent missionary

77. Here I accept the reading *Hellēnas,* "Greeks," "Gentiles," witnessed by P [74] a later correction of Sinaiticus, Alexandrinus, the original text of Bezae, and certain Fathers, as the correct reading. Vaticanus, later correction of Bezae, Laudianus, Leningrad (P), and other manuscripts read *Hellēnistas,* "Hellenists." Haenchen, *Acts* 365, n. 5, rightly holds that "Hellenists," standing in opposition to *Ioudaiois* ("to the Jews") in verse 19, makes no sense. My choice agrees with the first edition of *The Greek New Testament* (ed. Aland, 1966), and not the third edition (1975).

78. So, e.g., Haenchen and Meeks (*Acts* 355–63, 368–72; *Jews* 14). Note, in this regard, the whole thrust of chapters 11–15 in Acts, and especially the relationship between 11:19–26 and 15:1–2. Paul gives independent confirmation of the situation at Antioch in Gal 2:1–14. Haenchen and Meeks think that Luke purposely interposes the conversion of Paul and Peter's conversion of Cornelius between 8:1 and 11:19 to prevent the Hellenists from being directly and independently responsible for the beginning of the Gentile mission.

and not as an agent of the Jerusalem church under the Twelve. Haenchen (*Acts* 370–72) suggests that Barnabas was the one who made the fateful decision to convert Gentiles without circumcision.

Haenchen's reconstruction is certainly possible, and is followed in the main by Meeks-Wilken (*Jews* 14–15). A problem, however, arises: if Barnabas was such an independent Hellenist missionary,[79] the very founder of a circumcision-free mission to the Gentiles at Antioch, how does one explain his capitulation to Peter and James and his desertion of Paul during the conflict recorded in Gal 2:11–14? His submission to the Jerusalem authorities and his abandonment of Paul at such a critical juncture are more easily explained if Barnabas' activity at Antioch was from the beginning dependent on those same Jerusalem authorities. Therefore, while Haenchen's reconstruction remains a possibility, it seems more advisable to hold to the presentation of Acts 11:22–23. This need not prevent us from seeing Barnabas as a Hellenist and a follower of Stephen, though a more moderate Hellenist who remained in Jerusalem after the persecution and was acceptable to the Twelve. His delicate middle-man role between the Jerusalem authorities and the Hellenists at Antioch

---

79. Hengel, *Acts* 101–2, prefers to see Barnabas as a member of the "Hebrews" directed by the Twelve—one of the "Hebrews" sympathetic to the developments outside Palestine. Hengel does not think of Barnabas as simply an "inspector" sent from Jerusalem, but as one who moved to Antioch for theological and personal reasons. Of key importance is the definition of "Hellenists" whom Acts 6 distinguishes from the "Hebrews." Dictionaries interpret *Hellēnistēs* (an adjective peculiar to Acts and related to *Hellas*, "Greece," and *Hellēn*, "a Greek") as "Greek-speaking." Drawing on Acts, exegetes would add various qualifications in defining a Hellenist: (1) a Jew from the Diaspora; (2) resident in Jerusalem; (3) [in the case of a Jewish Christian] open to a circumcision-free mission to the Gentiles; (4) speaking *only* Greek, not Semitic; (5) heavily Greek-acculturated; (6) having an anti-Temple theology. Above, in discussing Group Four, the Introduction pointed to disagreement among scholars about these qualifications, and indeed the two authors of this volume disagree on the meaning of "Hellenist." I hold that Barnabas is a Hellenist; Brown is inclined to agree with Hengel. I accept the first three qualifications as well as the fifth, but have doubts about the others. As for (4), some Hellenists in Jerusalem may well have been bilingual; as for (6), whether or not Acts 7 represents the thought of the historical Stephen, I do not consider it proved that all Hellenists held anti-Temple views—especially when so much of the literary evidence comes from the post-70 era. Brown (pp. 6–7 above), arguing that Paul was not a Hellenist, places little emphasis on the first three qualifications, all of which apply to Paul. The last two are regarded by Brown as the most distinctively Hellenist.

may have prepared the way for his embarrassing position in the Antiochene clash of Gal 2.[80]

The church at Antioch soon grew large enough and, because of its Gentile converts, distinctive enough to receive a new designation from the Gentiles: Christians (*Christianoi,* Acts 11:26).[81] Interestingly, it is Ignatius *of Antioch* who is the only Apostolic Father to use the noun *Christianos* (though it also occurs in the *Martyrdom of Polycarp*).[82]

The next reliable piece of information[83] is the list of "prophets and teachers" at Antioch in Acts 13:1.[84] The five named are Barnabas (note his position at the head of the list), Lucius of Cyrene, Manaen (Menahem), who was a childhood companion of the tetrarch Herod Antipas, and Saul (placed at the end). That a childhood companion (*syntrophos*) of Herod should be a leader in the early days of the Antiochene church serves as a reminder that Christianity did not start out as a "slave" religion and did not entirely lack members from the higher strata of society. Given a leadership made

---

80. We cannot verify the information that Barnabas brought Saul from Tarsus to Antioch (Acts 11:25–26). Not surprisingly, Hengel, *Acts* 101–2, accepts its historicity, placing it "probably before the end of the thirties" (*Acts* 91). The event is in itself plausible, though Haenchen, *Acts* 367, suggests that Luke deduced it from the presence of the two men at Antioch in 13:1. The best we can say is that Barnabas and Paul were early leaders in the Antiochene church.

81. *Christianoi,* "followers or supporters of Christ," is best explained as a Latin title given to the disciples by Gentiles, perhaps the Roman authorities, who took *Christus* to be a proper name, not a title. The very fact of a special name indicates that the Gentiles perceived the Christians to be something more than merely a group of Jews, no doubt because of the Gentiles admitted to full membership without circumcision or full observance of the Mosaic Law. For other interpretations of the name, see Haenchen, *Acts* 367, n. 3; Downey, *History* 275, n. 19.

82. See Meeks, *Jews* 43, n. 80. Ignatius is also the first patristic writer to use the term "Christianity" (*Christianismos*), in *Magnesians* 10:1,3 (twice); *Romans* 3:3; *Philadelphians* 6:1.

83. The historicity of the famine collection (Acts 11:27–30), or at least its chronological placement by Luke, is called into question by many critics (see Haenchen, *Acts* 375–79; Funk, "Enigma" 130–36; and Jewett, *Chronology* 34). For unconvincing attempts to save something of Luke's order of events, see Jeremias, "Sabbathjahr" 233–38; Bruce, *Acts* 241; and Hengel, *Acts* 111–12.

84. On the question of the definition and function of NT prophets, see Hill, *Prophecy,* esp. 94–109 for the usage of Acts; also Dautzenberg, *Prophetie,* esp. 214, 53. The more natural reading of Acts 13:1 suggests that the persons named are both prophets and teachers; see Lemaire, *Les ministères* 58–59.

up of prophets and teachers, it is interesting to note that, when Peter comes to Antioch, what results is a structure of apostle(s), prophets, and teachers, a pattern also seen in I Cor 12:28 ("first apostles, second prophets, third teachers"). The Christian document called the *Didache,* reflecting perhaps some Syrian (or Egyptian?) church at a later date, also knows of itinerant teachers (*Didache* 11:1–2), apostles (11:3–6), and prophets (11:7–12). One should notice that, while the prophets and teachers of Acts 13:1 are attached to or associated with the "mission center" at Antioch, a number of them (at the very least) do not come from Antioch and are quick to go out on mission. Thus, while they may not be as "itinerant" as the teachers, apostles, and prophets of the *Didache,* they are not on the other hand necessarily "resident" leaders.[85] We shall have to ask later how the *Didache* material may fit into the development of the Antiochene church.

THE CLASH BETWEEN PETER AND PAUL

It is impossible, within the scope of this study, to give a detailed treatment of all the disputed points surrounding (1) the "Council of Jerusalem" described in Acts 15 and Gal 2:1–10 and (2) the clash at Antioch narrated in Gal 2:11–14, the latter being passed over in silence by Luke. With regard to methodological questions, almost all exegetes would agree that Paul's presentation in Galatians 2, while not free of a polemical bias, must be our primary source. Luke is interested in presenting a basically harmonious situation, with Antioch submitting readily to Jerusalem, with Jerusalem defending the mission to the Gentiles without circumcision, and with James as the chief and climactic spokesman for the circumcision-free mission.

As for settling the historical questions that concern us, Meeks-Wilken rightly point out that, for all the differences between them, the accounts of Paul and Acts do agree on certain key issues.[86] I list

---

85. *Ibid.* 58–61. Note that in the context of a mission out of Antioch, Luke, contrary to his usual terminology and perhaps because of his source, calls Barnabas and Paul "apostles" (14:4, 14). Since Barnabas and Paul have already been called prophets and teachers (13:1), this gives us the *Didache*'s designations of teachers, apostles, and prophets—all verified in Acts in the same persons.

86. The presentation that follows depends on the summary drawn up by Meeks, *Jews* 16–18, with some judgments changed and certain observations added. Note that

briefly both the main agreements and the accompanying disagreements.

(1) Representatives of the church at Antioch travel to Jerusalem for a meeting that has as its focal point the question of the conversion of the Gentiles to faith in Christ without circumcision. Even Paul, for all his defense of his independence, cannot mask the fact that the question is being brought to Jerusalem for a decision. Historically, Jerusalem did have a preeminent position and did enjoy special authority vis-à-vis Antioch.[87]

(2) The chief representatives of Antioch were Paul and Barnabas (if we may use the order of Acts 15:2). Galatians and Acts agree that Paul and Barnabas were not the only Antiochenes who went to Jerusalem. Luke speaks vaguely of "some others" (Acts 15:2), while Paul says specifically that the uncircumcised Titus, who turned out to be a test case (Gal 2:1,3), accompanied them. In Acts, the reason for the journey is that some unspecified "Judaizing" Christian Jews had upset the "integrated" congregation at Antioch by insisting that the Gentiles had to be circumcised as a condition for salvation. In the face of the resulting uproar the church appointed delegates to go to Jerusalem.[88] By contrast, Paul underscores his independence and initiative by affirming that he went up to Jerusalem "on account of a revelation" (Gal 2:2).[89]

(3) In neither account are the Christian Jews who were urging circumcision at the Jerusalem meeting identified with "the pillar apostles" or James in particular. It should be emphasized that no NT source ever claims that James demanded that Gentile converts be circumcised. Paul speaks vaguely of "false brothers, who sneaked in to

---

I do not accept the view of those who see in Acts 15 and Galatians 2 two different meetings in Jerusalem; for this opinion, see Dix, *Jew* 19–60.

87. See Holmberg, *Paul* 16–33. He emphasizes the need to distinguish between Paul's theological affirmations about his authority and historical events that indicate who actually wielded authority. Haenchen, *Acts* 464–65, makes similar observations; but he denies (wrongly, I think) that Paul recognized the Jerusalem apostles as arbiters or a court of appeal.

88. The verb *etaxan* ("appointed") probably has an official ring to it, though a milder translation, "it was arranged that . . .," is also possible.

89. These two reasons are not necessarily mutually exclusive; for instance, the decision might have been reached by the prophetic leaders of Antioch, (see Acts 13:1–3); so even Haenchen, *Acts* 464. Jeremias' attempt to explain Gal 2:2 through Acts 11:27–30 is not convincing; see footnote 83 above.

spy on our freedom" (Gal 2:4)—hardly the same group as the three "pillars" (James, Cephas, and John) who lead the Jerusalem church and who are introduced by name in verse 9 of Galatians 2. Acts identifies the Judaizers as Christian Jews from the Pharisee movement.[90]

(4) In any case, at a meeting the Jerusalem church issues the decision. Paul singles out James, Cephas, and John for special mention, implying perhaps a special meeting with them, though the three seem to have taken part in a larger meeting as well (Gal 2:1,4,6). Luke speaks of a formal assembly of the apostles and elders, in which Peter and James both speak. The final decision is reached by the apostles and elders in the name of the whole Jerusalem church.

(5) The decision reached is that the Gentiles do not have to be circumcised. Acts' placing of a decisive speech in the mouth of James probably reflects Luke's tendency to smooth over past differences in order to present a church united on basic theological questions.[91] The Antiochene missionaries are allowed to continue their circumcision-free mission to the Gentiles, while, according to Galatians, Peter continues the mission to the Jews.[92] It should be noted that, as far as we know, neither Peter nor James ever expressly repudiated the agreement about circumcision, though Paul feared that Peter's inconsistency at Antioch might effectively lead Gentile converts to accept circumcision. Both Acts and Paul also agree that "kosher" laws were an issue that was raised after circumcision. Acts has the issue raised at Jerusalem; Paul, at Antioch. Most exegetes agree that the "kosher" observances from Lev 17–18, imposed on Gentile converts in Acts 15:20,29, do not belong historically to the Jerusalem agreement between the pillars and Paul. Still, both Luke and Paul connect James with imposing kosher laws on Gentiles.

(6) Some time after their return to Antioch, Paul and Barnabas had a fierce disagreement which ended their partnership as missionaries. According to Galatians, Barnabas joins in the hypocrisy of

---

90. Haenchen, *Acts* 443–44, 458, sees the two distinct Judaizing groups (Acts 15:1,5) as the work of Luke. On the difficulty of identifying the "false brothers" (Gal 2:4) vis-à-vis "those who came from James" and "the circumcision party" (Gal 2:12), see R. E. Brown, *Peter* 26, including n. 58.

91. So Jervell, *Luke*, esp. 185–207.

92. On the precise meaning of "we to the Gentiles, they to the circumcised" (Gal 2:9), see Haenchen, *Acts* 466–67; Holmberg, *Paul* 29–32. This is the text that inspired the mosaics used as art on the jacket of this book.

Peter, who has withdrawn from table fellowship with Gentile Christians at Antioch because of pressure from members of the James party, who have recently arrived from Jerusalem. Paul rebukes Peter to his face. We are not directly informed as to the upshot of this, but certain subsequent events in Paul's career give us clues. Paul soon undertakes a lengthy mission into Asia Minor and Europe without Barnabas. He returns to Antioch only once for a brief visit (Acts 18:22). He never mentions Syrian Antioch again in his letters. Whatever relations he does have are with Jerusalem rather than with Antioch. Most glaringly, in Galatians 2 he is silent about who won the debate. We can reasonably infer from these facts that Paul lost the argument, found himself isolated at Antioch, separated himself from Barnabas, and undertook a wide-ranging mission with new coworkers.[93] Luke, as is his wont, mentions as a reason for the split only a personal dispute about taking along John Mark (Acts 15:36–41). Accordingly, Acts omits any reference to Peter's visit to Antioch, the pressure from the James party, and the resulting clash—perhaps deliberately, perhaps because Luke was confused about how all these events were related.

Treating the Jerusalem Council and its aftermath at Antioch, J. Schütz speaks of Antioch and Jerusalem as "two independent centers of Christianity."[94] That assessment may be too strong, if one considers which center had the decisive word when it came to a confrontation. A critical reading of the data in both Acts and Paul suggests that Jerusalem had a certain authority over Antioch and indeed, for all his protestations, even over Paul.[95] One cannot therefore agree totally with the judgment of Meeks-Wilken about Paul's course of action after the Antioch dispute: "Paul made himself independent of

---

93. So, following many others, Bornkamm, *Paul* 43–48; Haenchen, *Acts* 475–76. For a list of scholars who think Paul won the conflict with Peter at Antioch and of those who think Paul lost, see Holmberg, *Paul* 34, n. 117.

94. Schütz, *Paul* 138. Yet Schütz goes on to say that Jerusalem could nullify Paul's efforts, though not his gospel (p. 139—Schütz is treating the question of authority *from Paul's point of view*). Schütz admits that both Jerusalem and some Christians at Antioch thought Jerusalem's reasons for extending its discipline into Antioch must have been pressing (p. 152). But, if that be the case, is it exact to speak of "two independent centers of Christianity"?

95. So Holmberg, *Paul* 19–20. He summarizes on p. 35; "Up to and including the Apostolic Council and the Antioch Incident Paul has to receive authoritative words from the leadership of the Jerusalem church, which enjoys undisputed superiority of status." See Haenchen, "Petrus-Probleme" 55–67, esp. 63.

Antioch as well as of Jerusalem."[96] Antioch, yes; Jerusalem, no.[97] Throughout his later missionary journeys, Paul is concerned with collecting money for the Jerusalem church (see p. 110 below). Paul's churches also had poor people, but the Jerusalem church does not take up a collection for them. The relationship, while certainly bilateral, is not one of complete equality.[98]

The state of the Antiochene church after the departure of Paul must remain largely a matter of conjecture, though the portraits of the church we get decades later, first at the time of Matthew's gospel and then at the time of Ignatius, may offer some clues. Both Matthew and Ignatius depict one Christian community made up of Jews and Gentiles, defined over against both the Jewish synagogue and various dissident Christians (e.g., false prophets in Matthew, docetists and Judaizers in Ignatius).[99] One does not get the impression from either Matthew or Ignatius that there are a number of different, organized churches existing side by side in the same place. Unlike the NT epistles of John, for example, the gospel of Matthew does not suggest the existence of organized opposition by a group of schismatic Christians. Indeed, even at the time of Ignatius, we do not hear of any rival bishop (*episkopos*) or council of elders (*presbyterion*) among the dissidents or "heretics." It does not seem likely, then, that, after the departure of Paul, the Antiochene church broke into two totally separate groups of Jewish Christians and Gentile Christians. After Paul's departure, some Gentile Christians may have actually accepted circumcision; but the most likely outcome is that Gentile and Jewish Christians abided by the wishes of the James party by holding meals (and therefore probably eucharists) separately. Provided these restrictions were observed, neither James nor, *a fortiori*, Peter would demand circumcision. Therefore, some sort of fellowship (*koinōnia*)—however tenuous and uneasy—could be maintained. Indeed,

---

96. Meeks, *Jews* 17.

97. See Holmberg, *Paul* 56: Paul "and his work are still [even after the clash at Antioch] dependent on the recognition of the church which is the source and centre, not only of the Palestine Jewish Christian church but of *all* churches."

98. Berger, "Almosen" 197–98, rightly sees the collection as a sociological as well as theological expression of unity and community among the churches, but he denies any expression of Jerusalem's privileged position.

99. Some hold that, at the time of Ignatius, the docetists and Judaizers were the same people; see below pp. 79–80.

Paul's departure may have been precipitated by his desire to avoid an open schism. In the face of these divisions and tensions within the Christian community, Peter may have played a moderating role, helping to keep the compromise solution from degenerating into complete schism.[100] Peter's pivotal role at Antioch, holding the two groups of Antiochene Christians together, may be reflected in the prominence given Peter later in Matthew's gospel. In the Antioch of the late 40s and early 50s, the figure of Peter could (even in his physical absence) serve as a rallying point for Christians who felt antagonism toward either the "liberalism" of Paul or the "conservatism" of James.

No doubt it was not always easy to keep peace between the two groups with their conflicting viewpoints and programs. On the "left wing," the pro-Paul Gentile Christians would have preserved among themselves the desire for an unhindered universal mission, with baptism instead of circumcision as the initiation rite that made all equal members in the one people of God, and with Jesus rather than the Mosaic Law as the ethical touchstone of Christian conduct—in short, the type of missionary program outlined later in Matt 28:16–20. The various universalistic traditions enshrined in Matthew probably found their impulse and their incubator among this Antiochene group of Gentile Christians, to whom Peter would not be entirely unsympathetic.[101] These Gentiles would not be unaware of the fact that

---

100. Scholars of very different viewpoints agree on this mediating role of Peter, especially during and after the clash at Antioch. For instance, Holmberg, *Paul* 22, places Peter in the "middle" position, between the rigorism of Paul's Judaistic opponents and the liberalism of Paul. (One might question, though, whether James should be lumped together with Peter and Barnabas in the "middle," as Holmberg thinks. At least, pressure from *the James party* had impelled Peter and Barnabas to a course of action they would not have espoused on their own.) Similarly, Streeter, *Gospels* 504: "Antioch follows Peter and stands for the *via media* between the Judaistic intolerance of those who called James master and the all but antinomian liberty claimed by some of the followers of Paul." See footnotes 2 above and 446 below.

101. Despite some Lucan composition as to details and centrality, the basic story of Peter's conversion of a Gentile early in the 30s is probably historical, *contra* Haenchen, *Acts* 462–64. It occasions a dispute in Jerusalem which Luke would not be likely to have invented. Moreover, there was no reason for the Jerusalem Christians to see this extraordinary conversion, precipitated by charismatic phenomena, as a norm or program for a future universal mission without circumcision. In defense of the historical event, occurring before the Jerusalem Council, see Dibelius, "Conversion" 109–22; and Wilckens, *Missionsreden* 63. In I Cor 1:12 one party within the predominantly

Peter had modified his table practice not of his own accord, but under pressure from the James party.

On the other hand, the universalistic program harbored by the Gentile Christians would in practice be difficult to undertake with any great success as long as the James party on the "right" held the upper hand in the Jewish-Christian group and in the Antiochene church as a whole. While James himself, as far as we can know, never repudiated the agreement on circumcision, his party would have supplied the most comfortable haven for those who had opposed any circumcision-free mission. If these "right-wing extremists" of Group One (see Introduction above) could find shelter anywhere in the church, it would be under the Jamesian wing (roughly, Group Two), although ultimately they may have broken away entirely and become Ebionites and other marginal Jewish-Christian heretics. Perhaps these Antiochene Jewish Christians were the creators or bearers of the narrow, particularistic statements on mission found in Matt 10:5–6 and 15:24.

Such extremists did not, however, gain the upper hand at Antioch. Sometime after the departure of Paul, either Peter or perhaps even the Jamesian group, in a gesture of moderation, made closer fellowship between Jews and Gentiles possible. The price of the new compromise was the imposition of certain "kosher" observances on the Gentile Christians, observances now enshrined in the so-called "letter" of Acts 15:20,29 (repeated pointedly by *James* to Paul in 21:25).[102] The prohibitions against eating food sacrificed to idols,

---

Gentile Corinthian church (which in I Corinthians shows no particular tendency to Judaize) appeals to Cephas as their leader. Conducting missionary work in the diaspora, Peter would have been the member of the Jerusalem Twelve best known to Gentile Christians. Is it accidental that in Matt 15:15 Jesus explains *to Peter* that food does not render a person unclean (contrast Mark 7:17)?

102. Most critics rightly deduce from Gal 2:6,10, that the four prohibitions in the so-called "Apostolic Decree" come from a historical context other than the Jerusalem Council. Suggested by James and directly addressed to the Christians of Antioch, Syria, and Cilicia, the prohibitions may represent a more moderate policy developed by the James party after the departure of Paul from Antioch. Dibelius, "Council" 98–99, thinks that Luke knew of an actual document addressed to Antioch, Syria, and Cilicia. Haenchen (*Acts* 471) is vague on their origin: "These prohibitions must have come into force in a strongly mixed community of the diaspora, where Jewish claims were more moderate. . . ." This picture can be satisfied by an Antiochene church seeking to overcome the split occasioned by the quarrel of Paul, Peter, and James. Here we may

drinking blood from animals, eating meat from strangled animals, and maintaining incestuous unions (*porneia*), all come from Leviticus 17–18, in that precise order (footnote 3 above). They enunciate obligations which the Pentateuch considers binding on resident aliens—hardly a complimentary classification for Gentile Christians. Yet, despite the implicit insult, these provisions did aim at making some sort of common life possible for a church divided into ethnic groups. The very fact that the Gentile Christians would receive and obey these prohibitions indicates that a total split into two hostile churches had not occurred. It is quite probably from this imposition of Levitical prohibitions that the exceptive clause concerning incestuous unions (*porneia*) enters into the Matthean teaching of divorce (Matt 5:32; 19:9, where *porneia* is often translated as "fornication" or "unchastity").[103] Such a theory provides the kind of tradition history and "setting in life" that explains why the exceptive clause took shape only in the Matthean form of the teaching on divorce, as opposed to Mark, Q, the Lucan redaction, and Paul.

It is, however, somewhat simplistic to think of the Antiochene church after Paul's departure only in terms of left and right wings. Besides the moderating influence of Peter and the strengthened bond of fellowship represented by the Gentiles' acceptance of the four kosher rules, what helped keep the two wings of the Antiochene church together was probably the influence of another group, those Hellenist Jewish Christians who had taken part in the initial work of converting the Gentiles at Antioch. They had preceded Paul in this work; and, if we may take Stephen's speech in Acts 7 as a reflection of their theology, some of them were more radical in their critique of Juda-

---

have a shift in praxis leading from the church of Galatians 2 to the church of Matthew. For a recent summary of the question with full bibliography, see Catchpole, "Paul," who rightly sees that the Decree must come from a time when Paul was absent from the decision-making body in Jerusalem and that it presupposes that the decision about not demanding circumcision of Gentiles has already been made. But then Catchpole goes on to suggest that the Decree was not a mediating but a conservative proposal, and was the direct cause of the clash between Paul and Peter at Antioch. Catchpole's insights are better served if we see the Decree as a mediating position arising after the clash and Paul's departure from Antioch.

103. For the question of the Apostolic Decree's relation to the exceptive clause in Matthew, see Meier, *Law* 140–50, with the bibliography cited there; and *Vision* 248–57.

ism than was Paul. There is no reason to think that Paul's departure from Antioch caused all of these Hellenists either to leave the city or to change their theoretical stance vis-à-vis a Gentile mission. After both Paul and Barnabas left Antioch on mission, at least some of these more "liberal" members of the Hellenist group may have remained in the city. If so, they would have been basically in agreement with the Gentile-Christian group, even though they would technically be part of the Jewish-Christian group. What impeded them from openly joining forces with the Gentile-Christian group was the ascendancy of the James party, which Peter had not been able to resist and Paul had not been able to defeat. But what the apostles of the first generation could not do the Roman legions, the destruction of Jerusalem, the Jamnia movement, and the inner dynamics of Christian development finally conspired to achieve. For this we must move to our treatment of the second Christian generation at Antioch.

CHAPTER III

The Antiochene Church
of the
Second Christian Generation

(A.D. 70–100—Matthew)

L OOKING at the state of affairs in Antioch after the departure of Paul and looking at the situation reflected in Matthew's gospel (written in Antioch *ca.* 80–90), we are forced to the conclusion that the Antiochene church underwent some notable modifications between the 50s and the 80s of the first century.[104] It is essential to our purpose to inquire into the reasons for these changes and the results of the shift in existence the church experienced.

In what follows we shall try to sketch a viable hypothesis that takes into account: (1) the external factors that influenced the Antiochene church; (2) the factors internal to the church that made for change and tension; (3) the crystallization of individual streams of Christian tradition at Antioch, traditions that sometimes stood in tension with one another; (4) the gospel of Matthew as the evangelist's reply to all these factors and tensions; (5) the institutional means that Matthew's church had developed for teaching and insuring discipline, as reflected in the gospel.

---

104. Downey, *History* 288–92, appeals to reports of later Fathers like Justin, Irenaeus, and Eusebius in order to justify placing the Nicolaitans, Saturninus, and Menander at Antioch in the blank period between A.D. 70 and Ignatius. Since, however, the gospel of Matthew displays no great anti-gnostic tendency, one must place the rise of gnosticizing tendencies at Antioch close to 100. It was this threat in particular that precipitated the rise of the single-bishop at Antioch. Meeks-Wilken remain silent on the period, except for noting the break with the synagogue (*Jews* 18–19).

EXTERNAL FACTORS INFLUENCING CHANGE
IN THE ANTIOCHENE CHURCH

The single most important external event that influenced the course of the church at Antioch was the first Jewish War, along with the incidents preceding and following it.[105] Decisive for the future course of the Antiochene church were the death of James in Jerusalem in the 60s[106] and the destruction of Jerusalem in 70. The reason why these events should have had an impact on the Antiochene church is clear. Looking at Galatians and Acts, we notice a pattern: the problems at Antioch did not arise simply from within the community, but were largely occasioned by the opposition of at least some of the more conservative Jerusalem Christians. Luke claims that the disturbing teaching of some Christians from Judea/Jerusalem (see Acts 15:1,24) called forth the Jerusalem Council. From Gal 2:12 we know that the influence of men coming from James in Jerusalem precipitated the clash between Paul and Peter, made it expedient for Paul to leave Antioch, and moved Peter, Barnabas, and no doubt other Jewish Christians to separate themselves from table fellowship with Gentile Christians.

As has been suggested already, the fact that the James party gained the upper hand in Antioch as a result of the clash did not extinguish all liberal sentiment among the other groups. Once James was martyred by the Jewish authorities, and once the mother church in Jerusalem either fled into exile or was destroyed by the Romans, the decisive umbilical cord that had tied the Antiochene church to its Jewish identity and its Jewish past was severed. From that point on-

---

105. See Farmer, "Character." For the question of the fate of the Christian church at Jerusalem before and after A.D. 70, see von Campenhausen, *Jerusalem;* and Lüdemann, "Successors." The only clear fact about the Jerusalem church is that, whatever its precise fate during and after the Jewish War, it did not regain its former prominence in the decades immediately following the catastrophe of 70.

106. Diverse accounts are given in Josephus (*Antiquities,* 20.9.1; #200–203, though some claim this is a Christian insertion) and in Hegesippus' more legendary account, as recorded by Eusebius, *Hist.* 2:23.4–18. The date varies according to whether one follows Josephus (A.D. 62) or Hegesippus (*ca.* 66). On Hegesippus' presentation of James, see Zuckschwerdt, "Naziräat." It should be noted that legends about James' martyrdom pass (by way of Syrian Jewish-Christian heretics?) into Christian gnosticism; see "The Second Apocalypse of James" in Robinson, *Nag Hammadi* 254–55).

wards, the Jewish/Gentile groups of Pauline and Hellenist persuasion (Groups Three and Four in the Introduction above) could hope to make headway against the conservative elements on the "right," which had looked to James and Jerusalem for support. Yet even the conservative group at Antioch was not monolithic, for it contained members of Groups Two and One (see Introduction). The Jewish Christians of Group Two, having already compromised through the "Apostolic Decree" of Acts 15:23–29, might be willing to go farther to satisfy the Gentile Christians in this new situation. On the other hand, the extreme right-wing (Group One), finding itself unable to accept the post-A.D. 70 modifications, may have eventually left the Antiochene church to preserve in a Jewish-Christian sect what they considered to be the true heritage of James. Here we may have one source of the Ebionites, though the group may also have drawn supporters from remnants of Palestinian Jewish-Christian communities or perhaps even from Essenes attracted to Christianity.[107] Here also we may have part of the explanation why later Jewish-Christian heretical writings (e.g., the *Clementine Homilies* and *Recognitions,* the *Ascents of James*) champion James, exalting him over Peter and extolling him over against the enemy Paul[108]—a rather accurate picture of how the extreme right-wing would have interpreted the clash of Gal 2.[109] One wonders whether some of Matthew's attacks on the Jewish leaders may also have these proto-Ebionites in view.

Another external factor which could not be ignored by the Antiochene church after 70 was that, on the whole, the mission to the Jews had proved a failure, while the mission to the Gentiles was proving to be a relative success. Faced with this glaring fact, even

---

107. If the Ebionites come in part out of the church at Antioch, it is no accident that their own gospel, "The Gospel of the Ebionites," shows close resemblances to Matthew's gospel; see Vielhauer, "Jewish-Christian Gospels," esp. 153–55.

108. See Chapter X, section F below; and Martyn, *Gospel* 55–89, treating the Pseudo-Clementine literature and the *Ascents of James.*

109. It seems that through these Syrian Jewish-Christian heretics James also became a hero for certain Christian gnostic groups; see "The Apocryphon of James," "The First Apocalypse of James," and "The Second Apocalypse of James," in Robinson, *Nag Hammadi* 29–36, 242–48, 249–55. The judgment of Perkins is well founded: "The James Apocalypses draw heavily on Jewish Christian material and seem to have originated in a Syrian milieu . . ." ("Gnostic Christologies" 606, n. 48). See also the privileged place of James in "The Gospel of Thomas," logion 12, in *Nag Hammadi* 119.

conservative Jewish Christians at Antioch and elsewhere would find it more and more difficult to put obstacles in the way of a full-scale circumcision-free mission to the Gentiles. Increasingly, the Gentiles appeared to be the church's main if not only future, especially after the Jewish War.

The Jewish War would have also sharpened the tensions between Jewish Christians and Jews at Antioch. The debacle of the Jewish War led the surviving Jewish leaders, who were mostly of the Pharisaic persuasion, to reorganize, to codify, and to close ranks against common enemies. The beginnings of the Jamnia (Yabneh) movement, with its desire to impose a certain amount of uniformity on Judaism, would naturally put pressure on Jewish Christians to leave either the synagogue or the church.[110] Matthew's gospel certainly looks back to a past when Christians had experienced persecution from the synagogue. In this regard the *birkat ha-minim,* the cursing of Christians in the Eighteen Benedictions of the synagogue liturgy, is often mentioned. But there is no need to suppose that such a formal measure was necessary to bring about separation between Jewish Christians and the synagogue.[111] The fact that both entities, church and synagogue, were in a process of self-definition, consolidation, and codification of traditions is enough to explain the growing tensions, the persecution, and finally the separation. Especially at Antioch, where Jews had been harassed and even murdered by Gentiles during the time of the Jewish War—indeed, under the impulse of the Jewish apostate Antiochus—it is no wonder that Jews would

110. The prime example of the attempt to interpret Matthew's gospel as the Christian reply to Jamnia is Davies' *Setting.* In recent years, though, the work of such scholars as Neusner has made many researchers more cautious about what can be said with certainty of the early years of the Jamnia movement. For a short example of his voluminous labors, see Neusner, "Formation."

111. On the whole question of the persecution experienced by Matthean Christians, see Hare, *Theme* 54–56, treating the role of the *birkat ha-minim* in the exclusion of Christians from the synagogue. The *birkat ha-minim* was a curse directed against heretics (probably including Christian Jews). It was inserted into a key synagogal prayer, the Eighteen Benedictions, and had the effect of driving Christian Jews out of the synagogue. Hare thinks it unlikely that Matthew was written after the *birkat ha-minim* had been introduced into the Eighteen Benedictions; see p. 127. The unlikelihood would be greatly increased if the *birkat ha-minim* were to be dated not *ca.* 85 but rather around the beginning of the second century, since it is associated with Samuel the Younger who was active about the year 100. For a treatment of the recent literature, see the somewhat tendentious article by Kimelman, "*Birkat Ha-Minim.*"

have had little patience with non-conformist Jewish Christians who associated with Gentile Christians. It was simply a matter of time before the break with the synagogue came.

Perhaps some conservative Jewish Christians struggled valiantly to keep the bond with the synagogue alive, citing such logia as Matt 23:2–3: "The scribes and the Pharisees have succeeded Moses as teachers [literally, 'they sat in the chair of Moses']; therefore, whatever they tell you, do and observe." But the tide was against them. As Hare has ably argued, the break with the synagogue probably came before the writing of Matthew's gospel, a document that views the synagogue as an alien institution ("*their* synagogue" as opposed to "*my* church").[112] The break therefore would have taken place at some time between 70–85. Not only had the umbilical cord with James and Jerusalem been cut. By the mid-80s, the one remaining organizational link with Judaism, the connection with the local synagogue, disappeared for the Jewish Christians of Antioch. They were now adrift in a Gentile sea, heading towards a Gentile future.

We should not think that the Gentile Christians were free from harassment and persecution, simply because they had no connection with the Jewish synagogue. It was at Antioch that the disciples were first called Christians (Acts 11:26); this indicates that even in the 40s the Christian community was a well-defined group, clearly distinguishable from Jews who did not believe in Jesus. (At this early date, of course, Christian Jews and non-Christian Jews could sometimes find themselves in the same synagogue.) The new danger which arose after the break with the synagogue was that Christians could lose the protection of the category of a legal religion (*religio licita*), a protection that Judaism enjoyed and provided. The missionary and apocalyptic discourses in Matthew (10:5–42; chaps. 24–25) speak of opposition not only from synagogues but also from governors and kings, from both Jews and Gentiles (note the "to them [the Jews] and to the Gentiles" in 10:18; the "all the nations" in 24:9 and the "to all the nations" in 24:14).[113] The opposition from civil authorities would touch both Jewish and Gentile Christians and would naturally drive the two groups closer together.

---

112. Hare, *Theme*, esp. 104–5 and 151–58.
113. Cf. Meier, "Nations" 95, n. 3; and Thompson, "Perspective."

INTERNAL FACTORS FAVORING CHANGE
IN THE ANTIOCHENE CHURCH

The changed circumstances outside the church naturally called for changes within the church. By now, the Antiochene church had learned to live with a series of changes: the initial acceptance of a circumcision-free mission, the objection to such a mission (Acts 15:1,5), the acceptance of the mission (Acts 15:6–12/Gal 2:1–10), the restriction of the mission by refusal of table fellowship (Gal 2:11–14), and the compromise allowing table fellowship by observance of the four kosher rules (Acts 15:20,29). This compromise meant that for some time Jewish and Gentile Christians had been able to enjoy once again the full fellowship they had had in the church's earliest days. All could meet together for meals, eucharists, and other religious assemblies. This resumed fellowship created the natural stage for a slow process of mutual assimilation. Symbiosis gradually became osmosis. Persecution from the synagogue and the civil authorities only served to drive one group of Christians more firmly into the arms of the other. It was perhaps at this point that the extreme right-wing (Group One), no longer finding a home either in the synagogue or in the church, went its own way.[114]

The groups left in the Antiochene church in the 80s were thus the Gentile Christians (in ever increasing numbers), liberal Jewish Christians who preserved the ideals of Paul and the Hellenists, and the more conservative Jewish Christians who did not wish to break the bond of Christian fellowship and take the path leading to Ebionitism. These more conservative Jewish Christians found themselves in a unique plight. They had formerly had the upper hand; now they were definitely in the minority. They were too Christian to go back

---

114. It must be stressed, however, that no certain date can be assigned to the departure of the extreme right wing. It could have taken place after the composition of Matthew's gospel, for Ignatius still contends with a Judaizing group (see below in Chapter IV). The leave-taking could have been gradual or in a number of spurts. Yet, since by "extreme right wing" I understand those Jewish Christians who still opposed a circumcision-free Gentile mission, it is difficult to conceive of their remaining in the Antiochene church once Matthew became *the* gospel of the local church; see Farmer, "Character" 244. Of course, the theory and praxis of religious persons do not always exactly coincide—a possible situation for some time among the extreme right wing of the Matthean church.

to the synagogue and too much in the mainstream of Christianity to follow the extreme right-wing out of the church. They had shown themselves willing to compromise by agreeing to the "Apostolic Decree," but they were determined to hold on to their particular traditions. No doubt they viewed with some misgivings the large number of pagans now streaming into the church. Cut off from Jerusalem, cut off from the synagogue, how could they maintain monotheism, morality, and all the other aspects of their Jewish heritage which, in their view, made Christianity the true fulfillment of God's promise to Israel, and not another pagan religion? Despite all the changes after A.D. 70, or rather because of them, the church at Antioch still needed some way of synthesizing the various tendencies and groups which created tension within the community. This was the theological and pastoral problem Matthew had to face when he came to write his gospel.

DIFFERENT STREAMS OF GOSPEL TRADITION
IN THE ANTIOCHENE CHURCH

In the post-A.D. 70 period, the various viewpoints within the Antiochene church crystallized in different streams of gospel tradition, some written, some oral. Reflecting the theological tensions of the community, these various traditions presented Matthew with his gravest theological problem, yet also offered the elements of a solution. Matthew emerged as the "liberal conservative" who creatively redacted his sources in order to meet the identity-crisis of the Antiochene church. In order to appreciate Matthew's achievement, we must first examine his variegated, conflicting sources.[115]

(1) *The gospel of Mark* forms the backbone of Matthew's gospel. Written a little before or after A.D. 70, it seems to have been received quickly in the Matthean church. This is quite understandable if Mark's gospel came from Rome;[116] communications between the capital of the Empire and the capital of Syria were excellent. Especially after the destruction of Jerusalem, it was only natural for the

---

115. On the reconciliation of conflicting sources in Matthew, see Streeter, *Gospels* 512–15; Farmer, "Character" 245–47.

116. See the discussion in Chapter X, section C; also Pesch, *Markusevangelium* 1.12–14.

large Antiochene church to turn towards the church in the capital of the Empire, where the two significant figures of Antioch's early days, Paul and Peter, had both died martyrs. In the next generation, Ignatius will witness to the respect the Antiochene church felt for the Roman community.[117] If the tradition connecting the gospel of Mark with Peter was already known in the first century, this too would have aided the acceptance of Mark's gospel at Antioch. Some scholars, however, prefer a Palestinian or Syrian provenance for Mark's gospel.[118] While this seems less likely, it would certainly explain the rapid reception of Mark's gospel by Antioch.

In any event, at some date after 70, it seems likely that Mark became *the* written gospel used in the liturgy, catechesis, apologetics, and polemics of Matthew's church. As far as we know, it had at the time no competitor. Its sympathy for Gentiles and its critique of the Mosaic Law would make it especially acceptable to the Gentile Christians and the Hellenists. As time passed, however, it was only natural that the rough Greek, the even rougher theology, and the limited scope of the material would call forth a revision and expansion. Even before Matthew, corrections and additions may have been made as the text was read in public—not unlike the "targumic" or "midrashic" expansions of the rabbis. In this early period of Christianity, the written text was still very much enveloped in an evolving oral tradition.

(2) *The Q document,* of its nature hypothetical, is more difficult to deal with.[119] Whether or not the Q material can be traced to itinerant charismatics from Palestine,[120] much of the material seems very primitive and probably stems from an early attempt in Palestine to

---

117. Ignatius, *Romans* 3:1; 4:3, see below, pp. 182, 202.

118. Besides such authors as Marxsen and Kümmel, see Müller, "Rezeption."

119. By definition, Q is that material common to Matthew and Luke, but not found in Mark. The "Q document" is thus a hypothetical reconstruction accepted by many, though not all, NT scholars. Basically a collection of Jesus' sayings plus a few narratives, Q was a rudimentary document which may have circulated in the early church in various forms. See in particular Lührmann, *Redaktion;* Schulz, *Q;* Hoffmann, *Studien;* Edwards, *Theology;* Worden, "Redaction Criticism of Q"; Polag, *Christologie;* Vassiliadis, "Nature." On the symbol Q, see Neirynck, "Symbol"; Silberman, "Whence."

120. See the work on the sociology of the NT done by Theissen (now conveniently available in his *Studien*), esp. his "Wanderradikalismus" 79–105. For a more popular presentation, see his *Sociology.*

collect the logia of Jesus. Since Q never assumed the form of a finished gospel, its boundaries and content remained fluid; probably various recensions circulated. The eclectic nature of the Q collection would have facilitated its acceptance at Antioch; various groups could find in the words of Jesus something to bolster their position.[121] At the same time, it would be difficult for any group to reject what claimed to be nothing more than a catena of Jesus' sayings, presenting the radical moral demands, the eschatological prophecy, and the apocalyptic wisdom of Jesus. Whether a particular recension was brought to Antioch from Palestine, or whether Q itself was first redacted at Antioch, cannot be said. No doubt, even more than Mark, Q was by its very nature open to editorial changes in oral presentation.

(3) *The so-called M material* is simply an umbrella-term for all the traditions in Matthew's gospel not derived from Mark or Q. At times it is extremely difficult to separate M traditions from Matthean redaction.[122] There is not sufficient reason for positing an "M document," more rudimentary than Q.[123] The M material embraces traditions of the most varied sort, each strand reflecting a different viewpoint in the Antiochene church.[124] We may distinguish the following:

(a) The inheritance of the extreme Judaizers of Group One would be represented by the sayings rejecting a Gentile mission. Matt 10:5–6 reads: "Do not go to the Gentiles and do not enter a Samaritan city; go rather to the lost sheep of the house of Israel." And Matt 15:24 gives the prohibition a christological foundation: "I was not sent except to the lost sheep of the house of Israel." Such

121. Although Q manifests certain basic concerns (radical moral demands in the light of the apocalyptic crisis, the fate of the rejected prophets, the fusion of apocalyptic and wisdom, etc.), it seems doubtful that one can speak of a consistent redactional theology or of a "Q-community" which knew no other theological tradition (e.g., a passion-resurrection narrative). Equally doubtful is the attempt to assign logia to various stages of redaction.

122. For such an attempt in the key pericope of Matt 28:16–20, see Meier, "Questions"; Lange, *Erscheinen* (with full bibliography on 513–36); and Hubbard, *Redaction.*

123. As does Kilpatrick, *Origins* 36; to the contrary, see Schweizer, "Sondertradition."

124. Streeter, *Gospels* 512, unduly restricts M to a strain of Judaistic reaction against the Petro-Pauline liberalism in the matter of a Gentile mission and the observance of the Law. This is one strand in M, but not M as a whole.

sayings would mesh nicely with the primitive Q statement behind Matt 5:18/Luke 16:17: "Until heaven and earth pass away, not one *yod* or decorative flourish will pass away from the Law."[125]

(b) The James group (Group Two) that remained in the church would have stressed stringent observance of the Mosaic Law according to the teaching of Jesus. Hence, the moral material in the Sermon on the Mount that does not run counter to the Mosaic Law (e.g., 5:21–24, forbidding anger as well as murder; 5:27–29, forbidding mental as well as physical adultery; and the catechesis criticizing pagan prayer in 6:7–8) and the exhortation to remain subject to the authorities of the Jewish synagogue (23:2–3) might come from or have been preserved by the James group within the Antiochene church. Such an insistence on moral demands and moral authority could have been meant, in their eyes, to counter the danger posed by so many Gentiles entering the church.

(c) Traditions favoring the Gentile mission and opposing Pharisaic devotion to the Law might have been fostered by the "leftist" Hellenists allied with the Gentile Christians: e.g., the traditions behind the mandate for a universal mission in 28:16–20; the Magi story, representing the coming of the Gentiles to Christ, while the Jews fail to come; the rejection of the Pharisees in 15:12–14, which tells the disciples to "leave them [the Pharisees] alone; they are blind guides"; the M material in chap. 23 that criticizes the scribes and the Pharisees; and the critique of Jewish piety concerning alms, prayer, and fasting, in 6:1–6, 16–18. The Hellenists may also have been responsible for fostering the stringent moral demands that revoked the letter of the Mosaic Law: e.g., 5:33–37, prohibiting all oaths and vows; 5:38–39a, prohibiting all legal retaliation.[126] By handing on

---

125. Strained is the attempt by Farmer, "Character" 240–41, to read Matt 10:5–6 as a benign sanction of the division of labor between Peter and Paul, restricting the mission of the Twelve to Israel, while allowing others, like Paul, to go to the Gentiles. But this is to read something of Matthew's redactional setting (Matt 10:5a)—and indeed, a great deal more—into the isolated logion, which originally would have circulated independently. In itself the logion (10:5b–6) hardly suggests the benign limitation Farmer reads into it. As for Matthew's redaction, the *same* group that receives the limitation in chap. 10 also receives the universal mandate in 28:16–20. See Meier, *Law* 46–65, for the hypothetical original form of Matt 5:18.

126. Meier, *Law* 125–61, treats the Matthean antitheses with full bibliography up to 1975; see also Hübner, *Gesetz;* Hoffmann-Eid, *Jesus;* Piper, '*Love*'; Strecker, "Antithesen"; Dietzfelbinger, "Antithesen"; Dumbrell, "Logic."

such teaching they could answer the qualms of the James party about immorality and at the same time make a point about the imperfection of the Mosaic Law. Consequently, both the Jamesian and the Hellenist groups would be actively concerned about developing moral catechesis, a pressing need in a missionary church which so many pagans were entering. The final form of Matthew's gospel reflects this practical, pastoral need of the Antiochene church. All the different groups at Antioch would likewise be interested in preserving Petrine traditions, since historically the figure of Peter had proved to be a rallying point for the diverse wings of the community. As time went on, the growing strain and final break with the synagogue would impart an increasingly strong anti-Jewish tone to many of these M traditions.

It would be a mistake to think of Mark, Q, and M as three separate blocks of tradition which were combined for the first time by Matthew. The three main streams of tradition would have interacted regularly in liturgy, catechesis, and other church activities. M was the living sea of oral tradition in which Mark and Q floated and were steeped.[127] It may be that certain passages of Mark and Q had been altered by oral church tradition before Matthew ever wrote a word of his gospel. Particularly in the case of Q there is a strong possibility that a certain amount of M material was conflated with Q in written form. Hence, Matthew would have been working with this conflated, pre-Matthean form of Q.[128]

The development of traditions does not happen in a vacuum. With so many complicated strands of tradition circulating and growing in the Antiochene church, it was only natural that a group of teachers or scribes should arise to formulate, study, comment on, and teach the expanding Christian tradition. Acts 13:1 states that the earliest leaders of the Antiochene church were prophets and teachers (*prophētai kai didaskaloi*), who also conducted public worship (*leitourgountōn* in verse 2). This interaction between powerful, charis-

---

127. One must leave open the possibility that M contained stray variant forms of traditions also contained in Mark and Q. Some of the "minor agreements" of Matthew and Luke may be explained in this way.

128. So J. Brown, "The Form of 'Q' Known to Matthew," NTS 8 (1961–62) 27–42; Walter, "Bearbeitung" 246, n. 1; Schweizer, *Matthew* 12–14; Lührmann, *Redaktion* 11–23, esp. 18 and 21, n. 2; Hare, *Theme* 81.

matic preaching (prophecy) and Spirit-filled study of Scripture and catechesis (teaching), all in the context of liturgical celebration, would be the perfect matrix for what Stendahl has dubbed "The School of St. Matthew." One need not agree with all of Stendahl's thesis about Matthew's use of OT citations and the parallels with the Qumran literature to assent to his basic insight that Matthew's gospel comes out of a lengthy Jewish-Christian scribal tradition in Matthew's church.[129] Matthew may indeed be giving us a thumbnail self-portrait in the picture of the "scribe who has become a disciple of the Kingdom of heaven" (Matt 13:52). If Luke 11:49 preserves the original form of a Q saying which spoke of "prophets and apostles" (*prophētas kai apostolous*), it is significant that Matt 23:34 changes the reading to "prophets and wisemen and scribes" (*prophētas kai sophous kai grammateis*), almost an alternate version of Acts 13:1.[130] Matthew or the M tradition would not have had to warn Antiochene Christians not to covet the titles rabbi, teacher (*didaskalos*), and master (*kathēgētēs*) unless there were Christians at Antioch who might claim—or were claiming—these titles for themselves because of their prominent teaching position in the community (Matt 23:7–10).

It would be in this group of Christian scribes that the OT prophecies in their varied textual forms would have been studied and applied to Christian catechesis, apologetics, and polemics. When one considers the wide knowledge of different text-forms represented in the Matthean citations of the OT, it seems almost impossible that one man, starting on his own, could have enjoyed such a vast knowledge and command of textual variants. If one instead sees Matthew as coming at the end of and inheriting the work of a whole Christian

---

129. For a critique of the position of Stendahl (*School*) and further work on formula quotations (*Reflexionszitate*), see Gärtner, "Commentary"; Nepper-Christensen, *Matthäusevangelium;* Metzger, "Formulas"; Baumstark, "Zitate"; Fitzmyer, "Use of Explicit Old Testament"; Smith, "The Use of the Old Testament in the New"; Gundry, *The Use;* McConnell, *Law and Prophecy;* Rothfuchs, *Erfüllungszitate;* van Segbroeck, "Citations"; Cope, *Matthew;* R. E. Brown, *Birth.*

130. As Hummel points out (*Auseinandersetzung* 17), while Pharisees are totally rejected, Matthew does not think there is anything wrong with a scribe *qua* scribe. Rather, the Jewish scribes are enemies because they are Pharisees. This distinction may reflect the presence of scribes in Matthew's church, while the Pharisees are completely identified with the Jewish synagogue.

scribal school, which in turn drew upon Jewish learning filtered through Jewish Christians in the community, his achievement becomes more intelligible. The formula quotations of Matthew have their origin and home in the scribal school at Antioch. The prophets in the community, perhaps partly identifiable with the teachers or scribes, would proclaim and apply this learned reflection on Scripture in liturgical and other homiletic situations.[131] The formula quotations would be especially welcomed by the Jewish Christians in the Antiochene church, since such citations would help to anchor both the life and preaching of Jesus and the life and preaching of the church in the sacred writings and traditions of the Jews.

In a larger sense, of course, Matthew inherits not just the work of the scribal school but of all the bearers of tradition at Antioch. As his church faced a crisis of identity and unity, as the various groups within the church struggled to accept one another while pressure increased from the Jewish and Gentile worlds without, it was Matthew's task to embrace, reinterpret, and synthesize the competing traditions of Christian Antioch, to make them speak to a new day. It is now time for us to turn to Matthew's own work, a work of "inclusive synthesis."

MATTHEW'S GOSPEL AS A REPLY TO PROBLEMS FACING THE ANTIOCHENE CHURCH

Matthew's gospel must be seen as a theological and pastoral response to a crisis of self-identity and function in the Antiochene church, a crisis that was social and structural as well as theological in nature. A Christian community formerly under strict Jewish Christian control had suffered a traumatic break with some of the most vital religious symbols and institutional structures of Judaism:

---

131. Thus, the picture we get of the prophets and teachers at Antioch in Matthew's day would be somewhat different from the picture of the wandering teachers, prophets, and apostles in the *Didache* 11 – 13. The deep and intense study of the OT as well as of Christian traditions reflected by the work of the "School of St. Matthew" would demand a somewhat stable, sedentary group—something that the large urban setting of Antioch would make likely in any case. Of course, this would not exclude far-flung missionary work by individual prophets and teachers, after the manner of Paul and Barnabas.

the Temple, the holy city Jerusalem, and the local synagogue. Concomitant with this loss had been the loss of the revered mother church in Jerusalem, which had provided close ties with the Jewish past and Christian origins. Liberals and moderates had likewise lost their heroes, Paul and Peter. These major changes, all occurring in a relatively short time-span, created a crisis of identity: what is the church and how does it define itself over against both Jews and pagans?

Closely tied to this crisis was the crisis of authority within the church. As long as the church was tied to the synagogue, the authority of the Mosaic Law and the authority of the Jewish teachers in the synagogue could act as a support for moral teaching among Jewish Christians as well. Consequently, the question of authority, especially in moral matters, was not at first acute for Christians who belonged to a church with a markedly Jewish coloration. But, at the very time when the church saw an increasing number of Gentiles at her door seeking entrance, she also saw herself cut off from the synagogue, the bastion of traditional morality. How were moral teaching and the authority to teach morality in the church to receive a theological justification and basis?

That the problem is not a purely theoretical one for Matthew is indicated by references to the false prophets whose outward appearance is fine but whose deeds are evil (Matt 7:15–20), and to the charismatics who invoke the Lord Jesus, perform miraculous deeds of power, but do not perform the simple deeds of conforming to the will of the Father and the words of Jesus (7:21–27). The false prophets are mentioned again in the apocalyptic discourse, where the pointed remark is made that, because of the increase of immorality (*anomia*),[132] the love of the bulk of Christians will grow cold (24:11–12).

---

132. Here Matthew is fighting moral laxity, a practical, pastoral concern, *not* antinomianism, which is a theoretical denial of the validity of Law or moral obligation; so correctly Rohde, *Rediscovering* 58–59, *contra* Barth, "Matthew's Understanding" 74–75, 159–64. That *anomia* ("lawlessness") in Matthew need not mean antinomianism is clear from Jesus' accusation against the scribes and Pharisees in Matt 23:28: "Inwardly you are filled with hypocrisy and lawlessness [*anomia*]." *Anomia*, of which charismatic Christians and legalistic Pharisees can be equally guilty, is that inner rebellion against the will of God which the professionally religious hide by a flourish of pious or enthusiastic actions. See the use of *anomia* in the LXX to translate

Obviously, the crisis in institutional moral authority was being felt in Matthew's church in this period of transition.

It was to address the double crisis of church-identity and moral authority in the church that Matthew welded together the various traditions of Antiochene Christianity to form his gospel. His was a systematic attempt to "retrieve the tradition," to formulate a new Christian synthesis out of traditional materials, a synthesis which would provide his church with an adequate explanation of its origin and nature, as it tried to bridge the gap between a predominantly Jewish past and an increasingly Gentile future.[133] Matthew's approach is truly synthetic. Being a true "liberal conservative," he does not throw away the various strands of the old Jewish-Christian tradition. Rather, he absorbs them into a higher theological viewpoint, a higher synthesis. His aim is depicted clearly in the parable of the scribe who has become a disciple of the Kingdom of heaven: he is like a householder who brings forth from his storeroom things "new and old" (*kaina kai palaia,* 13:52). The all-inclusive approach is striking, but even more striking is the order. We would naturally expect "old and new." Matthew, the Christian scribe, understands the old order by the criterion of the new order, which is accordingly mentioned first. Such a hermeneutic is displayed perfectly in the formula quotations, where at times the OT text is manipulated according to the measuring rod ("canon") of the Christ-event. For example, in 2:6 Matthew adds the phrase "by no means" (*oudamōs*) to his citation of Micah 5:2—thus reversing the whole meaning of the OT passage!

Yet, while Matthew is intent on understanding the old by the norm of the new, he is equally firm on the need of preserving the old. While Mark 2:22 simply stresses that new wine is incompatible with old wine skins and must be poured into new skins, Matt 9:17 adds with broad-minded inclusiveness that, if this is done, then both types of skins will be preserved. That is his theological program: to pre-

---

such general Hebrew terms as *ʾāwen* (evil, wickedness), *ʿāwōn* (transgression, sin), and *pešaʿ* (rebellion, revolt).

133. For the idea of "retrieving the tradition," see Tracy, *Blessed Rage* and *Analogical Imagination;* for the idea of Matthew's gospel as "foundation myth," see Perrin, *New Testament* 164.

serve both the new and the old, from the proper hermeneutical perspective of the new. One can readily see how this program takes into account the needs of both Gentile and Jewish Christians within the Antiochene church. Let us examine briefly some elements in Matthew's hermeneutical program of synthesizing new and old.

(1) Matthew develops his own vision of *salvation history* in order to embrace both new and old.[134] Salvation history is divided into three periods: the time of prophecy in the OT, the time of fulfillment by the earthly Jesus, and the time of the universal mission by the church. This division enables Matthew to keep such stringent Jewish-Christian material as 10:5–6 and 15:24, which prohibit a Gentile mission. The prohibition of a universal mission is indeed affirmed by Jesus in Matthew's gospel—but only for the period of his public ministry. At the end of the gospel (28:16–20), the same Jesus, now risen, gives the same group of disciples the opposite command—a command to undertake a universal mission.

Matthew explains this turn-about by presenting the death-resurrection of Jesus as one powerful apocalyptic event, "the turning of the ages." To emphasize this theme, Matthew multiplies the apocalyptic motifs at both the cross, 27:51–54, and the empty tomb, 28:2–4.[135] At the cross an earthquake (the sign of God intervening in the end-time) opens the tombs and the holy ones of old are raised. At the tomb of Jesus on Easter Sunday, another earthquake (linking up with the death of Jesus) introduces the dazzling angel of the Lord who opens the tomb and announces the Easter message. The death of Jesus is the end of the old world; the resurrection of Jesus is the beginning of the new world.

This outline of salvation history allows Matthew to include narrow Jewish-Christian material in his gospel, although he presumably does not think that such material states the norm for his own day. He feels free, for example, to include the injunction to obey the scribes and Pharisees as the successors of Moses (23:2–3); this simply

---

134. For what follows, see Meier, "Salvation-History"; for other approaches, see Strecker, *Weg* 86–123; Trilling, *Israel* 102–5 and 137–39; Walker, *Heilsgeschichte* 111–13; Fischer, "Bemerkungen" 109–28; Frankemölle, *Jahwebund* 222; Hummel, *Auseinandersetzung* 168; Conzelmann, "Present and Future" 34, n. 34; Kingsbury, "Structure"; Thompson, "Perspective."

135. See Trilling, "Tod," and "Auferstehung"; Senior, "Death."

expresses for Matthew Jesus' willing acceptance of the restriction of his earthly mission to the land and people of Israel. Matthew's own view of the synagogue authorities, a view which seemingly indicates that a break has already taken place, is clear from such passages as Matt 16:12, "beware of the doctrine of the Pharisees and Sadducees" (contrast Mark 8:21); Matt 15:12–14, the Pharisees are "a plant . . . [which] my Father has not planted, [which] shall be uprooted; leave them" (contrast Mark 7:17); and Matt 21:43, "the Kingdom of God shall be taken from you and given to a people bearing its fruits" (contrast Mark 12:11–12).

These last citations also indicate another important function of Matthew's schema of salvation history: it portrays when and why Israel ceased to be the people of God and the church took its place. During his public ministry, Jesus addresses himself in principle only to the people of Israel, though certain exceptions (e.g., the healing of the centurion's servant in 8:5–13, the healing of the Canaanite woman's daughter in 15:21–28) point ahead to what will happen after the death-resurrection. The transferral of the Kingdom is promised in a Q logion that Matthew inserts into the story of the centurion's servant: "Many will come from the east and the west and will recline with Abraham, Isaac, and Jacob in the Kingdom of heaven. But the sons of the Kingdom will be expelled into the outer darkness" (Matt 8:11–12). The praise of the centurion's faith has been turned into a warning of the definitive rejection of Israel.

The tension between Jesus and Israel increases, especially from chap. 11 onwards. The threat of total rejection and the promise of a new people to take Israel's place is enunciated clearly in Matthew's addition to Mark's parable of the evil tenants of the vineyard: "The Kingdom of God will be taken from you and will be given to a people bearing its fruits" (21:43). In the passion the Jews unwittingly fulfill this prophecy, as no longer just the priests or the crowds but all the people (*pas ho laos*) cry out to a Pilate protesting his innocence: "His blood be upon us and upon our children" (27:25).[136] The transfer of the Kingdom takes place symbolically at the cross, where all the groups making up the Sanhedrin mock Jesus (27:41), while the centurion *and those standing guard with him* (Matthew's addition

---

136. Trilling, *Israel* 55–96, esp. 66–74.

to Mark in Matt 27:54, symbolizing the whole Gentile community) see the apocalyptic events and proclaim the crucified Jesus to be the Son of God, in the very words used by the disciples (cf. 14:33, "Truly you are God's Son"). At the conclusion of the gospel (28:16–20), the risen Jesus gives the missionary mandate to make disciples of "all the nations," with baptism instead of circumcision as the initiation rite into the people of God. The privileged place of Israel ends with the end of the time of the earthly Jesus.[137] The new period of the risen Jesus inaugurates the new time of the universal church.

As should be clear from this sketch, Matthew's view of salvation history and, in general, Matthew's theological problematic are not those of Paul. This is not surprising, considering that Matthew is writing at Antioch a generation after Paul and is facing the problems of a post-A.D. 70 church. One should therefore not attempt a false harmonization of Pauline and Matthean theology. By the same token, however, one should not too facilely posit opposition. Matthew's approach to the Law is certainly less abrasive and speculative than Paul's, and clearly lacks Paul's astounding claim that the Law is the occasion of sin. Yet, for all the theoretical differences, the practical results of Paul's theology and Matthew's theology are surprisingly similar. Both advocate a universal mission without circumcision imposed on the Gentiles. Both make radical moral demands centered on radical love. Both advocate the need for some church order while disliking any hint of tyrannical domination. Even in theological views there is some general agreement. Both see the death-resurrection of Jesus as the pivotal eschatological event of salvation history. Both hold on to the revelation of God in Jewish history and the Jewish Scriptures, while exalting the definitive revelation brought by Jesus Christ. Both advocate a relatively high christology, which has its impact on their view of the church. If Paul and Matthew cannot be simplistically harmonized, neither can they be played off against each other. As for missionary praxis as opposed

---

137. This need not mean that the Jews are not included in the missionary mandate to *panta ta ethnē* in Matt 28:19; see Meier, "Gentiles," in reply to Hare-Harrington, "Make Disciples." It may be significant that Matthew himself in 28:15 no longer speaks of Israel but only of "the Jews." After the death-resurrection, there is no chosen people Israel, only Jews, one people or nation (cf. 24:7) among many.

to a theory of Law, Paul and Matthew could probably have worked together in a mission to the Gentiles. Indirectly, therefore, Paul's heritage at Antioch was not completely lost. Matthew's inclusiveness was able to take in the practical if not the speculative aspects of Paul's vision.

(2) Closely allied to Matthew's hermeneutical tool of salvation history is the connection Matthew forges between the person of Jesus Christ, the church he founds, and the morality both teach. Indeed, this nexus between Christ, church, and morality could be called *the* specific characteristic of Matthew's gospel. [138]

Matthew constantly heightens the dignity, power, knowledge, and authority of Jesus as compared with the christology of Mark. For example, when Jesus comes home to Nazareth to preach in the synagogue, Matthew avoids all the Marcan statements which could impugn the power, knowledge, or status of Jesus (cf. Matt 13:53–58 with Mark 6:1–6a). In Mark 10:18, Jesus says to a flattering would-be disciple: "Why do you call me good? One alone is good, God." Matt 19:17 instead has Jesus reply: "Why do you ask me about what is good?" Similarly Matthew heightens the majesty of Jesus in the story of the stilling of the storm (cf. Matt 8:23–27 with Mark 4:35–41). Matthew's high christology is bolstered by the careful use of his two key christological titles, Son of God and Son of Man. The unique transcendent status of Jesus the Son receives perfect expression in his unique authority to teach (emphasized, e.g., by the astonishment of the crowds at the end of the Sermon on the Mount, 7:28–29). It is no accident that the object of this teaching is often moral instruction and general parenesis (especially in the five great discourses in chaps. 5–7; 10; 13; 18; 24–25; see also chaps. 11–12; 15:1–20; 17:24–27; 19; and 23). Christ becomes in Matthew the ground, the norm, the teacher, and the exemplar of morality.

Throughout his gospel, Matthew is intent on joining an ecclesiological motif to his central christological motif. Matthew will often take a Marcan or Q pericope which has a christological thrust; and, while heightening the christology he will also link to the christology

---

138. This is the main thesis of Meier, *Vision.*

an ecclesiological point.[139] The same christological-ecclesiological interest can be seen in the M material and Matthew's redactional compositions (1:21–23; the whole of chap. 18, esp. 18:15–20; and 28:16–20).

Obviously the church is tied to Christ insofar as Christ founds or builds his church (16:18). But, in the context of moral teaching, it is important to notice that Christ shares with his church his authority to teach, to make decisions, and to forgive sins. At the end of the healing of the paralytic, which vindicates the authority (*exousia*) of the Son of Man to forgive sins, Matthew reworks the Marcan conclusion to indicate that men in the church share this authority: "The crowds . . . glorified God, who gives such authority *to men*" (9:8).[140] The phrase "to men," which does not make too much sense in the narrative, is used by Matthew to stress that people in the church share the Son of Man's power to forgive sins. Similarly, Simon is not only made the rock of stability in the church (16:18) and the majordomo in the palace of Christ (16:19a). He is also given the rabbinic power to bind and loose, to declare certain acts licit or illicit, to declare them in keeping with or contrary to the teaching of Jesus (16:19b).[141] Peter is thus constituted, in Streeter's famous phrase, "the supreme Rabbi" of the church.[142] The local church in chap. 18 is likewise empowered to bind and loose, though the phrase here seems to refer more to disciplinary power, the power to admit to or exclude from the church.[143]

---

139. E.g., Matt 9:1–8, compared with Mark 2:1–12; Matt 16:13–20, compared with Mark 8:27–30; Matt 21:33–46, compared with Mark 12:1–12; Matt 22:1–14, the parable of the royal wedding banquet, compared with the Q parable preserved in its more original form in Luke 14:15–24, the parable of the great supper; Matt 27:24–26, compared with Mark 15:15.

140. See Held, "Matthew," esp. 175–78, 248–49.

141. For a full bibliography on Matt 16:17–19, see Burgess, *History*.

142. Streeter, *Gospels* 515. Notice how this bestowal of teaching authority on Peter follows immediately upon the rejection of the teaching authority of the "united front" of Judaism (Pharisees and Sadducees) in 16:1–12, esp. verse 12: "Beware of the teaching of the Pharisees and Sadducees."

143. On the difference between 16:18 and 18:18, see Bornkamm, "Authority" 46–48. Bornkamm rightly warns against viewing 18:15–18 as a rival tradition to 16:17–19; there is no rivalry, "not even in the sense of a historical sequence as though the congregation had replaced Peter" (p. 48). Contrast Schweizer, "Kirche," 159, who claims that the successor of Peter in the office of binding and loosing is the (local) community. This is to ignore the many differences between the two passages.

The concern with the church's power to teach reaches its climax in the final pericope of the gospel (28:16–20). In the missionary discourse of chap. 10, aimed at the limited mission to Israel during the public ministry, Jesus gave his disciples the authority to imitate him in proclaiming the Kingdom and working miracles—but teaching was notable by its absence (10:1–8). Only after the death-resurrection, in the great commission that extends the disciples' mandate to "all the nations," does Jesus give them the authority to teach all whatsoever he commanded during his earthly life (28:20).[144] This linking of Christ-church-and-morality, and the interweaving of these motifs with a particular vision of salvation history, all serve to provide a rationale for the origin and nature of Matthew's church. It is a rationale that defines the church's identity as the people of God and legitimizes its authoritative role in teaching morality to "all the nations." Just as God has transferred the Kingdom from Israel to a people bearing its fruits (21:43), so too He has transferred the teaching function from the synagogue to the church. Matthew's gospel thus helps his church to a new understanding of itself and its role which overcomes the traumas, crises, and divisions of the seventies and eighties.

(3) It is only natural that a group which is experiencing both rapid growth and a crisis of identity and function, and which moreover is interacting dialectically with other organized groups, should develop institutional organs of its own. It comes as no surprise then that the church at Antioch, as it grapples with its identity and role, as it engages in apologetic, polemic, and proselytizing activity among both Jews and Gentiles, and as it feels pressure from both the organizations of the synagogue and civil government, should find institutional ways of responding to its problems. Institutions may either betray or preserve the charismatic spirit of the group's origins, and no value judgment should be made before the facts are examined.[145] In the case of the Antiochene church, a number of institutional mo-

---

144. Matt 28:16–20 pulls together magnificently the three concerns of Christ, church, and morality. As Michel observed in "Abschluss" 21, this pericope is the key to the understanding of the whole of the gospel; see also Lohmeyer, "Mir"; Vögtle, "Anliegen"; Malina, "Literary Structure"; Kingsbury, "Composition."

145. See Holmberg, *Paul* 161–92.

tifs and concrete organs of authority are reflected in Matthew's gospel.

(a) The very fact that the gospel uses the word "church" (*ekklē-sia*) three times is significant.[146] The first-century Christians used the word to express their group-consciousness both early (2 times in I Thessalonians; 3 times in Galatians; 22 times in I Corinthians) and late (23 times in Acts; 3 times in I Timothy; 20 times in Revelation). The usage covered both the local church (e.g., I Thess 1:1) and the universal church (perhaps already in I Cor 10:32; I Cor 12:28; certainly in Col 1:18). The gospels, however, respect the archaic nature of their traditions. They do not use the word *ekklēsia*—the one exception being Matthew. Matthew uses *ekklēsia* once of the universal church (16:18) and twice of the local church (18:17). More significant still is the fact that the two passages involved speak of the authoritative act of binding and loosing, either by some official or by the whole local church. The term *ekklēsia* certainly means for Matthew the church as a visible structure and society, having authoritative officials and authoritative functions.

(b) Matt 16:18–19 has given rise to an endless flood of literature because of its use in later church doctrine and polemics.[147] At the same time, biblical scholars have often focused on the question of pre-Matthean tradition. All too often the problematic of the evangelist in his own time and place, the *redactional* question, is overlooked. Matthew, writing to meet the problems of a church in Syrian Antioch around A.D. 85, is certainly not concerned with the problem of whether a single-bishop in Rome is the successor of Simon Peter, especially since both Rome and Antioch around 85 do not seem to have known the single-bishop structure.[148] Rather, Matthew is pre-

---

146. For *ekklēsia* (church) in Matthew, see Schmidt, *"ekklēsia"*; Trilling, *Israel* 143–63; Frankemölle, *Jahwebund* 191–256.

147. See footnote 141 above.

148. The first epistle of Clement, written from Rome to Corinth *ca.* A.D. 96, envisions in Corinth a two-tier hierarchy of bishops/elders (*episkopoi/presbyteroi*) and deacons (*diakonoi*). Since the epistle takes this state of affairs for granted and sees it as willed by God, the natural presumption is that the same state of affairs prevailed in the Roman church; see von Campenhausen, *Ecclesiastical Authority*, 84–95, esp. n. 40. It is most significant that, while Ignatius (writing between 108 and 117) presupposes the presence of a monarchical bishop in the local church in all of his other letters, he is silent on the subject when addressing the church of Rome. Notice how usually the

senting Peter as the chief Rabbi of the universal church, with power to make "halakic" decisions (i.e., decisions on conduct) in the light of the teaching of Jesus. As Bornkamm points out, while the idea of admitting and excluding from the church (the main point of 18:17–18) may also be present in 16:18–19, the main thrust of 16:18–19 is Peter's teaching authority, his power to declare acts licit or illicit according to Jesus' teaching. Furthermore, this power extends to the whole of "*my* church," the whole church Jesus will build on Peter, not just some local assembly.[149]

Such, at least, is the meaning of this programmatic text in the present context of Matthew's gospel. It may well be that this Petrine tradition, preserved at Antioch, once referred to Peter's important function of giving stability and unity to the Antiochene church, strained as it was by the various tendencies of the 40s and 50s.[150] But, in the Matthean redaction, the sense is general and universal: Peter is the rock on which Jesus builds his church, period.[151] Matthew exalts the figure of Peter as *the* human authority for the church as a whole. Matthew thus proclaims the Antiochene tradition of Peter as the bridge-figure, the moderate center, to be the norm for the whole church, as opposed to those local churches, dissident groups, or sects which would appeal to a one-sided interpretation of the Pauline or Jamesian tradition as normative for the whole church.[152]

But does Matthew see any one individual in his own day functioning in this Petrine role, either at Antioch or elsewhere? Or does he understand Matt 16:18–19 as referring simply to the unique, sacred past? Is this vision of the one authoritative leader of the whole church just a fossil in the tradition, or could it be a hint that the monarchical episcopate is arising or will soon arise at Antioch? It is dif-

---

general salutation to the local church is soon followed by a mention of the church's bishop. There is no such sequence in Ignatius' letter to the Romans. On all this, see pp. 162–64 below.

149. Bornkamm, "Authority" 46; see Stendahl, *School* 28.

150. Downey, *History* 283, sees Matt 16:18 as expressing "the tradition of Antioch concerning the foundation of the church there. Thus the words in Matthew could form a basis for the claim of the church at Antioch to supremacy over Jerusalem." Perhaps Downey does not distinguish sufficiently between the sense of the isolated logion in the oral tradition and the sense it acquires in Matthew's redaction.

151. So rightly, R. E. Brown, *Peter* 100, n. 231.

152. See footnotes 100 above and 446 below.

ficult to reach any certitude on this point. To seek some further light
on this structural question, we turn to the second text using the word
ekklēsia, 18:17.[153]

(c) In theological disputes, Matt 18:17 has often been played off
against 16:18, but this procedure is wrong on a number of grounds.
First, it ignores the different contexts of the two sayings in Matthew's redaction: Matthew 16 contains the narrative of Peter's confession of faith near Caesarea Philippi, while Matthew 18 presents
Jesus' discourse on church life and order. Second, it ignores the difference in the meaning of *ekklēsia:* the church as a whole, over which
Peter is placed as "supreme Rabbi" in 16:18; the local church called
together by a member's appeal for adjudication and discipline in
18:17. Third, it ignores the difference in nuance[154] between "binding
and loosing" in 16:19 (chiefly the power to interpret the moral teaching of Jesus authoritatively) and "binding and loosing" in 18:18
(chiefly the power to admit to or exclude from the local church).[155]
What is especially intriguing about 18:15–20 is that we have a picture of a local church, presumably Matthew's church, engaging in
formal disciplinary action.[156] The problem of sin in the church is to
be settled in private, if possible. If the sinner refuses to correct his
ways, even when confronted with one or two witnesses, the local
church is called together to hear the case and act (presumably the

---

153. For a full treatment of Matthew 18, see Thompson, *Matthew's Advice;* also
W. Pesch, *Matthäus der Seelsorger* (Stuttgart: KBW, 1966).

154. As Bornkamm ("Authority" 46) points out, this is a difference in nuance
and emphasis; to a certain degree both meanings may be present in both texts.

155. Likewise often ignored is the secondary connection between 18:15–17 (in
the second person singular) and 18:18 (in the second person plural).

156. Commentators often point out the parallel to Qumran's disciplinary procedure; e.g., Gnilka, "Kirche" 51, 57, treats the inner structure of the Dead Sea Scroll
community, comparing Matt 18:15–17 with, notably, 1 QS 5:24 – 6:1 and CD 7:2–3;
9:2–3. Gnilka suggests that in the Christian assembly described in Matt 18:15–17 certain leaders would have had the final word. While that seems a common-sense approach, what is noteworthy is Matthew's silence about this aspect of the judicial
process. Interestingly, Corwin, *Ignatius* 83, suggests that we have the episcopal-pres-
byteral form of the discipline of Matt 18:17 described later in Ignatius, *Philadelphians*
8:1: "Therefore the Lord pardons all who repent, provided their repentance leads
them to union with God and the council of the bishop." Concerning Matt 18:15–17,
Thiering, "Mebaqqer" 70, arguing from the testing process in Deut 19:18, states: "The
involvement of the bishop cannot definitely be precluded." However, her general hypothesis suffers from questionable interpretations of both the Qumran and the NT evidence.

one or two witnesses of 18:16 would give testimony at the meeting, in keeping with Deut 19:15). The local church renders a decision; and, if the sinner refuses to abide by the decision, he is excommunicated (18:17).[157]

Of key importance here is the fact that no local leader or leaders are mentioned; the local church acts and decides as a whole. One might appeal to the presence of Peter in 17:24–27, just before the discourse on church life and order begins, and his reappearance right after this section on discipline in 18:21. However, Peter has a unique position vis-à-vis any other disciples in 17:24–27. Just enough money is provided for the payment of the tax for Jesus and Peter ("for me and for *you* [second person singular!] in 17:27). This argues for the conception of Peter not as a local leader but as the unique leader of the whole church, as in 16:18–19. Left with 18:15–20, the reader might be tempted to conclude that there are no local leaders in Matthew's church. Yet our survey of the gospel and of its antecedents at Antioch has indicated that this is not the case. Moreover, Peter is brought back in 18:21 to introduce the exhortation to forgiveness which acts as a restraint on the mechanism of discipline in the local church.[158]

Perhaps no leaders are mentioned in 18:15–20 because Matthew is intent on making sure that all members of the church share in important decisions, especially disciplinary decisions involving excommunication. If the grave step of excluding someone from the brotherhood has to be taken, all the members should be involved. Be-

---

157. The harsh "Let him be unto you as a pagan [*ethnikos*] and a taxcollector" (Matt 18:17) may indicate that the discipline stems from the days when the strict Jewish Christians had the upper hand. Notice the parallel in 5:46–47: "The taxcollectors ... the pagans [*ethnikoi*]." Matthew's hand, however, may be seen in the use of the relatively rare *ethnikos*, "pagan" (only four times in the NT) instead of *ethnē*, "nations," "peoples," "Gentiles." For Matthew, the *ethnē*, the uncircumcised, can be members of the church, but the *ethnikoi* are uncircumcised *pagans* who are not (yet) members of the church; so too Matt 6:7, which envisages pagan prayer practices as opposed to Jewish practices in 6:5. With three of the four NT uses of *ethnikos*, Matthew indicates his view of the church as a *tertium genus*, a third race, neither Jewish nor pagan (see Matt 21:43). The fourth NT appearance of *ethnikos* likewise refers to pagans as opposed to Christians; see the comment on III John 7 in R. Bultmann, *The Johannine Epistles* (Philadelphia: Fortress, 1973) 99, n. 12.

158. See Barth, "Auseinandersetzungen"; he suggests that Matt 13:24–30 and 18:21–35 act as a critique of the church's tendency to anticipate the final judgment in her discipline.

sides more theoretical reasons of ecclesiology, a practical reason
would demand full participation in making the decision: the discipline of "shunning" a fellow Christian would not be effective unless
all the other members agreed to implement the decision. At the same
time, Matthew's theological perspective is certainly at work here: the
local church is a family community of fellow servants (see 18:31a,
35;23:8c,11), all of whom must share in the authority and responsibility of decision-making. Of course, as often in NT documents, we
must reckon with the possibility that Matthew is giving not so much
a precise picture of what *does* happen in his church but rather what
he *wishes* to see happen. Instead of being a sober, sociological description of how Matthew's church usually acts, Matt 18:15–20 may
be a "performative" utterance telling all the members of the church
how they should act. But why should such an exhortation be necessary?

    (d) Matthew is obviously concerned about a type of nascent
"clericalism" that is threatening his church. It would make no sense
for him to warn his fellow Christians at Antioch to avoid ostenta-
tious religious clothing and paraphernalia (23:5), the desire for the
first seats at religious meetings (*prōtokathedrias* in 23:6), and the desire to be addressed with special titles (23:7–10), unless such practices were a real possibility or an actual reality in the Antiochene
church.[159] Who might have assumed these airs? The ostensible tar-
gets of Matthew's tirade are the Jewish scribes and Pharisees, precisely in their function as authoritative teachers of the people (23:2,
they sat on the chair of Moses, i.e., they succeeded to his teaching
position; and 23:3, their teaching is to be obeyed). This emphasis on
authoritative teaching is clear from the titles to be avoided: rabbi,
teacher, father, and master (verses 7–10). As we have seen, from its
earliest days, the Antiochene church seems to have been led by a
group of prophets and teachers (Acts 13:1). And such a college of
prophets and teachers (alias scribes or wise men) seems to form the
leadership in the Antioch of Matthew's day (13:52; 23:34). This college may also be identifiable with the "School of St. Matthew" sug-

---

    159. For details on the complicated tradition history of Matt 23:1–12, see Gar-
land, *Intention* 34–63; also Haenchen, "Matthäus 23"; Frankemölle, "Amtskritik";
Schweizer, "Kirche" 160.

gested by Stendahl.[160] Such powerful preachers and Spirit-led teachers and exegetes would tend to become the natural officiants at the church's liturgy. Indeed, the Antiochene prophets and teachers are said to engage in formal worship *(leitourgountōn)* in Acts 13:2. (One is reminded of the liturgical role of prophets and teachers, to which resident bishops and deacons are succeeding, in *Didache* 15:1–2, as well as the liturgical role of prophets in *Didache* 10:7; 13:3. *Didache* 11; 13:1–2 also mention the close connection between teachers, apostles, and prophets.) Matthew may see in all these tendencies the danger that a good and necessary leadership role will turn into domination, monopoly, and "clericalism." It is against such excesses and trappings arising among the official teachers in the church, and not against church leadership and teaching in itself, that Matthew directs his attack in 23:1–12.

And yet, looking at all of Matthew's "institutional" statements, one must admit a certain ambivalence in his approach. He extols the figure of the unique authoritative leader, Peter, the rock for the whole church. He presupposes a group of prophets and teachers in the Antiochene church, to whom he attributes real authority, as the parallel with Jewish scribes and Pharisees suggests. Yet he is extremely wary of the almost inevitable external trappings that leaders attract, and he exhorts his church to act and decide as a whole on disciplinary matters.[161] The ambivalence of Matthew's approach to

---

160. The "School" context, the threat Matthew sees of clerical domination, and the needs of a relatively large, expanding urban church like Antioch would all argue for a somewhat stable or resident group of leaders. That does not mean, however, that the more itinerant type of prophet has died out. On the contrary, Matt 10:41 seems to presuppose such a prophet. One might even see in Matt 10:41–42 a primitive church order: itinerant prophets (10:41a), just men, i.e., members or leaders of the local community who are distinguished by their zealous observance of the commandments (10:41b), and the little ones, i.e., the ordinary members of the community (10:42). Yet the sayings seem to be traditional, with many variations on the theme; cf. Mark 9:41; Luke 10:16; John 13:20; also Mark 9:37; Matt 18:5; Luke 9:48. This should make us cautious about drawing conclusions about church order in Matthew's own community, esp. from 10:41–42. Matthew may have gathered these logia at the end of his missionary discourse simply because of similarity of theme, as is his wont. On all this, see Schweizer, "Kirche," 138–70, esp. 156–59.

161. Garland *(Intention,* esp. 210–15) points out that the attacks on the scribes and Pharisees may actually be aimed at Christians falling into similar errors. However, in a desire to avoid anything "sub-Christian" in the gospel, Garland may minimize the lively, even fiery polemic between Matthew's church and the synagogue. As

church authority may be explained partly by the various traditions with which Matthew must work, partly by the fact that his church is a church in transition, a transition which has by no means ended,[162] but perhaps most of all by Matthew's own indecisiveness about how much authoritative leadership is good for his church. He admires the rock of 16:18–19 but seems unable or unwilling to have a local counterpart to this figure of universal ecclesiastical stability. Matthew's ambivalent treatment of church leadership may serve as a healthy reminder that we cannot expect the evangelist to have provided a perfect solution to each and every problem that the crises of Antioch put before him. Church history at Antioch did not end at A.D. 85. Matthew was to be a bridge, however unwittingly, to the emerging church catholic of the second century.

Meeks, *Jews* 19–36, shows, strained and polemical relations between Jews and Christians continued in Antioch, not only under Ignatius, but even into the fourth century.

162. See Thompson, "New Testament Communities."

CHAPTER IV

The Antiochene Church of the Third Christian Generation

(After A.D. 100—Ignatius)

Coming to the third Christian generation at Antioch, we have two possible witnesses: the seven letters of Ignatius of Antioch,[163] and a document called the *Didache* (more formally, "Teaching of the Twelve Apostles"), which sets forth rules for Christian morality and church order. Since Ignatius of Antioch obviously reflects Christianity in that city at the beginning of the second century A.D., we naturally turn to his letters first. Whether the *Didache* really comes from Antioch and belongs to Christianity's third generation is disputed, and so we shall treat the *Didache* separately, at the end of this chapter.

---

163. This study presupposes the authenticity of the seven letters of the so-called "middle recension," a position accepted by the vast majority of scholars today. We therefore accept as authentic the letters to the Ephesians, Magnesians, Trallians, Romans, Philadelphians, Smyrneans, and to Polycarp. As in the past, though, so too today there are those who claim that all or part of the middle recension is spurious. The most notable recent skeptics are Weijenborg, *Les lettres;* Joly, *Le dossier;* and Rius-Camps, *The Four Authentic Letters.* A review and critique of these works has been supplied by Schoedel, "Are the Letters of Ignatius of Antioch Authentic?" As for the date of the letters, Corwin, *Ignatius* 3, places them between A.D. 108 and 117 and lists other opinions in note 1 on the same page. Most authors are in general agreement with Corwin's dating.

A. Ignatius of Antioch

When we move from the church of Matthew to the church of Ignatius, we may be inclined to ask ourselves whether the latter could possibly be the descendant of the former. The vast differences between the church and theology of Matthew on the one hand and the church and theology of Ignatius on the other are so obvious that one wonders whether there are any connections whatever.

CHURCH STRUCTURE

The difference in church structure is especially striking. Instead of a group of prophets and teachers, who also probably led the liturgy, we find a clearly delineated three-tier hierarchy of one bishop, a group of presbyters (the council of elders or *presbyterion*), and a group of deacons (e.g., *Magnesians* 2–3).[164]

Clearly the bishop is *the* leader. Without him, nothing is to be done, no rite is to be celebrated, including baptism and the eucharist. We read in *Smyrneans* 8:1–2: "No one is to do anything with reference to the church without the bishop. That Eucharist is to be considered valid which is [celebrated] by the bishop or by a person he permits [to celebrate]. Wherever the bishop appears, there the assembly is to be, just as wherever Jesus Christ is, there is the catholic church. Apart from the bishop it is not lawful either to baptize or to hold the sacred meal [*agapē*]. But whatever he approves is likewise acceptable to God. . . ." The bishop is also the chief teacher in the church,[165] guaranteeing the unity of faith and the unity of the church. Significantly, nothing is said about a special group of prophets and teachers, probably because Ignatius has absorbed these charismatic

---

164. For a summary of Ignatius' statements about the members of the triple hierarchy in each of his letters, see Lemaire, *Les ministères* 163–78. For a summary of Ignatius' ecclesiology, especially in reference to the eucharist, see Paulsen, *Studien* 145–57.

165. And yet, as von Campenhausen notes (*Ecclesiastical Authority* 101), it is remarkable how little Ignatius actually says about the activity of teaching. Perhaps he is too busy doing it to make it an object of direct reflection. Certainly, it is presupposed in everything he says about the unity of faith and the danger of false teaching.

functions into himself as bishop—though in union with his council of elders.

How is one to conceive of the transition from the relatively loose structure of Matthew's church around A.D. 85 to the three-part hierarchy of Ignatius, which seems to be a *fait accompli,* at least at Antioch, by the second decade of the second century?[166] It seems that some further crisis or crises at Antioch had demanded a tightening up of church structures so that a united church could meet a common enemy. The most likely candidate for the role of catalytic crisis is the rise of gnosticism, especially in its docetic tendencies.[167] Since gnosticism posed a threat precisely on the level of teaching, it was only natural that the college of Christian teachers and prophets at Antioch should try to reorganize and unify itself to counter the gnostic doctrine more effectively.

If punitive measures against Christians under Domitian (81–96) reached as far as Syrian Antioch, civil persecution may have been another reason for consolidation of leadership in the face of crisis. Admittedly, we cannot be sure about persecution during the reign of Domitian (see footnotes 265, 338 below). But Ignatius' martyrdom does give definite proof that punitive measures did reach Antioch later in the reign of Trajan (98–117). Even apart from official imperial policy, local sporadic outbursts against Christians may have pushed the church towards increasing consolidation of authority.

---

166. Ignatius' letters presuppose the existence of the three-tier hierarchy in Ephesus, Magnesia, Tralles, Philadelphia, and Smyrna. Nevertheless, his incessant exhortations to be submissive to the bishop seem to indicate that the role of the single-bishop is relatively new in these churches. We should remember that we are seeing the hierarchies of the churches of Asia Minor through the eyes and vocabulary of Ignatius. The conceptions and vocabulary of some of the local leaders may have been different, as the letter of Polycarp to the Philippians suggests, esp. in its opening greeting; cf. Lemaire *Les ministères* 174–78.

167. "Gnosticism" is used here in a very general sense. It may well be that what Ignatius is battling should be labeled "proto-gnostic"; so Corwin, *Ignatius* viii, 11–14, who criticizes Schlier, *Untersuchungen,* and Bartsch, *Gut,* for supposing that there was a full-blown gnostic Redeemer myth which influenced Ignatius. Corwin is willing to admit that Ignatius was influenced by gnostic thought on revelation, but she claims that Ignatius does not show any awareness of the doctrine of an evil Creator God and the radical evil of matter. For references to docetic tendencies in Ignatius' opponents, see especially *Ephesians* 7:1–2; 16 – 19; *Magnesians* 11; *Trallians* 8 – 11; *Philadelphians* 2 – 7; *Polycarp* 3.

At any rate, *ca.* 100, one particularly gifted prophet-teacher came forth from the Antiochene college of prophets and teachers to take the "first seat" (*prōtokathedria*) so deprecated by Matthew (Matt 23:6; the evangelist was more a prophet than he knew).[168] This chief teacher and prophet (preacher), presiding over the college from which he emerged, received the designation "bishop" or "overseer" (*episkopos*). The remaining teachers and prophets were called "elders" or "presbyters" (*presbyteroi*), and their group or college was called a *presbyterion* (*Magnesians* 13:1; it is also called a *synedrion* in *Magnesians* 6:1 and *Philadelphians* 8:1). Ironically, the term Matthew wanted to mark the greatest leader in the church, "servant" (*diakonos,* Matt 23:11), was relegated to the assistants (deacons) who stood on the third and lowest rung of the hierarchical ladder—though bishop Ignatius does not hesitate to refer to them as "my fellow servants" in *Philadelphians* 4.

In the midst of all these distinctions, however, we should keep in mind that Ignatius is not depicting the faceless bureaucracy of some huge organization, with an all-powerful monarch secluded on a lofty pinnacle and jealous of his rights. It is of the essence of his vision of the church that all officials and members of the church cooperate in a living unity of reciprocal love.[169] Ignatius does not view his office as un-charismatic. Rather, in Ignatius we find a peculiar fusion of office and charism, perhaps because Ignatius has come forth from the college of prophets and teachers and still considers himself very much a man of the Spirit.[170] Moreover, when we read Ignatius' de-

---

168. Ignatius uses the participle *prokathēmenou* (presiding) of the bishop in *Magnesians* 6:1; yet he also uses it in the plural, *prokathēmenois,* presumably of the presbyters, in *Magnesians* 6:2. For Ignatius, the single-bishop presides in a collegial manner. The word *prōtokathedria* ("first seat") does not occur in Ignatius.

169. See von Campenhausen, *Ecclesiastical Authority* 102–6. On the central place of the ideal of unity in Ignatius, see Camelot, *Ignace* 20–55; Bartsch, *Gut* 77; and Paulsen, *Studien* 132–44. Von Campenhausen (97) suggests that the position of Antioch as the civil capital of Syria may have had some influence on the development of the Christian polity at Antioch; similarly, Corwin, *Ignatius* 44–45. Yet von Campenhausen (97–98) also stresses that Ignatius conceives of the church not as a legal-constitutional entity but rather as a living mystery.

170. For Ignatius as "a man of the Spirit," see Schlier, *Untersuchungen* 125–74; however, he ties Ignatius' pneumatic tendencies too exclusively to his theology of martyrdom. More balanced are von Campenhausen, *Ecclesiastical Authority* 102–6; and Bommes, *Weizen Gottes* 165–81. Ignatius' pneumatic character is already seen in his

mands that nothing be done without the bishop's approval, we should remember that the whole church at Antioch might be the size of a present-day parish, the bishop playing much the same role as a pastor.

To sum up, then: the presiding teacher-prophet at Antioch became the one bishop, the other teachers and prophets became the college of elders, and the other church workers became the deacons. Writing between A.D. 108–117, Ignatius can take this structure for granted in his own church as he attempts to shore up the position of the bishop in the churches of Asia Minor. The system of the monarchical episcopate has no doubt been operative at Antioch for a while before his letters are written. Hence we are forced to choose some date *ca.* A.D. 100 for the rise of the triple hierarchy at Antioch. The date has to be sufficiently before 108–117 to allow the new structure to become customary, and sufficiently after Matthew's gospel to allow for the development of one head presiding over the college. Whether Ignatius was the first monarchical bishop at Antioch cannot be known with certitude, but his silence about any predecessor would point in that direction.

THEOLOGY

The difference between Matthew and Ignatius is also clear in the area of theology, or, to restrict our consideration to a narrow focus, the area of *theological sources.*[171] Ignatius has imbibed a good deal of Pauline and Johannine thought, while alluding only infrequently to the OT.[172] It could be, of course, that, especially in the

---

second name, Theophorus ("God-bearer"), which von Campenhausen thinks Ignatius gave himself; the word is not found as a proper name before Ignatius. Ignatius stresses his own special spiritual knowledge in *Trallians* 5; cf. *Ephesians* 20. In *Philadelphians* 7:2, he states that the Spirit himself preaches through the bishop; see also his instruction to Polycarp on being spiritual in *Polycarp* 1:3; 2:2; 3:2. Interestingly, von Campenhausen, *Ecclesiastical Authority* 106, claims that one source of Ignatius' idea of the bishop as a "spiritual man" is the enthusiasm of the teachers and prophets who appear at the beginning of the history of the Antiochene church; cf. also Rathke, *Ignatius* 81; Paulsen, *Studien* 122–29.

171. Space does not permit a full treatment of Ignatius' theology; see Corwin, *Ignatius* 89–217; and the whole of Paulsen's *Studien*.

172. For Paul, see Rathke, *Ignatius, passim;* Corwin, *Ignatius* 66.

case of Johannine thought, it was Ignatius' gnostic or docetic opponents who introduced him to the thought-world of John, which Ignatius then turned against his adversaries.[173] What is most significant, though, is that Ignatius combines Pauline and Johannine thought with the Synoptic tradition, especially as represented by Matthew.[174] The result is a new theological synthesis at the service of mainstream Christianity. Ignatius represents the first attested attempt to blend the major streams of NT thought into a coherent viewpoint that articulates the faith of the church catholic (*hē katholikē ekklēsia*) as opposed to the gnostics (*Smyrneans* 8:2).[175] In this, the bishop-theologian Ignatius, in the first quarter of the second century, foreshadows the much greater synthesis of Irenaeus of Lyons, another bishop-theologian, in the last quarter of the same century.

At the same time, however, while Ignatius may be a theological predecessor of Irenaeus, from another vantage point he may be considered a theological successor of Matthew. For all their differences, Ignatius was moved by a theological crisis to take a direction similar to that of Matthew: to draw together venerable Christian traditions from different, even divergent streams, all in the service of the unity of the church as it entered a new period and faced a new crisis.[176] In

---

173. Corwin, *Ignatius* 68–70, thinks it is reasonable to suppose that Ignatius knew John at least in outline, even if it cannot be proved. For arguments that Ignatius knew John (but did not understand him), see Maurer, *Ignatius* esp. 100–2. Less convincingly, Corwin also thinks it likely that Ignatius knew the *Odes of Solomon*, the dating of which (first or second century?) remains problematic. Note Corwin's suggestion (102–3) that Ignatius was more aware of docetic dangers in emphasizing Christ's divinity than were the *Odes* or John. Certainly one can say that Ignatius knew Johannine tradition, whether or not he knew the Fourth Gospel in written form; similarly, Richardson, *Christianity* 261–71 and 275–80; see Schlier, *Untersuchungen* 176–77.

174. For Ignatius' knowledge and use of Matthew, see Chapter I above, esp. footnotes 57–58. All commentators agree that Ignatius stands closer to Matthew than to any other gospel. The dispute is whether he used our written gospel, Matthew's gospel in some other form, or Matthean oral tradition; see Schlier, *Untersuchungen* 178; and Paulsen, *Studien* 37–39, who hesitates. Corwin, *Ignatius* 94–95, lists all the events of Jesus' earthly life that Ignatius knew either from Matthew or from the general Synoptic tradition.

175. On the problem of the meaning of *katholikē* in *Smyrneans* 8:2, see von Campenhausen, *Ecclesiastical* 101. Lightfoot, *Apostolic Fathers* II 2.310–12, argues forcefully for the sense of "the general or universal Church, as opposed to a particular body of Christians"; similarly Funk, *Patres Apostolici* 1:282–83; Kleist, *St. Clement* 141–42.

176. Intriguingly, Corwin's description of Ignatius applies equally to the theological symbol of Peter and to the approach in Matthew's gospel: "Ignatius himself is

this at least, Ignatius of Antioch carried forward Matthew's theological program for the Antiochene church of the 80s. Even in Ignatius' particular theological emphasis, Matthew's gospel and the Synoptic tradition in general had a contribution to make. Faced with the docetic tendency of the gnostics, Ignatius had to emphasize the unity of the divine and human in Jesus Christ and especially the reality of Jesus' humanity. Here the Johannine traditions might not have been of the greatest help; the gnostics were quite comfortable with their brand of Johannine thought, as their subsequent history shows. While Matthew might lack the Johannine emphasis on preexistence and Logos, his concentration on the earthly life of Jesus provided a healthy counterbalance and so probably contributed more to Ignatius' thought than the small number of clear allusions to Matthew in Ignatius' letters might indicate.

DIVERSE GROUPS

Ignatius may also have inherited Matthew's theological problematic in that he had to deal with *both a "left wing" and a "right wing"* in his church. The "left wing" was made up of the docetists, among whom might have been some theological heirs of the Hellenists, especially if John is seen as a Hellenist gospel (see footnote 8 above). These people might also have imbibed gnosticizing tendencies from some of the many Gentiles entering the Antiochene church. The "right wing" was composed of a Judaizing group, perhaps partly made up of the remnants of the extreme right wing (Group One, Introduction) or of some of the Jamesian party from Matthew's day.

It must be admitted that not all critics agree that there were two different dissident groups in Ignatius' church, but C. Richardson, V. Corwin, and others seem to have the better part of the argument in

---

clearly the leader of a centrist party, which was maintaining a balance between the two extremes. . . . [Ignatius' theology] relies . . . on a strategy of inclusiveness. At least part of the time it is definitely irenic. . . . Ignatius declares that the saints and believers may be drawn from either the Jews or the heathen (*Smyrneans* 1:2). . ." (*Ignatius* 64). For a similar view of Matthew as a theologian seeking a middle path between two extremes, see Broer, *Freiheit,* esp. 125–26.

holding that there were two distinct groups of adversaries.[177] The "too high" christology of the docetists and their rejection of the Jewish Scriptures would be incompatible with the Judaizers' christology (which was probably low) and the Judaizers' devoted adherence to the Jewish Scriptures. Probably both groups considered themselves Christians and nominally acknowledged the bishop. We read in *Magnesians* 4:1: "It is fitting, then, not only to be called Christian but to be Christian; just as likewise there are some who call upon the bishop but who do all things without him." It may have been, though, that the Judaizers also used some other designation for themselves. In a context dealing with Judaizers, *Magnesians* 10:1 states: "For whoever is called by another name than this one [i.e., Christian] is not of God."

If we may judge from the relative infrequency of allusions to them in the letters, the Judaizers were less of a threat than the docetists, who were the main reason for dissension.[178] The latter had seceded from the church to the extent that they abstained from the eucharist (at least the one eucharist celebrated by the bishop) and the public prayer of the church. Whether the schism extended to every aspect of church life is not clear. The fact that Ignatius, during his journey to Rome, received word that peace had been restored to the Antiochene church (*Philadelphians* 10:1; *Smyrneans* 10–11; *Polycarp* 7) may indicate that the situation was not as "frozen into irreconcilable opposition" as we might think.[179] We hear nothing of bishops or elders at the head of the dissident groups. For Ignatius, the word bishop of its very nature means the focal point of unity. It would seem, then, that the schism had not reached the point of sepa-

---

177. See Richardson, *Christianity* 78–81; and Corwin, *Ignatius* 52–61. Rathke, *Ignatius* 85, remains undecided; he simply notes that Bauer and Maurer held for only one heresy, while Bartsch and von Harnack held for two. A similar reserve is shown by Paulsen, *Studien* 143–44.

178. Because they are not mentioned with frequency (explicitly only in *Magnesians* and *Philadelphians*), the exact nature of the Judaizers remains obscure. *Philadelphians* 6:1 may indicate that some Judaizers were actually uncircumcised Gentiles. The debate between the relative priority and authority of the OT and the gospel in *Philadelphians* 8:2 reminds one of Matthew's problematic of the *kaina kai palaia* (the new and the old: Matt 13:52 and 9:17). Corwin's view (*Ignatius* 61) that the Judaizers stem from Essene Jews who had fled to Antioch and were attracted to Christianity lacks adequate proof. See footnote 432 below.

179. So Corwin, *Ignatius* 54; see Schoedel, "Theological Norms."

rate, organized churches. Rather, Ignatius had inherited, in a more developed form, the tensions present in the Antiochene church from the days of Peter and Matthew. In short, we can say that, for all the differences and radical changes, links between the Antioch of Matthew and the Antioch of Ignatius are still discernible. The church of Ignatius of Antioch is not a totally new creation, springing up out of nothingness.

B. The Didache

Throughout this treatment of the question of Christianity at Antioch, only passing references have been made to the *Didache*. The reason for this is that the problem of the date and place of composition for the final form of the *Didache*—to say nothing of its complicated tradition history, especially with regard to the Doctrine of the Two Ways—is still hotly debated among scholars.[180] From a methodological viewpoint, therefore, it is unwise to introduce the *Didache* into a hypothesis resting on three groups of documents (Galatians [supplemented by Acts], Matthew, and the letters of Ignatius) for which the dating and place of origin can be fixed with a higher degree of probability.

To be sure, no one denies that the *Didache* evidences obvious contacts with Matthean traditions.[181] As usual, the debate revolves around whether the *Didache* knew and/or used the written gospel of

---

180. To sample opinions: The place is *Syria* for Altaner, Audet, Köster, Quasten and Streeter (or Palestine); and *Egypt* for Glover, Kraft (final redaction), Vokes (or Syria), and Vööbus. The date is A.D. 50–70 for most of the Two Ways (Audet); late first century for major redaction (Giet); *ca.* 100 (R. E. Brown, Streeter [except interpolations]); after 100 for final redaction (Kraft); 100–150 (Altaner, Köster); not before 150 for some parts (Layton); and 175–200 (Vokes). Moreover, there are different theories on how *Didache* developed and was interpolated. Köster, for instance, distinguishes five individual sections. Such diversity of opinions would make the use of the *Didache* for the construction of my hypothesis hazardous. For similar methodological reasons, I have avoided making the basic hypothesis dependent on the *Ascension of Isaiah,* the *Ascents of James,* the *Epistle of Barnabas,* the pseudo-Clementine literature, and the *Epistola Apostolorum.*

181. Cf. Köster, *Überlieferung* 159–241, for a full treatment of the parallels; Streeter, *Gospels* 507–11; Massaux, "L'influence." See Glover, "Didache's Quotations."

Matthew.[182] Simply from the theological slant of some of the *Didache*
material parallel to Matthew, it seems more likely that the *Didache,*
at least in its final form, is later than Matthew's gospel and uses the
gospel. In some of the material paralleling Matthew, there is a falling
away from the intense, uncompromising radicalism of Matthew's
moral vision. One need only compare the tone of the Sermon on the
Mount in Matthew 5–7 with the accommodating remark at the end
of the Doctrine of the Two Ways: "For if you can bear the whole
yoke of the Lord, you will be perfect; but if you cannot, do what you
can" (*Didache* 6:2). One is reminded, by way of contrast, of Matt
5:48 ("You are therefore to be perfect, as your heavenly Father is
perfect") and Matt 11:28–30 ("Take my yoke upon you . . . for my
yoke is easy, my burden light").[183]

According to Matthew, Christian pious practices such as fasting, while recommended, are to be carefully purged of the ostenta-
tion and legalism of the "hypocrites" (Matt 6:1–18). The *Didache,*
while rejecting the fasts of the "hypocrites" on Mondays and Thurs-
days, falls into the same sort of legalism by stipulating fasts on
Wednesdays and Fridays (*Didache* 8:1). The difference between Judaism and Christianity in fasting is reduced to a matter of dates rather than of a total conversion of religious outlook. Rubrical concerns
and expansions have grown up around Matthean liturgical material:
the triadic formula of baptism (Matt 28:19, "baptizing them in the
name of the Father, and of the Son, of the Holy Spirit") is followed
by a discussion about what sort of water is to be used (*Didache* 7:1–2:
preferably cold, running water, though other water may be used

---

182. Interestingly, Köster, who regularly argues against use of a written gospel in
the early Apostolic Fathers, is nuanced on *Didache:* "The result, therefore, is that the
compiler of the *Didache* already knew a written gospel, but did not use it himself;
rather, he only referred to it. That written gospels (Matthew and Luke) were already
used at the time of the *Didache* as collections of the Lord's sayings is proven by their
use in *Did.* 1, 3ff. The *Didache* therefore presupposes the existence of the Synop-
tics. . ." (*Überlieferung* 240). Glover, "Didache's Quotations" 13, holds that the *Didache* does not use our gospels but rather the *written* sources of Luke and Matthew
(contrast Köster's stress on *oral* tradition). Emphatic in their insistence that the *Didache* did know and use Matthew's gospel are Massaux, "L'influence" 40–41; Layton,
"Sources" 369–70 (for the *Didache* 1:3b – 2:1); Vokes, *Riddle* 115, 119, and 208.

183. Here I disagree with Stuiber, "Das ganze Joch," who argues that *Didache*
6:2–3 is an addition to the Teaching of the Two Ways by a Jewish author who is trying
to attract Gentiles to Diaspora Judaism.

when necessary). The Matthean form of the Lord's Prayer (Matt 6:9–13) is concluded with a doxology and a command to recite the prayer three times a day (*Didache* 8:2–3). From such internal considerations, it seems that the moral and liturgical material, at least in its redacted form, is later than Matthew and represents a decline from Matthew's radicalism.

If the final form of the *Didache* is later than Matthew, then it seems impossible to place this final form at Antioch in Syria. In the *Didache* resident bishops and deacons (nothing is said about elders or presbyters) are beginning to replace the itinerant prophets and teachers as instructors in the faith and as liturgical officers. The *Didache* has to urge that the bishops and deacons be respected on a level of equality with the prophets and teachers. Since, as we have seen, one has to posit the beginning of the tripartite hierarchy of one bishop, a college of elders, and deacons at Antioch around A.D. 100, the embryonic two-tier hierarchy of the final form of the *Didache* must be placed elsewhere.[184]

For all these reasons, it is not advisable to call on the *Didache* to help fill in the picture of the development of the Antiochene church from Barnabas through Matthew to Ignatius. If, however, the *Didache* does come from somewhere in Syria (instead of Egypt, as some claim), then one should note the interesting parallel between a "church order" originally dependent on prophets and teachers who perform the liturgy (*Didache* 15:1–1; cf. 10:7) and the early structure of prophets and teachers at Antioch. The similarity in the order and choice of words is striking. Acts 13:1–2 reads: "Prophets and teachers . . . while they were worshiping [*leitourgountōn*]"; *Didache* 15:1 reads: "For you, they [i.e., the bishops and deacons] too conduct [*leitourgousi*] the liturgy [or 'service,' *leitourgian*] of the prophets and teachers." Yet, by the time of the Matthean church, there seems to be a fairly stable group of teachers at Antioch with a scholarly bent, not exactly the itinerant, charismatic, and sometimes money-hungry prophets and teachers who form the older type of church order in the *Didache*. The difference is quite understandable if Matthew's church order grew up in cosmopolitan Antioch, while the *Didache's*

---

184. The surprising lack of any concern about a docetic crisis would also argue for some place other than Ignatius' Antioch.

church order represents a more rural situation.[185] It may be, then, that the *Didache* represents a primitive church order, also seen in Acts 13:1–2, which was preserved in its original form in some churches in Syria for a much longer time than it was preserved at Antioch. While even in the second century the church reflected in the *Didache* is only beginning to see a resident two-tier hierarchy replace the older form of itinerant prophets and teachers, the church at Antioch is already accustomed to the three-tier hierarchy of Ignatius.

We are left with something of a paradoxical situation: while some of the theological and liturgical traditions of the *Didache* show expansion upon and perhaps decline from those of Matthew's gospel, the church structure remains more primitive than that of Ignatius. Perhaps the one point of relevance for our study of the Antiochene church is the possibility that at the very end of the first century the college of prophets and teachers at Antioch developed briefly into a two-tier system of bishops (or elders) and deacons as a transitional stage on the way to the threefold hierarchy. But, while it is a possibility suggested by the data in the *Didache,* it must remain a pure surmise. We cannot be certain exactly how the college of prophets and teachers in the Matthean church evolved into the Ignatian system of bishop, elders, and deacons.

---

185. So Kraft, *Apostolic Fathers,* 3.77: "Probably it [the *Didache*] also comes from a semirural rather than a large urban environment—thus the itinerant ministry, the basically agricultural-pastoral symbolism and economy (esp. ch. 13), although 'trades' are also in view (12:3f.)."

CHAPTER V

Summary—Peter, Matthew, Ignatius, and The Struggle For a Middle Position

OUR study has shown how important Syrian Antioch was for the development of Christianity in its first hundred years. If in later patristic history Antioch proves to be a center of both Christian theology, exegesis, and church power, a center that affects the church throughout the whole of the Roman Empire, the seeds of its subsequent lofty status are already present in the first century. It is at Antioch that the disciples are first called Christians. It is at Antioch that the first organized circumcision-free mission to the Gentiles is undertaken. It is from Antioch, with its embryonic theology, structures, and liturgy, that Paul goes forth on his mission. It is at Antioch that traditions about Peter as the rallying point of church unity are fostered. It is at Antioch that Matthew overcomes a basic crisis in the church's identity and role by drawing together divergent traditions into the masterful theological synthesis of his gospel, the Synoptic gospel favored by the second-century church. It is at Antioch, in and perhaps before the tenure of Ignatius, that a new challenge to church unity is met with the three-tier hierarchy. It is at Antioch that Ignatius develops a theological synthesis, holding to the unity of the divine and human in Christ and holding to the unity of the local church and of the church catholic (*hē katholikē ekklēsia*). Peter, Matthew, and Ignatius all had to undertake a delicate balancing act between left and right as they struggled for a middle position in what was to become this universal church.

It was also from Syrian Antioch that both the gospel of Matthew and the theological justification of the monarchical (single) episcopate moved out into the larger Christian community spreading throughout the Roman Empire. Both that gospel and that hierarchy were to have a decisive effect on the Christian church in the second century—and indeed, in all subsequent centuries. Matthew's gospel, the gospel most cited or alluded to by second-century Fathers, was to have a significant impact on the christology and ecclesiology of the later church. Its resonant, rhythmic language and its carefully structured pericopes were especially suited to liturgy and catechesis. And so it is no wonder that the Matthean form of the Lord's Prayer and the beatitudes, to cite but two examples, triumphed in both formal church teaching and popular piety. In this sense, it is fitting that it became "the first gospel" in the canon, and in the memories and hearts of many Christians.

Likewise, by the end of the second century, the single-bishop form of government had triumphed in the major churches of the Roman Empire. In this joint triumph of Matthew's gospel and the three-tier hierarchy there may be a historical irony. Reading Matthew's strictures against clericalism in Matt 23:1–12, one wonders what the evangelist would have thought if he had seen the victorious march of both his gospel and the theology of the monarchical episcopate throughout the churches of the Roman Empire, as the twin gifts of the church at Antioch. My own guess is that the underlying passion present in both Matthew and Ignatius, the passion for drawing together and synthesizing divergent theological traditions and structures for the sake of Christian unity, would have reconciled the great liberal-conservative evangelist to the new wine skins demanded by the new wine, provided both new and old were properly preserved.

One final surmise may be in order as we conclude this treatment of Antioch and move on to Rome. We have ended our survey of Christian Antioch with Ignatius, writing his letters as he is led to Rome for martyrdom. Could it be that it was from the revered martyr Ignatius that the Roman church first learned about Antioch's twin gifts to the Christian world: the monarchical episcopate and the gospel of Matthew? Up until the time of Ignatius it seems that the Roman church had known neither contribution. Perhaps the martyred bishop from Antioch bequeathed to Rome more than a personal example of courage. With such a surmise—and it can be nothing more than a surmise—let us turn to study the Roman church.

PART TWO

<u>ROME</u>

by
Raymond E. Brown

W E HAVE SEEN that Antioch was the first great city of the Roman Empire to become a center of the Christian movement, and in that sense could be called the cradle of worldwide Christianity. We have far less information in the NT about the origins of the church in Rome, although a case will be made that Christianity came to the capital of the Empire in the early 40s and thus no more than a decade later than Christianity came to Antioch. We have no convincing evidence that either Antioch or Rome was a church founded by a well-known apostle, but strangely Peter and Paul played a significant role in both. In Chapter II above, John Meier showed that the struggle between Peter and Paul at Antioch had serious implications for the future of Paul's ministry as he withdrew from that city, and also for the future direction of (Petrine) Christianity in Antioch. As for Rome, we do not know when Peter came there. Paul came as a prisoner in the early 60s—an arrival after a long and perilous sea journey that Luke announces with masterful understatement, "And so we came to Rome" (Acts 28:14). More important than the coming of either apostle was the fact that both were martyred in Rome in the mid-60s.[186] Thus Peter and Paul whose theological ways had parted at Antioch were joined in their final witness to Christ in Rome. This meant that the church in the capital of the Empire could claim the

---

186. For the factuality of this martyrdom, see p. 124 below. It is not important for our purposes to debate the exact year of the martyrdom (within the range 64 to 67), or which apostle died first—the ancient traditions give conflicting reports. See O'Connor, *Peter.*

heritage of the two most prominent apostles known to us from the NT. The prominence thereby achieved was already an essential part of the Roman story within thirty years of the event; for the twofold apostolic witness would be mentioned *ca.* A.D. 96 by Clement writing from Rome (5:3–5), and a decade or two later by Ignatius writing to Rome (4:3). Simplifying the relation of Peter and Paul to the development of the Roman church, Irenaeus (*Adv. haer.* 3.3.3) a century after the martyrdom could speak of Peter and Paul *founding* the Roman church. Ultimately such a distinguished base in apostolic martyrdom would play no small role in making Rome the most prominent episcopal see in the church catholic.

Essential to the discussion that follows will be an analysis of the kind of Christianity that came first to Rome and took root there. From Roman, Jewish, and Christian sources I shall attempt to show that the dominant form of Christianity at Rome in the 40s and early 50s was probably one close to Jerusalem and Judaism (Chapter VI). Then, as was done with Antioch, the story of the Roman church will be carried through three generations (footnote 16 above). Towards the end of the *first generation* (*ca.* 58) we have the letter of Paul to the Romans which can test the reconstruction of early Roman Christianity just mentioned (Chapter VII). At the beginning of the *third generation* (*ca.* 96) we have a letter written from Rome to Corinth by Clement, a letter that expresses Roman ideals in reference to how a Christian community should function (Chapter IX). Just as with Antioch, the principal problem concerns the *second or in-between generation,* covering most of the last third of the first century. The gap (Chapter VIII) can be filled in with I Peter written from Rome probably *ca.* 80–90, and with the Epistle to the Hebrews possibly written to Christians in Rome sometime after 70. A supplementary chapter (X) will consider evidence from a half-dozen other works that may help to fill in the picture, in part by tracing the trajectory of Roman Christianity into the second century. Nevertheless, my main concentration will be on the four works, Romans, I Peter, Hebrews, and *I Clement,* and the likelihood that they show a consistent Christianity in a forty-year period (58–96)—a Jewish/Gentile Christianity more conservative in its preservation of the Jewish Law and cult than the Christianity of Paul in Galatians. Indeed, as with Antioch, so also with Rome, this Jewish/Gentile Christianity can plausibly be related to the image of Peter. The Paul of Romans (milder than the Paul of Galatians) was ultimately associated with the developed Petrine trajectory, so that Peter and (a somewhat domesticated) Paul could serve in that order as "pillars" in the developing church catholic (*I Clem.* 5:2).

CHAPTER VI

The Beginnings of Christianity at Rome

B ECAUSE we do not have direct evidence on this topic and must infer from passing references, it is wise to begin with a brief summary of the history of Judaism in Rome, and then turn to how Christians may have fitted into the picture.[187] That background will enable us to speculate intelligently on the type of Christianity that may have flourished at Rome.

JUDAISM IN ROME

With understandable exaggeration, the Jewish historian Josephus, writing toward the end of the first century of the common era, boasts: "There is not a community in the entire world which does not have a portion of our people" (*War* 2.16.4; #398). Certainly there were large Jewish colonies in the main cities of the Empire, and far more Jews in the diaspora (area outside Palestine) than in Judea and Galilee. Commercial cities seem to have had the greatest attraction for Jewish migration, and because of that Jews came to Rome long after they were a major factor in Alexandria and Babylon. It must be remembered that Rome's power was not initially based on commerce, for the initiators of Roman expansion were hard-headed Italian farmers who learned to be soldiers. Ironically, as Rome became a world power, its own agriculture went into decline; and the

---

187. As stressed by Gager, *Kingdom* 128ff., diaspora Judaism offered a blueprint for Christian adaptation to the Greco-Roman world. A knowledge of the former is essential for understanding the latter. That this applies to Rome in particular is shown brilliantly by Wiefel, "Jewish."

native Romans came to depend on an inflow of the wealth and produce of the world that could be brought up the Tiber to the last navi-
gable landing, which is Rome. In that development Jews came to
Rome—the first city in Europe known to have had a Jewish presence. Some came as captives or slaves from Roman campaigns in the
eastern Mediterranean area;[188] others came as merchants.

Our oldest reference to Jews in Rome is dated *ca.* 139 B.C. when
the praetor Gnaeus Cornelius Hispanus "compelled the Jews . . . to
go back to their own homes."[189] An attempt has been made to associate this action with the embassy that had been sent to Rome by Simon Maccabeus, the Jewish royal high priest, *ca.* 140 B.C. (I Macc
14:24). In any case, the reference to going back to their native country may indicate that sojourners or merchants rather than Roman
residents were involved.[190] Certainly by the early part of the next century there were many Jewish immigrants, a number enlarged by the
captives brought to Rome by Pompey in 61 B.C. after his conquest of
Palestine. The importance of the Jewish colony in Rome was attested
in 59 B.C. as Cicero defended in court a prestigious scoundrel, Lucius
Valerius Flaccus, whose administration in the Roman province of
Asia had been marked by a large accumulation of personal wealth.
In particular, he was accused of stealing gold from the Jews. Cicero,
a member of the Optimates or aristocratic party at Rome, had no
reason to love the Jews who favored the Populares or people's party
and eventually supported Julius Caesar. In the trial Cicero used anti-
Semitic prejudice to support his client: "You know how large a
group they are, how unanimously they stick together, how influential
they are in politics. I shall lower my voice and speak just loudly
enough for the jury to hear me; for there are plenty of people to stir

---

188. Philo, *De legatione ad Gaium* 23 #155, states that at Rome most of the
Jews lived in the Trans-Tiber region and were emancipated captives who were not Roman citizens.

189. Reported by Valerius Maximus, *Factorum ac dictorum memorabilium*
1.3.2—an account written two centuries later in the time of Tiberius and preserved in
epitomes. The section concerned deals with the rejection of foreign religion: Hispanus
is said to have banished Chaldean astrologers, and the epitome of Julius Paris adds the
reference to the Jews. The charge against them involved proselytism to the worship of
Jupiter Sabazius; it may represent Roman confusion between the worship of Yahweh
Sabaoth and a Phrygian cult.

190. See Leon, *Jews* 3–4. This work is a model of sobriety in evaluating the evidence, and for this chapter I am greatly indebted to it. Helpful also is Penna, "Juifs."

up those Jews against me and against every good Roman."[191] Even if we allow for oratorical exaggeration, Cicero's "grandstanding" would make no sense unless there was in Rome a considerable Jewish presence of some political import.

The Jewish support of Caesar, and the luck of the Herod family in Judea in ultimately opting for the winning side in the wars that followed Caesar's assassination[192] brought Jews special privileges (Josephus, *Antiquities* 14.10.1–8; #185–216). These included relaxation of rules governing the *collegia* or private associations, so that Jews could freely assemble for cultic or common meals. They had permission to raise money for the support of the Jerusalem Temple, exemption from military service, and their own courts. Although there was some prejudice against them in the capital (as witnessed in Horace's sarcasm about the credulousness of Jewish religion), by the first century A.D. there were some 40,000–50,000 Jews in Rome.[193] An expulsion of Jews from Rome that occurred under Tiberius in A.D. 19 may well have been sparked by the increasing success of Jewish proselytism, converting even a lady of senatorial family.[194] Aelius Sejanus, a virtual dictator under Tiberius, conducted an active anti-Jewish cam-

---

191. Cicero, *Pro Flacco* 28 #66–67.

192. Suetonius, *Julius* 84.5, reports how greatly the Jews mourned the death of Caesar. The synagogues of the Augustesians and Agrippesians were named after the Emperor Augustus and his son-in-law, Marcus Agrippa.

193. Leon, *Jews* 15. Penna, "Juifs" 328, gives the lowest count I have seen: 20,000 at the time of Nero. Although they occupied the Trans-Tiber area, there were fewer Jews in Rome than in Alexandria, where Jewry occupied two of the five districts and numbered hundreds of thousands. (See Lieberman, "Response" 122–28; he points out, however, that relatively little is known of Alexandrian Jewry and that much of its literature was preserved by Christians.) Edmundson, *Church* 7, estimates that there were about 4,500,000 Jews amid a total empire population of 54 to 60 million, or one out of every thirteen people. Leon, *Jews* 135, reports estimates of 6 to 7 million Jews in the empire, plus a million in Babylon; but such estimates are very uncertain.

194. In this deportation Judaism again seems to have been mixed up with an Oriental cult (Isis). About 4000 Jews were conscripted for military service in Sardinia, and *the rest* were supposed to have been expelled from Italy. But since Jews who were Roman citizens could not have been expelled without a trial, Leon, *Jews* 18–19, suggests that only foreign Jews were involved. For an astute analysis of the conflicting accounts of Josephus (*Antiquities* 18.3.5; #81–84), Tacitus (*Annals* 2.85.5), Suetonius (*Tiberius* 36), and Cassius Dio (*History* 57.18.5a), see E. Mary Smallwood, "Some Notes on the Jews under Tiberius," *Latomus* 15 (1956) 314–29. She opts for the year 19 with Tacitus and Cassius Dio (not 31 with Josephus), and for proselytism as the cause with Cassius Dio (and not mere fraud with Josephus).

paign at Rome[195] before his political fall in A.D. 31. Early in his reign (41–54) Claudius rebuked the Jews of Alexandria for fomenting sedition but reaffirmed the special privileges of the Jews. The expulsion of Jews from Rome *ca.* 49 will be discussed below. Nero's second wife, Poppaea, was favorable to Judaism and may even have been converted (Josephus, *Antiquities* 20.8.11; #195). Even during the Jewish revolt in Palestine against Rome in the late 60s Jewry in Rome does not seem to have been troublesome, for not a single hostile action by the Roman government in the capital is reported at this period. After the fall of Jerusalem Vespasian did not revoke the privileges enjoyed by the Jews, except that the money formerly levied for the support of the Jerusalem Temple was now converted into a poll tax on the Jews (*fiscus judaicus*) for the support of the Temple of Jupiter Capitolinus in Rome. Titus, who captured Jerusalem and destroyed the Temple, thought of making Berenice, his Jewish mistress, empress of Rome and was dissuaded only when threatened with the resentment of the Roman aristocracy.[196] Domitian, although more rigorous than his predecessors in enforcing the *fiscus judaicus,* never revoked the other ancient Jewish privileges.

A particular aspect of Roman Judaism deserves special attention, namely, its close political and intellectual affiliation with Jerusalem and Palestine. As Leon (*Jews* 240) points out, most of the Jewish residents in Rome had originally come as immigrants or captives from the Palestine/Syria area, as far as can be discerned from the available evidence. The Maccabean/Hasmonean high priests of Jerusalem initiated Jewish contact with Rome some 140 years before Christ. The later Hasmonean priests supported Julius Caesar against Pompey, and the Judean king Herod the Great eventually became an ally of Octavian Augustus. After the death of Herod the Great, the kings in Jerusalem or tetrarchs in Palestine were appointed (or removed) with the acquiescence of Rome. The close bond between the Herodian family and the Caesars was cemented by the rearing of the Herodian princes in the imperial court as personal friends of the future emperors. Thus, in the late 30s and early 40s A.D. a kingdom in Palestine rivaling that of his grandfather (Herod the Great) was giv-

---

195. Philo, *De legatione ad Gaium* 24 #159–60.
196. Cassius Dio, *History* 66.15.4; Suetonius, *Titus* 7.1–2.

en to Herod Agrippa I through the patronage of his friends Caligula and Claudius. The Jewish historian Josephus, after the fall of Jerusalem, lived out his life in Rome as a client of the Flavian Emperors, whence his adopted name Flavius. The emperor Titus brought to Rome in the 70s the Jewish king Agrippa II and his sister Berenice who became Titus' mistress.

Intellectually, even after the destruction of Jerusalem by the Romans, there was a constant interchange between Palestinian Judaism and Roman Judaism.[197] During the reign of Domitian (81–96) four famous rabbis are supposed to have come from Palestine to Rome to preach in the synagogues and debate with pagans and Christians: Rabban Gamaliel, Joshua ben Hananiah, Eleazar ben Azariah, and Aqiba.[198] The Talmud speaks of Todos (Theudas, Theodoros?), a Palestinian sage who taught in Rome and was spiritual leader there, probably in Hadrian's time (117–138). He instituted the practice whereby the Jews of Rome ate a roasted lamb the first night of Passover, a practice objected to by Palestinian rabbis: "Were you not Todos, we would put you under the ban" (Babylonian Talmud, *Pesahim* 53a). Later Midrashim (*Canticle Rabbah* 8:5; *Psalms* 28:2) preserve the memory of Paltion who continued in the footsteps of Todos and served as a Palestinian teacher in Rome. During the reign of Antoninus Pius (138–161), the Roman school of the Palestinian Matthias ben Heresh was respected by the Palestinian rabbis; but famous rabbis still came from Palestine to Rome to give guidance on spiritual matters, e.g., Simeon ben Johai and Eliezer ben Jose.[199]

Although most of the Jewish evidence given above pertaining to Jerusalem's intellectual and spiritual influence on Rome dates from the period after the fall of Jerusalem (A.D. 70), there is an interesting Christian confirmation in Acts 28:21, written in the 80s but describing a situation in early 60s. When Paul gets to Rome, he is met by the local leaders of the Jews who say to him, "We have received no

---

197. Lieberman, "Response" 129–31: "We must not forget the influence of the Palestinian scholars on the life of the Roman Jewish community." He points out that Palestinian Jewry seems to have had more respect for Roman Jewry than for that of Alexandria.

198. Leon, *Jews* 35–36. The text of Jerus. Talmud *Sanhedrin* 7(14):19 (ed. Venice 25d) may point to Eliezer ben Hyrcanus, instead of Eleazar.

199. Leon, *Jews* 38.

letters from Judea about you"—an implicit indication from Luke
that Roman Jewry looked to Jerusalem for guidance.

Christianity in Rome

Date. The story of the prominent Jewish community at Rome
has been narrated to make intelligible the suspicion that it would not
have been long before Jews who believed in Jesus and who were making converts in other cities of the Empire, like Damascus and Antioch, made their way to such a promising missionary field.[200] To
determine more precisely the date of the advent of Christianity in
Rome we must proceed backwards from the first datable references.

But before I begin that task, I wish to dispose of a question that
has haunted the study of Roman Christianity, namely, *unverifiable
evidence* about Peter and Paul at Rome. That the two apostles were
in Rome is relatively clear from Ignatius, *Rom.* 4:3, who refers to Peter and Paul giving orders to the Romans. From *I Clement* and other
(later) evidence it is generally admitted that Peter and Paul died in
Rome (A.D. 64–67) as martyrs in the persecution of Christians under
Nero. Indeed, it is plausible that Peter died by crucifixion in the Circus of Nero south of Vatican Hill (in which vicinity he was buried)
and Paul died by beheading on the Ostian Way, as commemorated
by subsequent churches and shrines.[201] As for the career of the apostles at Rome before the martyrdom, there is no reason to doubt the
information in Acts 28 that Paul came to Rome for the first time as a
prisoner *ca.* 61 and remained there in prison for at least two years

---

200. The practice ascribed in Acts to Paul of first going to the Jews of an area
and only later (sometimes after rejection) to the Gentiles is quite plausible and receives
some confirmation from Romans' reiterated "Jews first, then Gentiles" (1:16; 2:9–10).

201. Under the main altar of St. Peter's basilica has been discovered the *tropaeum* or *tropaion* (commemorative shrine) mentioned by Gaius, a Roman presbyter
(?), about A.D. 200: "I can point out the trophies of the apostles; for if you go to the
Vatican or to the Ostian Way, you will find the trophies of those who founded this
church" (Eusebius, *Hist.* 2.25.7). However, the *tropaeum* marks the place where the
death and burial were honored, not necessarily the exact place of burial. The claim
that the bones of Peter were found is dubious. See O'Connor, *Peter* 135–206; R. T.
O'Callaghan, BA 12 (1949) 1–23; 16 (1953) 70–87; and G. F. Snyder, BA 32 (1969) 1–
24; Walsh, *Bones.*

(till 63). We have no accurate knowledge of Paul's relation to Rome between that imprisonment and the time of his death.[202] As for Peter, we have no knowledge at all of when he came to Rome and what he did there before he was martyred. Certainly he was *not* the original missionary who brought Christianity to Rome (and therefore *not* the founder of the church of Rome in that sense). There is no serious proof that he was the bishop (or local ecclesiastical officer) of the Roman church—a claim not made till the third century. Most likely he did not spend any major time at Rome before 58 when Paul wrote to the Romans, and so it may have been only in the 60s and relatively shortly before his martyrdom that Peter came to the capital.[203]

The paucity of hard evidence in the preceding paragraph indicates why in studying the history of Roman Christianity we do not turn first to the Peter and Paul stories, but rather to the more general information supplied by the Roman historian Tacitus (*Annals* 15.44). While Nero was away from the capital in A.D. 64, beginning on July 19th and lasting for nine days, the greatest fire in Rome's history broke out and destroyed in whole or in part ten of Rome's fourteen districts. Nero quickly returned to the city and began the attempt to rebuild Rome from the ashes. Despite the imperial munificence in this rebuilding, the sinister suspicion that the Emperor himself had instigated the fire could not be eliminated (and still troubled Tacitus over fifty years later). Thus some months after the fire:

> To suppress this rumor Nero created scapegoats. He punished with every refinement of cruelty the notoriously depraved group who were popularly called Christians. The originator of the group, Christ, had been executed in the reign of Tiberius by the procurator, Pontius Pilate. But, in spite of this temporary setback, this pernicious superstition

---

202. It is generally assumed that he was freed from imprisonment, left Rome for further missionary travels, and ultimately returned for a second imprisonment that led to his death. That the travels were to Spain (Rom 15:24; *I Clem.* 5:7) is more likely than the visit to Asia Minor and Greece that scholars have constructed on the basis of the post-Pauline Pastorals, a visit unknown to the author of Acts (20:25,38).

203. On all these points O'Connor, *Peter* 207, shows excellent judgment: "Nothing can be determined, however, about when he came to Rome, how long he stayed, or what function or leadership, if any, he exercised within the Roman Church."

had broken out again, not only in Judea (where the mischief had originated) but even in the capital city [Rome] where all degraded and shameful practices collect and become the vogue.

First, Nero had self-acknowledged members of this sect arrested. Then, on their information, large numbers [*multitudo ingens*] were condemned—not so much for their arson as for their hatred of the human race. Their deaths were made a farce ... so that despite their guilt [as Christians] and the ruthless punishment they deserved, there arose a sense of pity. For it was felt that they were being sacrificed to one man's brutality rather than to the public interest.

From this description by Tacitus[204] we learn three interesting facts pertinent to the origins of Roman Christianity: (1) by A.D. 64 it was possible to distinguish between Christians and Jews at Rome; for there is no memory of a persecution of Jews by Nero in connection with the fire even though their Trans-Tiber district was not burned and so they could have been plausible scapegoats;[205] (2) There was a large number of Christians in Rome;[206] (3) Even pagans made a connection between Christianity in Rome and its origin in Judea.

If there were many Christians in Rome in the mid-60s, how much before that time had faith in Christ arrived on the scene? Paul's letter to the Romans, usually dated *ca.* A.D. 58, implies that the Christian community in Rome had already been in existence for a considerable period of time, since Paul says he has been wishing "for many years" to visit (15:23). That this span of time is not pure

---

204. *Annals* 15.44. In discussing this difficult text, Fuchs, "Tacitus" 69–73, argues on textual and logical grounds that the original read: "popularly called Chrestians [*Chrestianos*]." Tacitus, because of his own career in Asia, knew the correct spelling; but the populace connected this group with the riots in Rome fifteen years earlier "at the instigation of Chrestus." See footnote 208 below.

205. It has been suggested that such a move was blocked by the pro-Jewish sentiments of Nero's wife Poppaea.

206. The *multitudo ingens* of Tacitus cannot be dismissed simply as narrative exaggeration; for *I Clement,* in connection with the deaths of Peter and Paul which had occurred in the author's own generation (5:1–2), writes of a great multitude (*poly plēthos*) of the chosen who suffered and were gathered to join the two apostles (6:1).

rhetoric is suggested by Paul's gratitude to God that "the faith of the Romans is being reported all over the world" (1:8). Such flattery would be absurd if he were writing to a weak community recently founded. Thus the Roman community must have existed by the early 50s.

Evidence in Acts 18:2–3 suggests that we must move the date back still farther. There we are told that when Paul came to Corinth (A.D. 49–50), he found lodging with Aquila and Priscilla, a Jewish couple "who had recently come from Italy because Claudius had ordered all Jews to leave Rome." Almost certainly Aquila and Priscilla were Jews who already believed in Jesus and came from Rome as Christian Jews. They are subsequently described as Christian missionaries and their conversion by Paul is never reported—a strange silence if they had become Christians after Paul came to live with them. Moreover, granting that this couple had just been expelled from Rome (because of inner Jewish fights as we shall see), it is most dubious that if they were not Christians, they would have exposed themselves to possible trouble in their new residence by offering hospitality to a Jewish Christian missionary who was stirring up the synagogues.

The presence of Christian Jews in Rome in the 40s could explain a tantalizing statement by Suetonius, *Claudius* 25.4, that Claudius "expelled Jews from Rome because of their constant disturbances impelled by Chrestus [*impulsore Chresto*]." Suetonius' phrasing would make one think that Chrestus or Chrestos was a troublemaker among the Jews in Rome. The name is attested as a Roman name,[207] but how would a pagan Roman have caused such internal friction among Jews as to cause expulsion? If one theorizes that Chrestus might have been a Jew, among the several hundred names of Roman Jews known from the Jewish catacombs and other sources, no instance of "Chrestus" appears. On the other hand, in the second century (the period when Suetonius was writing), both "Christus" (Christ) and "Christianus" (Christian) were often written

---

207. In the *Corpus Inscriptionum Latinarum* 6.10233 the name P. Aelius Chrestus appears (A.D. 211). Prof. Morton Smith has pointed out to me *Chrēstos* as a nickname *ca.* 340 B.C. in Plutarch's *Life of Phocion* 10.2 (see 10.5).

with an "e" instead of an "i" following the "r."[208] One wonders whether Suetonius might not be giving us a garbled memory of struggles among the Jews over Christ. The possibility that Roman Jewry could be so divided springs from the fact that, unlike the Jews in Antioch and Alexandria, the Roman Jews seemingly had no centralized control. For instance, in Alexandria the government of the Jewish community was entrusted to a *gerousia* (or committee of *archons* representing the several synagogues) presided over by an ethnarch.[209] Similarly, the Jewry of Antioch was presided over by a type of ethnarch (see p. 31 above). But the Jews of Rome, attending some dozen different synagogues, had no single spokesperson or overall ruling body.[210] This means that Christian preachers could have made headway in individual synagogues, without meeting concerted resistance. If some synagogues accepted with tolerance the proclamation that Jesus was the Messiah while others rejected it, there may very well have been a squabble among the Roman Jews over Christ and no centralized authority to settle it. From his treatment of the Jews in Alexandria, we know that Claudius would not have tolerated such dissension; and Tiberius had already given him the precedent of ex-

---

208. See F. Blass, *Hermes* 30 (1893) 465–70; H. Janne, *Annuaire de l'Institut de Philologie et d'Histoire Orientales* 2 (1934—Mélanges Bidez) 531–53; and Fuchs, "Tacitus" 71. Tertullian, *Apologeticum* 3.5 (CC 1.92) and Lactantius, *Divinae institutiones* 4.7 (PL 6.464–65) comment on the ignorant pronunciation of "Christus" as "Chrestus." Yet Codex Sinaiticus used *Chrest-* for *Christ-* in Acts 11:26; 26:28; I Peter 4:16.

209. See Appelbaum, "Organization" 474. Also E. Schürer, *A History of the Jewish People in the Time of Jesus Christ* (5 vols.; Edinburgh: Clark, 1885–90) 2.2 §31, pp. 244–45.

210. This was pointed out by E. Schürer, *Die Gemeindeverfassung der Juden in Rom in der Kaiserzeit* (Leipzig: Hinrichs, 1879), but subsequently denied by such competent scholars as J. Juster, G. La Piana, and S. Baron. However, the thesis that the Roman gerousiarch presided over only the council of an individual congregation and that there was no overall ethnarch was carefully argued by Frey, "L'ancien Judaïsme" cvi-cxi. Leon, *Jews* 167–70 accepts the argumentation, as does Appelbaum, "Organization" 498–501. There were some eleven to fifteen synagogues at Rome (Leon, *Jews* 135–66). We should probably abandon attempts to relate the *Eleas* Synagogue (meaning "of the olive") with the reference in Rom 11:17–18 to Gentiles being grafted onto the olive tree of Israel, and the Synagogue "of the Hebrews" with the destination of the Epistle to the Hebrews. The latter may simply have been the first Hebrew (Jewish) meeting place at Rome; the meaning of the former is uncertain since a place name may be involved.

pelling Jews from Rome. Suetonius does not specify the number expelled, but presumably Luke's statement that "Claudius had commanded *all* the Jews to leave Rome" is an exaggeration—this would have been a massive expulsion of some 50,000 people! (The silence of Josephus about the expulsion militates against what would have been a major anti-Jewish episode; and Cassius Dio, *History* 60.6.6., specifically denies a general expulsion of Jews.) It would be more reasonable to assume that Claudius exiled those Jews who were the most vocal on either side of the Christ issue, an action that would explain the expulsion of Aquila and Priscilla whom we know later to have been vigorous Christian missionaries. Neither Suetonius nor Cassius Dio supplies us with enough information to date the expulsion; the later writer Orosius would date it to A.D. 49. Orosius is not famous for his impeccable accuracy,[211] but such a date receives some confirmation from Acts. If we accept it as reasonable, we have persuasive information that by 49 the Christian mission had been in Rome long enough to cause serious friction.

That is as far back as our more convincing evidence takes us. Two other uncertain indications have been used to date Christianity in Rome to the early 40s. The first stems from the report in Acts 12:17 that after his imprisonment at Jerusalem by King Herod Agrippa I (who ruled in Judea 41–44), Peter departed from Jerusalem "and went to another place." Many have speculated that he went to Rome and founded the church there. This idea may be reflected in the chronology of Eusebius and Jerome which gives Peter a twenty-five year stay in Rome (A.D. 42–67).[212] But there are many objections to this thesis: the traditions that Peter founded the church at Rome are late, and there are contradictory traditions.[213] In Paul's flattering letter to the Romans, he never mentions Peter or apostolic

---

211. *Historia adversus Paganos* 7.6.15 (CSEL 5.451) refers to the ninth year of Claudius (41–54, hence 49) but cites for support Josephus, who does not mention the incident!

212. For the literal acceptance of such tradition, see Barnes, *Christianity* xii, 13, 24: Peter arrived in Rome on May 20, 42 and died there June 29, 67! Linus and Cletus were auxiliary bishops who governed Rome when Peter was absent for the Jerusalem meeting in 49–50.

213. See O'Connor, *Peter,* for details.

foundation—items that could have helped his praise of Roman faith. Luke is fascinated by Peter's missionary activities and is greatly interested in the faith getting to Rome as a symbolic goal—it is almost inconceivable that if he knew Peter had gone to Rome at the time described in Acts 12:17, he would not have mentioned it. Christianity may well have reached Rome in 42 (and hence given rise to the misunderstanding that Peter, who helped to "found" the church by dying there in the 60s, had already come in 42); but we do not know who brought it. The likelihood is that Peter did not become a major figure in the Roman church for two more decades. The second item sometimes used to date the beginnings of Roman Christianity concerns Pomponia Graecina, wife of Aulus Plautius the conqueror of Britain (Tacitus, *Annals* 13.32). She was judged and found innocent by her husband on the charge of "foreign superstition." After the murder of Julia, daughter of Drusas, through the intrigues of Messalina, Pomponia wore the attire of a mourner for 40 years. It has been calculated that she would have gone into mourning about A.D. 43, and some have wondered whether she did not adopt the newly arrived Christianity and its asceticism. In the catacomb of Callistus an inscription mentions Pomponius Graecinus and suggests that later some members of the family were remembered as Christian. Nevertheless, the evidence for Pomponia as a Roman Christian in the early 40s is largely by inference, and the "foreign superstition" could have been Judaism or another Oriental religion.[214] Thus the contention that Christianity reached Rome in the early 40s remains an unverifiable probability; that it had reached Rome by the late 40s or early 50s is virtually certain.

Origin. What was the origin of Roman Christianity? According to Acts, for the first two Christian decades, Jerusalem and Antioch served as the dissemination points of the Gospel. Because of his interest in Paul, the author keeps us well informed of missions to the West moving out from Antioch, but there is never a suggestion that a mission went from Antioch to Rome. (Indeed, in the first 15 chapters of Acts the only mention of Rome/Roman is 2:10 which notes

---

214. For contrary views, see Edmundson, *Church* 85–86, and Leon, *Jews* 252.

the presence of Roman Jews at Jerusalem on the first Pentecost.[215] There are no arguments from Acts for a site other than Jerusalem as the source for Roman Christianity, and Acts 28:21 relates that Jews in Rome had channels of theological information coming from Jerusalem. The picture of Roman Judaism I have given earlier in this chapter shows that the Jerusalem-Rome axis was strong, and Tacitus seems to have thought Christianity came to Rome from Judea.

In the subsequent chapters I shall examine various NT and early Christian works as support for the contention that Roman Christianity came from Jerusalem, and indeed represented the Jewish/Gentile Christianity associated with such Jerusalem figures as Peter and James. The earliest and principal body of Roman Christians, then, would have belonged to what was called Group Two in the Introduction (p. 3 above), namely Christians who kept up some Jewish observances and remained faithful to part of the heritage of the Jewish Law and cult, without insisting on circumcision. It will be my contention that only this type of Christianity makes sense of the first-century Christian works directed to and emanating from Rome.

---

215. It is sheer imagination to contend that these went back to Rome and planted Christianity there immediately after Pentecost. Those described in the list of foreign Jews in Acts 2 were *resident* at Jerusalem; yet the list may be a Lucan theological creation to foreshadow the eventual spread of Christianity from Jerusalem throughout the Roman Empire.

CHAPTER VII

The Roman Church
near the End of the
First Christian Generation

(A.D. 58—Paul to the Romans)

TOWARD the end of the 50s Paul wrote, seemingly from Corinth, "to all the beloved of God in Rome" (Rom 1:7). Although for years he had wanted to go to Rome (1:13; 15:23), Paul would be coming for the first time after taking to the saints in Jerusalem money raised in a collection in Macedonia and Greece (15:25–26). Paul is apprehensive about the reception of this collection in Jerusalem and asks Rome's prayers and help that it may be successful (15:30–31). He hopes to preach the gospel in Rome when he comes (1:15); but evidently he is contemplating only a brief stay, for he is on the way to Spain (15:24,28).[216]

A LETTER SHAPED by ROMAN CHRISTIANITY

All the other undisputed Pauline letters are written to communities evangelized by Paul, and no one doubts that each of those letters shows a knowledge of the church addressed. The fact that Paul

---

216. Note the geographical order: to Jerusalem first, then to Rome, and on to Spain. Did Paul intend to complete the oval and return through North Africa to Jerusalem (J. Knox)? Certainly the progress of the action envisaged in Romans is less linear than in Acts where the overall movement is from Jerusalem to Antioch, then to Cyprus, Asia Minor, and Greece, and to Rome as the climax. I favor the chronology whereby Romans was written in the winter of A.D. 57–58, but nothing in this book is affected by a chronology that dates Romans a year or two earlier.

had never been to the imperial capital and the somewhat general tone of Romans have caused a major debate as to whether Paul knew the situation at Rome and was addressing himself to it in this letter.[217] Obviously the question is of major importance for any attempt to reconstruct Roman church history in NT times.

A preliminary issue concerns chap. 16 of Romans which contains greetings from Paul to some twenty-five named people. If Paul knew so many people in Rome, presumably he knew something about the Roman church. But scholars have argued that he could not have known by name so many people at a church he had never visited, and that the chapter was not originally part of the letter. This theory gains support from sixth-century Latin textual evidence for a 14-chapter form of Romans (a form already known to Tertullian and Origen and thus ca. A.D. 200) and from the third-century Beatty Papyrus 46 as evidence for a 15-chapter form of Romans. Since Prisca and Aquila are named in 16:3 and they are known to have been in Ephesus in the mid-50s (I Cor 16:19; Acts 18:24–26), and since Epaenetus is mentioned in Rom 16:5 as an early convert in Asia, one theory, popular since the last century, is that chap. 16 was originally written to Ephesus as a letter of recommendation[218] for Phoebe (16:1). Indeed, some would suggest that there were two forms of the letter,[219] Rom 1–15 sent to Rome, and Rom 1–15 adapted for Ephesus through the addition of 16.

Although the view that chap. 16 does not belong to Romans has wide following, especially in Germany, the recent study by Harry Gamble has shown comprehensively the weakness of the textual and structural arguments used to support it. Chapter 15 is clearly Pauline and is closely related to 14, and so there are really only two possibili-

---

217. Those who think Romans is not essentially concerned with the situation at Rome (but is a general tractate, or a last will and testament, or a letter to Jerusalem, or a reflection on Paul's own situation in Greece and Asia Minor) include: Bornkamm, Bruce, Cranfield, Dodd, Drane, Karris, J. Knox, J. Lightfoot, T. W. Manson, Michel, Munck, and Nygren. Among those who think there is a major concern with the situation in Rome are: Bartsch, Baur, Beker, Dahl, Donfried, Harder, Jewett, Gamble, Minear, Preisker, and Wiefel.

218. An *epistolē systatikē* or *literae commendaticiae.*

219. This is best developed by T. W. Manson, "St. Paul's Letter to the Romans—and Others," in his *Studies in the Gospels and Epistles,* ed. M. Black (Manchester Univ., 1962) 225–41; reprinted in Donfried, *Romans Debate* 1–16.

ties: a 15-chapter Romans or a 16-chapter form. Not only is there weak textual evidence for the 15-chapter form (weaker than for the 14-chapter form), but the ending of chap. 15 would be anomalous as the conclusion of a Pauline letter. The pattern in 16:17–24 of hortatory wishes, peace, greetings, and grace-benediction is, in content and order, exactly what is to be expected as the conclusion of a Pauline letter.[220] The formal considerations confirm the overwhelming textual evidence in support of chap. 16 as an authentic part of Romans. The contention that 16:1ff. has the appearance of a commendatory letter means nothing as regards the issue under discussion, for frequently notes of commendation were found *within* the conclusions of lengthy ancient letters.[221] As for the number of people greeted in chap. 16, paradoxically the argument that Paul would not send so many greetings to an unfamiliar community is demonstrably wrong. The letters that Paul sent to familiar communities which he had founded do *not* contain extensive greetings to named people, presumably because the already existing relationship does not require special attention to individuals among the recipients. Therefore, the numerous greetings in Rom 16 would not be customary in a letter to a familiar community like Ephesus, but only in one to a community like Rome where the acknowledgment of people known to or by Paul [222] would be of help to Paul as an implicit recommendation—these people were well known among the Roman Christians while Paul was not.

As for those named, it is not implausible that Aquila and Priscilla (Prisca) were in Rome in the late 50s. They had come to Corinth from Rome at the time of Claudius' expulsion of Jews (*ca.* 49) and had a residence there when Paul arrived on the scene *ca.* 50 (Acts 18:2–3). A year and a half later they left Corinth with Paul and went to Ephesus (Acts 18:11,18–19). According to Acts 18:26 and I Cor 16:19 they were still in Ephesus in the year 54 when Paul returned from visiting Jerusalem and Antioch, and in early 57 when he

---

220. Gamble, *Textual History* 84–95.

221. See Chen-Hie Kim, *Form and Structure of the Familiar Letter of Recommendation* (Missoula, Mont.: Scholars Press, 1972); and Gamble, *Textual History* 85.

222. Nothing in chap. 16 forces us to think that Paul had met or traveled with everyone whom he names. See footnote 236 below.

wrote I Corinthians from Ephesus; indeed, they had a church in their house. But in mid-57 riots broke out in Ephesus against Christians, so that Paul left (Acts 19:23 – 20:1). Imitating their procedure at Corinth, Prisca and Aquila may have left at the same time and returned to Rome. (Claudius had died in 54, and the first years of Nero's reign were popular and benevolent—a quinquennium of good government.) Nor is there a problem if, when Paul wrote to Rome in early 58, there was a church congregation meeting at their house, as seemingly in several other households (Rom 16:5,11,14,15), some of them owned by Jewish Christians. Presumably the Jews driven out of Rome in the disputes over Chrestus in 49 would not have lost all their property, and their houses may have been maintained for them by friends. Moreover, it is likely that after 49 Christians of Jewish origin were no longer welcome at many or all Roman synagogues,[223] and their community meetings would have moved to the houses of the better-off Christians. Such a separation may explain why in 64 Nero could distinguish between Christians and Jews, even though both were "foreign superstitions."

Many of the names given in Rom 16 fit the Roman scene quite well. As for "Aristobulus," a grandson of Herod the Great who bore that name seems to have lived out his life at Rome, while a "Narcissus" was a powerful Roman freedman under Claudius. I do not mean that Paul was writing to those individuals, but perhaps to people connected with the households. Indeed, J. B. Lightfoot has shown that the twenty-five names of Rom 16 are attested and hence quite plausible in the Rome of the early Christian centuries.[224] (Of course the names may be plausible elsewhere in the Empire as well, but at least no argument against the Roman direction of chap. 16 can be drawn from them.) Thus, overall the 16-chapter form of Romans has every reason to be considered as original. The 14-chapter and 15-

---

223. A possible exception would have been the Jewish Christians who insisted on circumcision for their Gentile converts. See p. 126 below. Roman Jewish synagogues may have met in houses rather than in separate buildings.

224. Lightfoot, *Philippians* 174–77; also W. Sanday and A. C. Headlam, *A Critical and Exegetical Commentary on the Epistle to the Romans* (ICC; 2nd ed; New York: Scribners, 1926) 418–19; and Wiefel, "Community" 112. Six of the 25 names are Latin; the rest are Greek. Many are typical of slaves and freedmen, and thus may represent Jews and non-Romans who had employ in the great Roman houses. Clearly those whom Paul calls "kin" (Andronicus, Junias, Herodion) are Jews.

chapter forms were early abbreviations in order to make the letter less particularly directed to one church so that it could be read easily in the churches of other places and other times.[225] Such a movement is already apparent in the Muratorian Fragment (probably late second century) which speaks of one Pauline letter as different in the sense that it envisions the whole church.

More important than the dismissal of the arguments against the pertinence of chap. 16 is the reasoning that the whole 16-chapter letter makes sense only if Paul *did* know Roman Christianity and was writing a letter applicable to his relationship to that community. Even scholars who insist that Romans is a situational letter sometimes argue that, since in A.D. 49 Claudius had expelled Jews from Rome because of their fights over Christ (p. 100 above), the Christianity addressed by Paul at Rome was largely Gentile Christianity[226]—an affirmation often made *with the assumption that the designation "Gentile Christianity" tells us something distinctive about the views held at Rome.* I would insist parenthetically that it is quite implausible that all Christian Jews were expelled from Rome by Claudius—only those zealous enough to be involved in disturbances (wherefore evangelists like Prisca and Aquila). Nevertheless, by the late 50s Gentiles may well have been the majority among believers at Rome, and Paul may be addressing himself chiefly to that group (see 1:5–6,13,14; 15:16).[227] But that possibility tells us nothing about the relationship or the attitude of these Gentile Christians toward Judaism.

---

225. The same goal explains the (poorly attested) textual omission of the address to Rome. See N. Dahl, "The Particularity of the Pauline Epistles as a Problem in the Ancient Church," in *Neotestamentica et Patristica,* ed W. C. van Unnik (O. Cullmann Festschrift; SuppNovTest 6; Leiden: Brill, 1962) 261–71.

226. See Beker, *Paul* 61; Wiefel, "Community" 111; Schelkle, "Römische" 400. Preisker, "Problem," thinks that Jewish Christians were arguing against Gentile Christians.

227. Among the older commentators on Romans, Baur argued that it was addressed to Jewish Christians, while Jülicher, Pfleiderer, and Zahn argued for a Gentile Christian address. In wrestling with the problem that much of Paul's argument in Romans is a dialogue with Judaism and yet he addresses himself to Gentiles, Beker, *Paul* 75–76 (who is admirably insistent on the situational character of Romans), postulates that Rome had a mixed community of Jews and Gentiles. To be sure, but so must every one of the four groups described in the Introduction above have been mixed. The crucial issue is the theological outlook of this mixed Jewish/Gentile Christianity.

Many scholars, basing themselves on Paul's warning to the Gentiles not to boast over against the Jews (11:18; 12:3), assume that the Gentile Christians of Rome despised Jewish Christians and had little to do with them. To my mind that theory ignores one of the clearest indications in Romans about its purpose. Paul knows that he is not appreciated by some at Jerusalem because of his preaching that Gentile Christians are free of the Law, especially when that preaching has been phrased in heated rhetoric against law-observant Jewish Christians and their Gentile converts, as it was in Galatians. Paul is writing to the Roman Christians with the request that they should strive together with him by prayers on his behalf that the collection of money that he has raised will be acceptable in Jerusalem (15:30–31). The importance of the Jerusalem collection in Romans is widely recognized by scholars, even to the point of maintaining that the arguments presented in Romans are a dress rehearsal for what Paul will say in Jerusalem.[228] Yet, the further point must be made that evidently Paul thought the Roman Christians would be swayed by the same arguments that he was formulating for Jerusalem. If Roman Christianity was characterized by Gentiles who boasted of their superiority over Jewish Christians, why should Paul think that Roman help and prayers would make acceptable his service to the Jewish Christian saints in Jerusalem? (Acts 21:20–21 cannot be far wrong in its description of Jerusalem Christianity presided over by James: Many thousand Jews have believed; "They are all zealous for the Law.") More plausible is the thesis that Paul appealed for Rome's help because *the dominant Christianity at Rome had been shaped by the Jerusalem Christianity associated with James and Peter, and hence was a Christianity appreciative of Judaism and loyal to its customs.*[229] I shall develop arguments for this thesis below; but it is interesting to find it confirmed by Ambrosiaster, one who lived in Rome and wrote *ca.* 375. In his commentary on Romans (PL 17.46) he re-

---

228. J. Jervell, "The Letter to Jerusalem," in Donfried, *Romans Debate* 61–74. The German orig. is in *Studia Theologica* 25 (1971) 61–73.

229. Although I shall often speak of "James and Peter," I recognize that within Group Two (Introduction) James was more conservative than Peter and that Peter was more directly concerned with the Jerusalem mission to Gentiles in the diaspora, so that for Rome Peter was more the embodiment of Jerusalem Christianity than was James.

ports that the Romans "received the faith although with a Jewish bent [*ritu licet Judaico*]."[230]

The non-situational approach to the Romans Epistle as if it were a general Pauline theological treatise or a general *apologia* for Paul's ministry is wrong in not recognizing sufficiently the directional signals in the Epistle. Yet, some truth may be allowed for such an outlook on Romans when it is complementary to a situational approach, so that there is a convergence of motivation.[231] True, Paul is gathering together his views about God's plan for Jew and Gentile. True, he is doing this in a more nuanced and balanced way than in previous writings. True, he is indirectly defending his apostolate. But all of this may be because he writes this letter when he is on his way back to a dominantly Jewish church in Jerusalem that he has antagonized, and because the Roman church he addresses is quite similar to Jerusalem in its respect for Law and cult. As an apostle who has developed a skill in preaching to Gentiles, he makes a nuanced summary of position and an *apologia* to the Roman community (ethnically largely Gentile) and thus hones what he will ultimately say to Jewish Christians of the same persuasion in Jerusalem. If he is successful with the Romans, he can gain a persuasive ally helping to make him and his collection acceptable in Jerusalem, and acceptance in Jerusalem will ultimately make Paul acceptable when he comes to Rome after Jerusalem.

BACKGROUND OF ROMANS

The closeness of Galatians to Romans has long been recognized, sometimes with the bland explanation that in Galatians Paul was saying in a more excited and preliminary way what he would say with greater calm and balance in Romans. More forthright is the analysis of Wilckens: "On the whole, the position in Romans is a revision of the polemical position of Philippians and Galatians."[232] To

---

230. I am indebted for this reference to Msgr. Jerome Quinn of the St. Paul (Minn.) Seminary.

231. N. Dahl, cited by Beker, *Paul* 92; "The relationship between theology and missionary activity is as intimate in Romans as in any of Paul's letters, but the perspective is different."

232. "Entwicklung" 180. See also Beker, *Paul* 95–99; Ward, "Example."

test that claim let us reflect briefly on the probable impact of Galatians. In narrating his own career Paul made clear that James and Peter maintained fellowship with him on the principle of not insisting on circumcision for Gentile converts (2:9). He boasted, however, that he withstood Peter and the men from James on the question of observing Jewish food laws, and indicated that they were not straightforward about the truth of the Gospel. He also spoke of these great figures as "so-called pillars" who made no difference to him. The opponents in Galatia that Paul was encountering were clearly to the right of James and Peter, for these Jewish Christian missionaries were insisting on circumcision (5:2–3).[233] Yet in the savagery of Paul's attack he seems to lump his opposition to them with his earlier opposition to Peter and James! Can we imagine that the Galatian adversaries did not capitalize on Paul's contempt for the Jerusalem authorities and happily try to pretend that they stood with Peter and James against Paul? Since we know that there were Jewish Christians at Jerusalem who insisted on circumcision, would not the Galatian Jewish Christians have sent back a report of Paul's comments to Jerusalem, complete with his derogatory statements about the principal figures of the Jerusalem Church? Well may Paul have feared that even his pacifying gesture of raising money for the Jerusalem church would not be acceptable.

What Paul condemned in Galatia was the insistence that *Gentiles* be circumcised so that Christ could be accepted as fully effective (5:1–12). According to Acts 21:21, the rumor among the Jewish Christians in Jerusalem was that Paul was teaching *Jews* (who came to believe in Christ) to forsake Moses, not to circumcise their children, and not to observe their Jewish customs. Some may dismiss the Acts report as Lucan confusion; but a distorted report of what Paul wrote to the Galatians, such as the adversaries would have been likely to make, could very well have led to such a view. Consider Paul's words in Gal 3:19, denigrating the Law as "ordained by angels through an intermediary"; in 4:24, portraying the Sinai covenant as one of slavery; and in 5:2, "If you receive circumcision, Christ will be

---

233. According to the classification of Jewish/Gentile Christianity given in the Introduction above, the Galatian adversaries were representative of Group One, while James and Peter represented Group Two, and Paul was of Group Three.

of no advantage to you." Such broadsides, combined with sarcasm about Peter and James, might well upset even the more moderate Christians at Jerusalem.[234]

If echoes of Galatians would have reached Jerusalem, and if Roman Christianity was influenced by the Jerusalem Christianity of James and Peter, it is not unlikely that Pauline phraseology similar to that in Galatians reached *Rome* as well. Indeed, the view of Paul attributed to Jerusalem Christians in Acts 21:21 may have been shared by many Roman Christians. This would explain why in Romans Paul shows apprehension not only about the reception of the collection at Jerusalem, but also about his reception at Rome. Some of Paul's fellow workers from the missions in Asia Minor and Greece were now in Rome, e.g., Urbanus, and the couple Prisca and Aquila (Rom 16:3,4,9). The greetings extended so carefully to such people may have been Paul's way of encouraging Roman Christians to consult them about what he really held and not to be dependent on rumors. As Gamble has argued,[235] Romans 16 lays heavy emphasis on the relationship of named individuals to Paul; for he is tying himself to them and them to him: "Those singled out for greeting are claimed by Paul as his advocates within the community." In 16:17 Paul raises the fear that some may create dissensions at Rome. Actually, the dissensions might well center on whether the genuine Paul is the one presented by his Jerusalem adversaries or by those who have been involved in one way or another with his mission.[236]

But Paul needs more than favorable representation by sympathetic friends; he needs to state clearly and with balance where he really stands on the value of Judaism for Christians, Jew and Gentile alike. That is why Paul does not send to Rome merely chap. 16 as a letter of commendation, but chooses to incorporate the commendations of his friends in a long statement explaining his gospel of justification. Even if phrases like "more balanced" and "more complete

---

234. Although Galatians is the most violent of Paul's letters on the subject of the Law, Philip 3 is also intemperate, since there he attacks "dogs" and evil-workers who mutilate the flesh.

235. *Textual History,* 92.

236. If there are those in Rom 16 whom Paul greets without having met them personally, they may have been converts made by Paul's own converts and friends and thus people whom he could trust to be sympathetic.

and reflective" catch some of the contrast between Romans and Galatians, they do not do justice to the real possibility that Paul had *learned* in the period between the two letters (55–58?). In Chapter II above, John Meier has plausibly suggested that Paul lost at Antioch; it is possible that Pauline heated overstatement caused him to lose in Galatia as well. There he was faced with ultraconservative Jewish Christians and their Gentile converts who insisted on circumcision. At Corinth he seems to have encountered Gentile Christians who had no respect for the Law. (The incident in I Cor 5:1–5 concerns *porneia* or cohabiting within degrees of kindred forbidden by the Law—seemingly one of the very aspects of the Law on which James insisted according to Acts 15:20,29). Perhaps a wiser Paul now found himself closer to Peter and James than he was when he was at Antioch in 50 or when he wrote Galatians (*ca.* 55?). Of course, here I am proposing what is virtually heresy in the eyes of many Pauline scholars: namely, that Paul was not always consistent in his major epistles; that Paul even changed his mind; that the defiant Paul of Galatians was exaggerated; and that something is to be said for the position of Peter and James over against Paul on observance of some Jewish customs (so long as the observances were not looked upon as necessary for salvation). It is curious that sometimes a radical scholarship that has been insistent on the humanity of Jesus balks at any real indication of the fallible humanity of Paul!

Observations from the Text of Romans

The background I have suggested needs to be tested by what Paul actually says in Romans. Let us begin by noticing the gingerly politeness of Paul in this letter. When he writes of Judea and Jerusalem, he distinguishes carefully between the unbelieving Jews and the Jewish Christians: the latter he twice (Rom 15:26,31) calls "saints." (Indeed, according to Rom 11:5, all Jewish Christians are a remnant chosen by God.) This is quite different from Galatians where he stresses his independence of those who were apostles before him (1:17), attacks some of the Jewish Christians at Jerusalem as "false brethren," and is sarcastic about the leaders of the Jerusalem community as those who were reputed to be something and so-called pillars (2:4,6,9).

As for the Roman community, it consists of saints beloved of God (1:7) whose faith is proclaimed in the whole world (1:8).[237] Paul recognizes fully the high quality of the Christianity that exists in Rome even though he was not its source: "I myself am satisfied about you, my brothers, that you yourself are full of goodness, filled with all knowledge and able to instruct one another" (15:14). Indeed, he fears only adversaries who may create dissension "in opposition to the doctrine which you have been taught" (16:17).[238] In other words he acknowledges that the Romans received a valid form of the gospel. If they received it from Jerusalem and from more conservative Jewish Christians than Paul, he is not making the mistake of Galatians where, by implication, he made it possible to join all shades of adversaries as the preachers of "another gospel" (Gal 1:6–7) by charging even Peter and the men from James (two named figures who had given him the right hand of fellowship) with not being straightforward about "the truth of the gospel" (2:14). If that word has reached Rome and if there anti-Paulinists are saying that Paul would not consider the Roman church properly Christian[239] since it

---

237. In 1:9–10 Paul says, "For God is my witness ... that without ceasing I mention you always in my prayers, asking that somehow by God's will I may now at last succeed in coming to you." It is tempting to speculate that the delay in Paul's plan to visit Rome let his adversaries spread the word that he despised the Christian community there and did not want to have anything to do with it because of its strong allegiance to Judaism. Yet Rengstorf, "Paulus" 452, is probably right in arguing against Michel that Paul is using a tradional epistolary opening formula that is not overly indicative of the history of those addressed, e.g., Philip 1:8, "For God is my witness, how I yearn for you."

238. Gamble, *Textual History* 53, points to this as a connection with the body of Romans (6:17: "the pattern of teaching to which you were committed"), so that we have another argument for not dissociating chap. 16 from the rest of the epistle. The word "teaching" is sufficiently broad to cover what the Romans received from unnamed missionaries.

239. Judge and Thomas, "Origin" 81–82, contend: "The Christian community in Rome was built up mainly through the migration of converts from the East, without any regular organization or public preaching"—therefore launched as a "church" only after Paul arrived. G. Klein, "Purpose" 47–49, maintains that Paul did not consider the Roman community a properly founded church since an apostle had not been involved, and that is why he wanted to preach there. I disagree strongly. *First*, we do not know who founded the church at Rome or how it functioned; but if it came from Jerusalem, the founders had as much contact with apostolic Christianity as did those who founded the church at Antioch! I Corinthians 15:11 ("Whether it was I or they, so we preach and so you believed") shows that Paul is more interested in the content of the gospel than in the pedigree of the missionary. *Second*, the praise of the Roman

had been evangelized by those loyal to men whom he despised, Paul is countering that subtly but clearly. The statement in 16:16, "All the churches of Christ greet you," since it must convey a greeting from the churches Paul founded,[240] places the church at Rome on the same level as them. A similar function is played by Paul's strategic use of the first person plural[241] joining the Roman Christians with him and his Christians: All of us were baptized into the death of Christ and we walk in the newness of life (6:3–4); Jesus was put to death for our trespasses and raised for our justification (3:24–25).

When he is describing his own role, Paul is remarkably nuanced. The opponents in Galatia apparently questioned Paul's right to be called an apostle. Although he is being more diplomatic in Romans, he can never let that be called into question, even by Christians evangelized through a descendancy from James and Peter (who were apostles before Paul: Gal 1:17,19). Yet, a desire not to seem arrogant explains the difference in tone between Gal 1:1 ("Paul an apostle—not from men or through men, but through Jesus Christ and God the Father") and Rom 1:1: "Paul, a slave of Jesus Christ called to be an apostle." Moreover, unlike his custom in all the other undisputed letters, Paul associates no one with himself in the opening address in Romans. There are well known figures with him while he is sending the letter (16:21–23), especially Timothy who is mentioned in the opening of many Pauline letters; but the authority of this letter rests on Paul. When he goes to Jerusalem, he will have to defend himself on what he has preached, not on what others would say; and it is important to make clear to the Romans that he and he alone is responsible for the views he will advance. If he writes this letter explaining to the Romans the roles of Jews and Gentiles in

community as one whose faith is proclaimed throughout the world is irreconcilable with the thesis that Paul denied it was a proper church. This is similar to the praise Paul gives to a church he himself founded: "Your faith in God has gone out everywhere" (I Thess 1:8). *Third,* chap. 16, which is an original part of Romans, acknowledges the existence of house-churches (16:5,16); and an attempt by scholars to allow the presence of churches at Rome but to deny the title of church to the whole community lacks justification. (The use of "saints" rather than "church" at the beginning of Romans [1:7] proves nothing—see Philip 1:1.)

240. The abstract, impersonal tone of such a greeting makes it unlikely that the addressees of chap. 16 were a Pauline church such as Ephesus.

241. See Rengstorf, "Paulus" 458.

Christ, he is careful to state that it is not because he thinks they are poorly or inadequately instructed (15:14). Rather it is a compulsion placed on him by God: "On some points I have written to you very boldly by way of reminder because of the grace given me by God to be a minister of Christ Jesus to the Gentiles in the priestly service of the gospel of God" (15:15–16). If Paul is coming to Rome, let no one say that he is doing so because he wants to set the Romans straight about the gospel which hitherto they had heard only from men (contrast Gal 1:11: "The gospel preached by me is not man's gospel"). Indeed he is hesitant to preach where others have laid the foundation of the community (15:20); but he is under divine obligation to preach to Gentiles wherever they are, including Rome (1:14–15). He will only be bringing the fullness of the blessing of Christ's gospel (15:29) as he passes through on the way to Spain, enjoying their company and asking godspeed (15:24).[242] The formula, "I exhort" or "I beg" (*parakalō*) that Paul uses in giving advice to the Romans (12:1; 15:30) is typical of diplomatic style; and Jewett[243] uses this as one of the many proofs that Romans should be classed as an ambassadorial letter, i.e. one in which the rhetoric is not simply flowery or urbane but an essential step in demonstrating the author's adherence to the values of his listeners. The suggestion that Paul writes one way in Galatians and another way in Romans disturbs purists, but matches Paul's own claim in I Cor 9:22: "I have become all things to all, that I might by all means save some." Well did H. Chadwick[244] write in comment on that verse that Paul shows "an astonishing elasticity of mind, and a flexibility in dealing with situations requiring delicate and ingenious treatment which appears much greater than is usually supposed."

---

242. Although the circumstances were quite different, the Paul who wrote this was also the author of II Cor 13:10: "I write this . . . in order that when I come I may not have to be severe in my use of the authority which the Lord has given me for building up and not for tearing down." Were the Romans who were reading this letter familiar with the reputation of a Paul who wrote fierce letters threatening what he might do in the name of apostolic authority when he arrived on the scene?

243. "Romans" 11–12, drawing upon the work of C. J. Bjerkelund, *Parakalō: Form, Funktion und Sinn der parakalō-Sätze in den paulinischen Briefen* (Oslo: Scandinavian Univ. Press, 1967).

244. " 'All Things to All Men' (I Cor. ix 22)," NTS 1 (1954–55) 261–75, esp. 275.

Most commentators on Romans (e.g., Barrett, Dodd, Kuss, O. Michel) recognize that Paul wished to assure his readers of his orthodoxy. But for our purpose of diagnosing the nature of Roman Christianity, it is interesting to note what Paul thought would convince his hearers of orthodoxy. In 1:3–4 he summarizes "the gospel of God" (1:1) to preach which he has been especially chosen: It is the gospel concerning God's Son "who was born of the seed of David according to the flesh, designated Son of God in power according to a Spirit of Holiness as of resurrection from the dead." Critical scholarship recognizes that here Romans is offering a Jewish Christian formulation of the gospel that would be familiar to the readers. In other words, Paul, who is so zealous against other gospels (Gal 1:6–9), seeks to win the heart of the Romans by offering a gospel formulation that is not his own but is already known to them almost as a creedal expression, with the hallmark of Jewish origin.[245] Later on in the letter Paul implicitly defends his orthodoxy by proposing views and then recoiling from them in horror. In 3:8 he asks, "And why not do evil that good may come—as some slanderously charge us with saying." Plausibly the slander is an exaggerated echo of teaching similar to Gal 3 that the Law brought out transgressions and placed under a curse all who could not live up to it, and that Christ redeemed from this curse. Paul's opponents could accuse him of holding that transgressions offered a greater opportunity for the grace of Christ. If Paul rejects this as slander, it is because he thinks his hearers in Rome will be pleased to know that he is not indifferent to what is forbidden by the Law (see also the rhetorical question in 6:1). In Rom 3:31 he asks, "Do we overthrow the Law by faith? By no means! On the contrary, we uphold the Law." Once again he thinks this will please his recipients who surely must be well disposed to-

---

245. For disputes about the precise translation and meaning, see R. E. Brown *et al.*, *Mary in the New Testament* (New York: Paulist, 1978) 34–40. Jewish origin is indicated by the reference to Jesus as "Son of David" and by the expression "Spirit of Holiness," which reflects a Semitic genitival structure (in place of Paul's normal and better Greek expression "Holy Spirit"). Jewish background is also indicated by the lapidary statement in Rom 3:30, "The one God will justify the circumcised and the uncircumcised by faith," if that echoes the basic Jewish prayer, the *Shema:* "Hear, O Israel, the Lord our God is one." Does Paul assume that the Christians of Rome know and pray this prayer? See Mark 12:29 where Jesus makes it the first commandment (in what may be a gospel addressed to the Romans; consult Chapter X, section C, below).

ward the Law. As Wuellner and Jewett have shrewdly observed, Romans belongs to a demonstrative literary genre wherein Paul affirms values recognized by the audience and thus establishes community with the audience.[246]

But is not the thesis of a moderately conservative Jewish/Gentile Christianity at Rome, sympathetic to Jerusalem, refuted by the warnings to the Gentiles not to boast (p. 110 above)? How does one answer the objection that surely this implies a Christianity at Rome that looks down upon Jewish observances?[247] In my judgment, these warnings are also directed against a slanderous view of Paul. There was a Jewish/Gentile Christianity that regarded Judaism as displaced by Christianity and vigorously rejected Jewish customs and feasts (Group Four in the Introduction, p. 6 above). Paul's intemperance in Galatians may have led some to classify him in that (Hellenist) category. The warnings to "the strong" in Rom 14–15 may be addressed to more liberal Christians in Rome who would claim Paul in their camp because he had the reputation of allowing his converts to eat all types of food without observing Jewish customs (Gal 2:12) and of making fun of those who considered it an important religious issue what they put into "their belly" (Philip 3:19). But in dealing with Corinth Paul had learned, to his sorrow, that freedom can lead the "knowledgeable" to be insensitive toward those who do not share their enlightenment. In I Cor 8:8–9 he had to lecture his own converts: "We are no worse off if we do not eat, and no better off if we do. Take care lest this liberty of yours become a stumbling block to the weak!" It is, then, a wiser Paul who writes to Rome in an even more delicate situation where those sensitive about food may be a majority among Christians,[248] and the minority may think they share

---

246. Wuellner, "Rhetoric" 166; Jewett, "Romans" 6. For how such rhetorical questions as those cited above reflect misinterpretations of Paul's own teaching, see Harder, "Anlass" 15–16. Certainly Harder (18) is right that Paul is not simply challenging Gentile libertines.

247. Of course, there are also directives against Jews who boast about their superiority over Gentiles (Rom 2:17ff.).

248. Diagnosing the situation in chaps. 14 – 15 is complicated because of the description in 14:2: "The weak eats (only) vegetables." Is this a fact or a pejorative generalization by the more liberal who consider themselves "strong" because they can eat all things with religious impunity? Could such a generalizaton arise from a few ultra-conservative Gentile Christian converts of Group One (Introduction above) who were

Paul's view by looking down on them as weak. In Rom 14:1ff. Paul dissociates himself from such a divisive attitude. Similarly, by chastising Gentile boastfulness and describing the Gentile Christians as a wild olive stock grafted into the cultivated olive tree of Israel (11:24), by insisting that God has not rejected His people (11:1), and by predicting the ultimate conversion of all Israel, Paul is refuting such radical Christianity *not primarily because it dominates at Rome but because he has been falsely charged with holding it*—a charge that would make him *persona non grata* to the majority of Roman Christians. What Paul affirms of Jewish values in Rom 9–11, then, is not an attack on prevailing Roman Christianity but a confirmation of it! Origen (PG 14.854–55) was perfectly right when he observed that Paul points out faults in the faith of Galatia but not in the faith of Rome.[249]

I proposed above (p. 114) the possibility that Paul had become more mature and truly changed his mind in Romans when compared with the earlier Paul of Galatians. Therefore, while Paul may justifiably have characterized some of the views attributed to him as slander, at other times in Romans he would be struggling to modify views that he once actually expressed. This struggle, implicit to be sure, would also confirm my evaluation of the audience addressed in Rome. If, according to Gal 2:11–12, Paul fought at Antioch with Peter and the men from James over their too strict observance of the food laws so that they would not eat with Gentiles, in Rom 14:3 he seems to take a more pacific attitude toward strict observers. "Let him who eats not despise him who abstains." In Gal 5:2 Paul said, "If you receive circumcision, Christ will be of no advantage to you." There seems to be more than a moderated tone in Rom 3:1–2: "What advantage is there in being a Jew? Or what benefit in being circumcised? Much in every way. To begin with, the Jews are entrusted

---

so anxious about not eating meat that Jews regarded as impure (either in itself or through contact with idols) that they abstained from meat altogether? Remember Paul's rhetoric in I Cor 8:13: "If food causes my brother to stumble, I will never eat meat again."

249. In later church history Paul's positive attitude helped Rome to be seen as a norm for the faith of the world. Indeed, many Fathers saw such Pauline confirmation as a reason for putting Romans first in the canon of Pauline epistles. See Schelkle, "Römische" 395–99.

with the words of God."[250] The Paul, who in Galatians distinguished himself as having a mission to the uncircumcised while the Jerusalem "pillars" were for the circumcised, says in Rom 15:8: "Christ became a minister of the circumcision to show God's truth, in order to confirm the promises given to the fathers." Again, in Gal 3:10,13,23,24 Paul wrote, "All who rely on observing the Law are under a curse ... Christ redeemed us from the curse of the Law. ... Before faith came we were under the restraint of the Law. ... The Law was our custodian until Christ came." There are strains of the same thought in Rom 3, but the chapter ends on a different tone (3:31): "Do we nullify the Law by this faith? Not at all; rather we uphold the Law." And in Rom 7:7,12,14,16 Paul denies that the Law is sin: "The Law is holy. ... The Law is spiritual. ... The Law is good." No longer does Paul state, as he did with insistence in Gal 3:19–20, that the Law was given by angels.[251]

Perhaps the change may be summarized under the heading of Paul's attitude toward salvation history. In his commentary on Galatians in the Anchor Bible, J. Louis Martyn will eloquently (and correctly) contend that the Paul of Galatians really does not see God's dealing with humankind as a history of salvation, i.e., a salvation already offered in what we call the OT dispensation, coming to a climax in Christ. Rather in Galatians there is an apocalyptic contrast between a previous realm of slavery, sin, and curse which was marked by the impotency of the Law, and a new realm introduced by Christ and marked by freedom and grace.[252] The apocalyptic element is present in Romans too; for Rom 5:8,10 describes people before the death of Christ, including Jews, as sinners and enemies of God, and 5:13,20–21 states that the Law made it possible for sin to be counted and to increase. But this negative view of what preceded Christ is

---

250. Contrast the Hellenist outlook on Jesus' relation to the Jews: "You do not have His word abiding in you" (John 5:38).

251. Very good on the comparison of the two epistles is Wilckens, "Entwicklung" 180–85.

252. Already Beker (*Paul* 73) has showed an openness toward such a view: "Paul's response to that [Galatian] crisis had created the impression that the place of the Jew in salvation-history was a purely negative one and had in fact become obsolete with the coming of Christ." For ways in which Martyn would go beyond Beker, see his review of Beker's book in *Word and World* 2 (1982) 194–98.

tempered elsewhere in Romans and modified toward at least a partially salvific-history outlook, particularly in chaps. 9–11. Many
modern scholars (Sanday, Dodd, Bultmann) who prefer the Paul of
Galatians would classify Rom 9–11 as an appendix, distraction, or
idealistic interlude interrupting the main thought of Romans (which
they read in harmony with Galatians). But Beker,[253] who thinks that
"Romans gives a much more balanced picture of Israel in salvation-
history," argues that Rom 9–11 can be read as the climax of the epistle thus interpreted. Certainly the magnificent praise of the Israelites
in 9:4–5 (which might embarrass a modern Jew as ecumenically insensitive) gives a positive value to the past history of Israel under the
Law: "To them belong the gift of sonship, the covenants, the gift of
the Law, the cult, and the promises. To them belong the patriarchs,
and from their race according to the flesh came the Messiah." A
sense of salvific sequence is found in 15:8–9: "Christ became the servant of the circumcised because of God's fidelity in fulfilling the
promises given to the patriarchs." The refrain in Rom 1:16; 2:9,10,
"First Jews, then Greeks," is closer to salvation history than to apocalyptic, especially when we add to that refrain the "finally all Israel"
of 11:26. Unlike Galatians which focuses on the obsolescence of the
Law, Romans concentrates on the relation of two peoples in God's
plan of salvation.[254]

AFTERMATH: PAUL IN ROME:

In the next chapter I shall take up the continuity of some
themes of Romans in I Peter. (This continuity lends support to the
case I have made for the moderately conservative character of Christianity that became dominant at Rome, a Christianity associated
with Jerusalem and with James and even more so [in the heavily
Gentile mission] with Peter.) But let me conclude this chapter by

---

253. *Paul* 89. Paul's seeming rejection of salvation history in Galatians may ultimately have worked against his own "gospel." There are many passages in the Law
and the prophets offering life to Israel if the Law is observed (e.g., Deut 30:15–16). If
there really was no such salvific opportunity offered by God before Christ, how can
Gentiles trust the divine promise of life that Paul attaches to belief in Christ? See
Ward, "Example."

254. Beker, *Paul* 71.

some reflections on the immediate aftermath of the letter that Paul wrote to Rome in the late 50s. I have pointed out above that in part Paul was writing self-defensively, worried that he would be acceptable in neither Jerusalem nor Rome. Acts 21:17–26 reports that there was serious opposition to Paul when he did get to Jerusalem at Pentecost of 58 because he had a reputation among some Jewish Christians for propaganda against *their* observing the Law. James himself treated Paul as a brother (even if James reiterated the view not shared by Paul that Gentile Christians should observe specific Jewish food laws). Nevertheless, when Paul attempted to show good will by going to the Temple, the Jews rioted against him; and their continued opposition led the Romans to send him to Rome as a prisoner. As he drew near (*ca.* A.D. 60?), some Roman Christians came out of the city thirty or forty miles, as far as Tres Tabernae and even Forum Appii (Acts 28:15), to greet Paul and give him courage. Thus, if one can depend on this information in Acts, the Paul who wrote Romans found acceptance both by the part of Jerusalem Christianity represented by James and also by the leaders of Roman Christianity. The latter detail finds some confirmation from the statement in *I Clement* 5:2–7, written some thirty-five years later, which refers to "the good apostles Peter and Paul" as examples of "the greatest and most righteous pillars [of the church]." Notice both the association of the two names and their order. Paul had referred to Peter in the late 40s as one of "the so-called pillars" and boasted that he withstood Peter face to face, charging him with not being honest about the truth of the Gospel (Gal 2:9,11,14). Yet in the memory of the Roman church Paul is associated closely with Peter as an example of that very feature of architecture that he once railed against! The order of the two names in *I Clement* betrays the established rank of the two men in Roman evaluation; for Ignatius of Antioch, writing to Rome (4:3) about a decade after *I Clement,* uses the same order in referring to Peter and Paul as apostles in the Roman church.[255] Although Rome was not a Pauline church, evidently the letter to the Romans was well enough received to make the majority of Roman

---

255. Toward the end of the second century, Irenaeus, *Adv. haer.* 3.3.2, associates Peter and Paul (in that order) in the foundation and constitution of the Roman church.

Christians recognize Paul's claim to be an apostle comparable to Peter (Gal 2:7–8).

Nevertheless, the implications in *I Clement* about the death of Peter and Paul[256] indicate that all did not go smoothly at Rome for the two apostles, both of whom seem to have been in the capital in the early 60s. What they suffered is presented as an example of death because of "jealous zeal and envy." (Chap. 4 of *I Clement* gives seven examples of "jealous zeal" doing serious harm in the OT period; chaps. 5–6 give [seven?] examples of the same in the Christian period.[257]) If Peter and Paul died in the persecution instituted by Nero, then deduction from Tacitus, *Annals* 15:44, suggests that the "jealous zeal and envy" refers to betrayal by their fellow Christians:[258] "The first [Christians] seized who made a confession were convicted, and then *upon their evidence* a great multitude." Matthew 24:10 shows that Christians did deliver up one another to the authorities; and that "envy" was sometimes the cause is clear from Philip 1:15–17 where Paul writes as a prisoner that "some preach Christ *out of envy* . . . thinking to bring affliction on me in my imprisonment."[259]

---

256. *I Clement* 5:4–7, which discusses Peter and Paul, does not say explicitly that they were martyred at Rome; but Cullmann, *Peter* 91–110, has shown that such a martyrdom is the most reasonable interpretation. (See also his earlier study, "Les causes.") *I Clement* 5:2 prefaces the reference to Peter and Paul with the affirmation that the greatest pillars were persecuted to the point of death, and 6:1 follows it by associating them with others "among us" who were tortured. Polycarp, *Philip.* 9:2, clearly understood the phrase about Peter in *I Clem.* 5:4 ("the place which was his due") to refer to Peter's going to heaven and thus, implicitly, to death. The argument that Rev 11:3–13 refers to the martyrdom of the two apostles in "the great city" of Rome is less clear. The *Ascension of Isaiah* 4:2–3 (early second century?) describes figuratively Peter being delivered into the hands of the king who has slain his own mother (Nero). Overall the evidence supports the judgment of A. von Harnack and H. Lietzmann that the martyr Peter was buried on Vatican hill and the martyr Paul on the Ostian way, as tradition has insisted.

257. The examples seem consistently to involve jealousy on a fraternal or compatriot level.

258. Cullmann, *Peter* 102–10 makes this point well: "The magistrates were encouraged by the attitude of some members of the Christian Church, and perhaps by the fact that they turned informers, to take action against others." See also Beaujeu, "L'incendie" 293. *I Clement* was written as a warning that *inner Christian quarrels* reach "also those who dissent from us so that . . . you are creating dangers for yourselves" (47:7). Pliny, *Letters* 10.96 confirms that denunciation of Christians by Christians was standard Roman investigatory technique.

259. This evidence would be all the more relevant if Philippians were written during Paul's Roman captivity; see Chapter X, section A, below.

Who may have been the fellow Christians who so hated Peter and Paul? All the evidence points to Jewish Christian missionaries insistent on circumcision (Group One in my classification on pp. 2–3 above). In II Cor 11:12 Paul speaks of the "danger" he has suffered "from false brothers," and Gal 2:4 identifies the circumcision-insistent Jewish Christians whom Paul faced at Jerusalem in the late 40s as "false brothers." Although they did not succeed in swaying the Jerusalem "pillars" against Paul at that time, the ultraconservative Jewish Christians remained his enemy, propagandizing against him in the early 50s in Galatia and Philippi. According to Acts 21:20, when Paul came to Jerusalem in the late 50s, the Jewish Christians "zealously jealous for the Law" were spreading false rumors about him. Although Paul was advised by James to go to the Temple to refute those rumors, the Jews rioted against him[260] and that led ultimately to his being transported to Rome as a prisoner. In Rom 16:17–18 Paul feared that dissension was being sown in Rome by opponents of the moderate Jewish Christian doctrine which had been preached at Rome. His reference to the dissenters as serving not the Lord "but their belly" makes clear that he is thinking of extremists insistent on circumcision (see Philip 3:2,19). Seemingly after Paul got to Rome, these dissenters hated him enough ultimately to denounce him to the Romans. The evidence with regard to opposition to Peter is less extensive, but the Christians "of the circumcision party" were unfriendly to him as well. According to Acts 11:2–3, after Peter baptized Cornelius (in the late 30s?), they criticized him in Jerusalem on his openness to Gentiles. Acts 15:5–11 and Gal 2:1–9 make clear that Peter disagreed with the position on circumcision taken by the "false brothers" or Christian Pharisees in the Jerusalem meeting of the late 40s. Yet, after that meeting, according to Gal 2:12, Peter drew back from Paul's position on the Jewish food laws because he "feared the circumcision party." Certainly the image of Peter projected in I Peter written from Rome (in the 80s?) would not have been appreciated by Jewish Christians insistent on circumcision, for I Pet 3:18 implies the inability of the Law to make people righteous.

---

260. Acts does not make an explicit connection between the Jewish Christian opposition to Paul in Jerusalem (21:20–25) and the riot against him by the Jews (21:27–35), but is it not likely that the Jews learned of Paul's teaching from Jewish Christians who disliked him?

Thus, there is impressive evidence that ultraconservative Jewish Christians criticized, propagandized against, and endangered Peter and Paul in the 40s and 50s, especially in Jerusalem.[261] Granted my thesis that Roman Christianity came from Jerusalem in the 40s, even if the majority position in Rome was a moderate Jewish/Gentile Christianity favorable to Peter (and more conservative in tone than the early Paul), is it not probable that at least a minority representation of circumcision-insistent Christianity came as well and made Gentile converts? That would explain why in Romans, although Paul was "bending over backwards" to show his closeness to moderate Jewish/Gentile Christianity, in the early chapters he repeated his opposition to any insistence on the circumcision of the Gentiles. I mentioned above that in the persecution of Nero no blame was put on the Jews. May not the Jewish Christians and their circumcised Gentile converts have considered themselves Christian *Jews,* and may not the "evidence" given to the Roman authorities (Tacitus) have consisted in distinguishing between themselves and Gentile Christians who had been converted to Jesus without circumcision? If such evidence, prompted in part by dislike ("jealous envy") of the missionary policies of Peter and Paul, led to the death of the two apostles,[262] one can understand why later Roman tradition would have glossed over the differences between the thought of the two men and have joined them together as "pillars" and even foundations of the Roman Church. The listing of Peter first may signify that his was the position in regard to Judaism that was closest to the mainstream of the Roman church.[263] Paul's remarks in Romans, however, seemingly enabled him to be appreciated as sufficiently moderate; and perhaps his earlier, more radical reputation as one who saw no value in circumcision and the Law received more understanding when the

---

261. Cullmann, *Peter* 53, points to *I Clem.* 5:4, "Peter, who because of unrighteous zeal suffered not one or two but *many* trials," as a suggestion that Peter suffered not only from ultraconservative Jewish Christians on the right but also from the Hellenists on the left. However, Acts 6:1–6 points to zealous "Hebrews," not to Hellenists, as the source of trouble dividing the Jerusalem Christian community.

262. *I Clement* 5 gives greater length to the description of all that Paul suffered, perhaps because there was greater "jealous zeal" directed against him than against Peter. Certainly Paul would have been the greater enemy for ultraconservatives.

263. An alternative or additional reason for listing Peter first may have been that he died first, as Cullman, *Peter* 94–95, thinks, or that he was an apostle first.

intolerance of circumcision-insistent Jewish/Gentile Christianity became apparent in the persecution.

Nevertheless, the instinct of Rome against too radical a rejection of the Jewish heritage revived in the mid-second century through opposition to Marcion. After all, despite his angry tone and his apocalyptic dualism between the Law and Christ, the Paul of Galatians still held that the Law came from God (through angels). Marcion went further in the rejection of salvation history by having a demigod responsible for the Law in contrast to the true God who gave us Jesus Christ. The fact that Marcion made Paul, one of the two apostles of Rome, his theological hero and the center of the NT canon did not save Marcion from expulsion by the presbyters of Rome *ca.* A.D. 144 (Epiphanius, *Panarion* 42; PG 41.696D).

CHAPTER VIII

The Roman Church
in the
Second Christian Generation

(A.D. 65–95—I Peter and Hebrews)

T WO WORKS, I Peter from Rome and Hebrews written to Rome, supply some information about Rome in the period between the Epistle of Paul to the Romans (*ca.* 58) and *I Clement* from Rome (*ca.* 96). Neither of these intermediary works can be assigned a certain date; but one cannot be far wrong in placing them in the period between the late 60s and the early 90s, with the suspicion that both may belong to the 80s.

A. The First Epistle of Peter

Some preliminary issues must be discussed before we turn to those aspects of the epistle that reflect on Roman church history.

DATE AND DESTINATION

To a great extent the date of this work depends on two issues: (1) Was it written at the onset of a Roman persecution as echoed in 4:12–14, "The fiery ordeal which comes upon you to prove you . . . when you are reproached for the name of Christ"?[264] If so, a logical

---

264. Some would connect the "fiery" with the fire of Rome that led to Nero's persecution or even to his burning of Christians. (Conversely, W. Rordorf, "Die ner-

date of composition would be the eve of one of the known persecutions: the local persecution of Christians in Rome by Nero (*ca.* 64), or the persecution in some areas late in Domitian's reign (90s),[265] or the repression in Bithynia under Trajan (*ca.* 112). However, the impressive study by John Elliott, *A Home for the Homeless,* shows that the language of I Peter may reflect simply the hardships of an alienated community rather than a full-scale persecution.[266] (2) Was it written by Peter and, therefore, in his lifetime (which ended in the mid-60s)? Various arguments have been offered to disprove the authorship by Peter claimed in 1:1 (also 5:1: a witness to the sufferings of the Messiah), e.g., a Greek style too good for a Galilean fisherman; OT quotes from the Greek (LXX) version rather than the Hebrew; strong echoes of Pauline thought. Most of these objections can be countered, especially with the hypothesis of a secretary or collaborator.[267] Since in 5:12 the author states, "I have written to you briefly through [the help of] Sylvanus," the coauthor or scribe theory is not fanciful. Also one must note that nothing in the letter is directly contrary to Petrine authorship, i.e., no anachronisms or historical inaccuracies.[268] Nevertheless, depending chiefly on their sense of where this epistle would best fit, most modern authors, even those inclined

---

onische Christenverfolgung im Spiegel der apokryphen Paulusakten," NTS 28 [1982] 365–74, thinks that Christian apocalyptic speculation about the destruction of God's enemies through fire caused the Romans to think that the Christians set the fire to destroy Rome.) The "name of Christ" may also be significant since Tacitus, *Annals* 15.44, states that those blamed for the burning of Rome "were popularly called Christians"; Pliny, *Epistles* 10.96, speaks of "those who were accused before me as Christians."

265. For the evidence that there was persecution of Christians *in some areas* of the empire in Domitian's last years, see Goppelt, *Apostolic* 109–10; Grant, *Augustus* 79–80; Barnard, "St. Clement" 5–13. Seemingly there was no empire-wide persecution.

266. Such alienation was evidently dangerous enough to open the possibility of Christian apostasy. In reference to Pontus and Bithynia (two regions addressed in I Peter), Pliny, *Epistles* 10.96, states that about twenty years earlier than 110 (thus about 85) Christians had fallen away. Some would use this to support a date of 85 as plausible for I Peter.

267. Articles by N. Brox. *Biblische Zeitschrift* 19 (1975) 78–96, and F. Neugebauer, NTS 26 (1979–80) 61–86, are recent restatements of the arguments pro and con Petrine authorship.

268. Best, *I Peter* 59—an admission all the more important because Best does not think that Peter wrote it.

to be cautious (for example, Best and Elliott), opt for a period
around the 80s and after Peter's lifetime. In that case the epistle
would have been written by someone who considered himself a disciple or adherent of Peter, not unlike Sylvanus.[269] The discussion below
will illustrate the general ambiance of I Peter, and it will become apparent why I too incline toward the post-Peter pseudonymous explanation and a date in the 80s. Yet I insist that it is not absolutely
crucial for a reconstruction of Roman church history to know
whether we are hearing in I Peter a voice from the mid-60s or the
mid-80s, i.e., a voice from the Roman church when Peter was about
to die or after he had died.[270]

That Rome was the place of authorship has few doubters. In
5:13 the author refers to the church as "the co-elect at Babylon";[271]
and, especially after Rome had conquered Jerusalem and destroyed
the Temple in 70, even as Babylon had done 600 years before, the
symbolism of Babylon for Rome became frequent in Jewish and
Christian circles.[272] (That, by the way, is an argument for dating I
Peter after the 60s and Peter's lifetime.) Already in the early second
century Papias had the tradition that I Peter was composed at Rome
(Eusebius, *Hist.* 2.15.2).

More disputed is the precise geographic area intended in the address: "To the exiles of the diaspora in Pontus, Galatia, Cappadocia,
Asia, and Bithynia." Despite the Jewish language of "diaspora," the
addressees are clearly Gentiles as remarks about their past indicate
(2:9–10; 1:14,18). But in the places named is the author referring to

269. Most often Sylvanus is invoked in the scribe hypothesis with Peter as the
real author or coauthor. Yet there is no compelling reason why a nameless Petrine
disciple need be preferred over Sylvanus in the pseudepigraphical hypothesis where
the disciple would be the whole author, writing after Peter's death and using his name
and authority. Elliott, *Home* 270–91, makes a strong case for relating I Peter with a
Petrine circle at Rome.

270. Goppelt, *Petrusbrief* 50, 63–64, dates I Peter to A.D. 65–80, after Romans
but before Hebrews. It was not written by either Peter or Sylvanus, although they may
have influenced the tradition it presents.

271. For the feminine "elect" used for a church, see R. E. Brown, *The Epistles of
John* (AB 30; Garden City: Doubleday, 1982) 653–55. I am assuming that I Peter is a
unified letter and that 4:12ff. belongs to what precedes. See Best, *I Peter* 20–28.

272. Rev 14:8; 16:19; 17:5; 18:2,10,21; *II Baruch* 11:1; 67:7; *Sibylline Oracles*
5:143,159.

the Roman provinces that constitute most of Asia Minor,[273] or to more restricted areas reflecting ancient national origins? The former thesis (provinces) would mean that some regions of the Pauline missions were included (e.g. Galatia); the latter leaves open the possibility that mostly northern Asia Minor is meant—an area where Paul had not worked. Elliott's reconstruction of the recipients as predominantly rural Christians in backwoods areas of northern Asia Minor finds some support from Pliny who about the year 110 sought out Christians in the Bithynia area and found them scattered "through villages and rural areas."[274]

If one accepts the hypotheses that the recipients had been evangelized by people other than Paul and that Christianity had been their religion for a number of years, one must raise the question of why a letter would be sent to them from *Rome* bearing the name *Peter*. Some suggestions are not very plausible, e.g., that an imperial persecution loomed and the church at the capital of the empire could best give advice, or that Peter was pope and could write with authority anywhere in the church.[275] Since Ignatius in the Introduction to his *Romans* speaks of the church at Rome as preeminent in love, Elliott thinks that Rome may have been "the locality where this concern for Christian love, hospitality and cohesion was particularly evident and fostered."[276] One may add another possible answer, however. If this area addressed in Asia Minor had not been evangelized by Paul, it may have been evangelized from Jerusalem by missionaries representative of moderate conservative Jewish Christianity who associated themselves with Peter.[277] We know that Jewish Christian

---

273. An argument against this is that Pontus and Bithynia constituted one province, so that the splitting of the names would be curious.

274. *Epistles* 10.69.9; Elliott, *Home* 63–64.

275. The development of the papacy at Rome is related to the image of Peter in the NT, but it would be anachronistic and simplistic to think of the historical Peter functioning as a later pope. See R. E. Brown, *Peter* 8, 19–20, 167–68.

276. *Home* 163, a thesis previously advocated by von Harnack.

277. Within Jerusalem Christianity (Group Two in the Introduction above), all our evidence indicates that Peter was the one among the Twelve most open to the Gentiles, and so he may have been the patron of the Jerusalem mission to the Gentiles in the diaspora. James would have been the patron of the Jerusalem mission to Jews whether at Jerusalem or in the diaspora—note that the Epistle of James (1:1) is addressed to the *twelve tribes* (Jewish Christians) in the diaspora. A. Schlatter, *Der Brief*

missionaries of an even more conservative bent were at work in the
50s converting Gentiles in *Galatia,* and Paul's attack on them suggests that they were claiming the support of Jerusalem and perhaps
invoking the names of Peter and James. Of the other four of the five
regions named in I Peter 1:1, three (*Cappadocia, Pontus,* and *Asia*[278])
are mentioned in the list of Acts 2:9, a list that some think is programmatic of what Luke knows to have been the spread of Jerusalem
Christianity, a list that ends with Rome. Thus, the main reason for a
letter from Peter and Rome to northern Asia Minor may be that
both regions shared the same type of Christianity, which had its origins in Jerusalem. The "co-elect" at Rome that sends its greetings
(5:13) and the elect that receive the letter (1:1) may be part of the
"brotherhood throughout the world" (5:9) because they had the
same missionary parenthood. It is tempting to speculate that with
the fall of Jerusalem and the flight of Jewish Christians (who regarded James as their hero) from Jerusalem, Rome where Peter had died
became a main spokesman (or spokeswoman, since "the co-elect of
Babylon" is feminine) for a Christianity that remained strongly appreciative of the Jewish heritage without insisting on circumcision or
the Sabbath.[279] This would explain why Rome writes Corinth[280] cor-

---

des Jakobus (Stuttgart: Calwer, 1932) 67–73, and others have argued for a close relationship between the epistles of James and I Peter, a relationship that would reflect
positively on the Jerusalem-Rome axis that I have proposed. Selwyn, *First Epistle*
439–58, argues for parallels between Matthew and I Peter; these lend support to the
contention of this book that Antioch and Rome had a related Christianity (through
Jerusalem origins and through the role of Peter).

278. According to Acts 16:7, in the early 50s Paul tried to go to Bithynia and
Asia but was prevented by the Spirit. Did this check have anything to do with Paul's
belief that his apostolate was not meant to take him where others were preaching
Christ (Rom 15:20–21; II Cor 10:15–16)? Reicke, *Epistles* 72, thinks that in the 60s
the Christian mission in Asia Minor was already divided, with the southeast under
Antioch and with the northern area under the influence of Rome. I would speak rather of Pauline and non-Pauline areas, with Jerusalem, and eventually Rome, having influence on some of the latter.

279. Goppelt, *Apostolic* 126, says of Rome: "To a certain extent the successor of
Christian Jerusalem . . . she thus assumed the responsibility for the other churches."
This would have been facilitated when toward the end of the first century the name of
James and the memory of Jerusalem were coopted by the more extreme Jewish Chris-
tians (Group One, Introduction) who insisted on circumcision. See p. 207 below.

280. During his lifetime Peter had a following at Corinth (I Cor 1:12; 9:5).

rectively about A.D. 96 (*I Clement*) and why Ignatius can write to the Romans *ca.* 110: "You have taught others" (3:1).

THE JEWISH ASPECT OF I PETER

More important for our purposes than speculation about the origin and quality of Christianity among the recipients of I Peter is what the letter tells us about the Christianity of the Roman senders. Let us begin our analysis of that by looking at I Peter's appreciation of the Jewish heritage of Christianity.

Every commentary on I Peter reports long debates among scholars about whether chap. 1 (and part of chap. 2) represents in whole or part a baptismal homily, a baptismal liturgy, a baptismal hymn, or a baptismal confession. If we leave aside the minor differences, such suggestions imply something that would receive wider consent, namely, that the opening of I Peter offers a fundamental way of looking at Christian conversion and the status of Christian life. This presentation of Christian basics is very heavily influenced by the OT to the point that the exodus, desert wandering, and promised land motifs from the Pentateuch have simply been taken over and imaginatively reapplied to the conversion of Gentiles to Christ. If that desert experience made the slave tribes from Egypt into a people, nay God's people, so has Christian conversion made the Gentiles who were once no people into God's people (I Peter 2:10).

Let me illustrate this briefly. If the Hebrews who left Egypt were told to gird up their loins for quick departure (Exod 12:11), the Gentile Christian recipients of I Peter are told to gird up their mind (1:13). If in the desert the Israelites murmured and wanted to go back to the fleshpots of Egypt (Exod 16:2–3), the recipients of I Peter are warned about the passions of their former ignorance (1:14). Moses was ordered to tell the people whom God was making His own, "Be holy; for I, the Lord your God, am holy" (Lev 19:2); the same charge is quoted to the recipients of I Peter (1:15–16). Christian life is described as a time of exile with the hope of an inheritance yet to be attained (I Peter 1:17; 1:4), echoing Israel's desert wandering before it reached its inheritance in the promised land. Redemption and even the paying of a ransom were figures of speech used to describe

God's liberation of His people from Egypt (Exod 6:5–6; Deut 7:8; Isa 52:3), and so it is not surprising to find in I Peter 1:18: "You know that you were ransomed from the futile ways inherited from your fathers." The Israelites made a calf and worshiped it as the god who brought them out of the land of Egypt (Exod 32:1–4), a calf made with the silver and gold the Hebrew women got from their Egyptian neighbors at the time of the tenth plague (11:2); yet, in fact, the Hebrews had been spared from that plague by the blood of the unblemished passover lamb marking their houses (12:5–7). The echoes of this appear in the continuation of I Peter 1:18: ". . . ransomed not with perishable things such as silver and gold, but with the precious blood of Christ, like that of a lamb without blemish or spot."

One could continue (and below I shall do so in terms of the language of cult), but the analogies between the Israelite and the Christian salvific experiences are patent. Clearly such an instruction had its origin, however far back, in reflections that had a great appreciation of the Jewish heritage. One can scarcely imagine that it was shaped by Jewish Christian missionaries who shared with the Paul of Galatians a dualistic approach, applying the language of sin, slavery, and curse to the Israelite dispensation of the law given to Moses on Sinai. Such a presentation of Christian fundamentals as we find in I Peter is much more in harmony with a salvation history view whereby the divine kindness in the dispensation of Moses to Israel has been enlarged and increased in the dispensation of Christ to the Gentiles.

I Peter and Pauline Thought

General relationship. In treating the letter to the Romans in the last chapter, I argued that therein Paul presented a different face from the Paul of Galatians, one much more favorable to the Jewish heritage. As regards the Roman origin of I Peter, the correspondence of that letter with a moderate Paul is significant. First of all, even though the letter is presented as the work of Peter,[281] the only two

---

281. The strength of various Pauline features has led some scholars to argue that I Peter was originally presented as a letter of Paul but that someone misread the (hypothetically) abbreviated name *PS* in 1:1 as PETROS instead of PAULOS. This is most unlikely. Granted the number of Pauline letters, and granted the Pauline theology and named Pauline companions in this letter, a scribe filling out such an abbrevia-

people associated in the letter with Peter are people who had been associated with Paul. *Sylvanus* of I Peter 5:12, the purported secretary, is the Silas of Acts 15:22,27 who was sent from Jerusalem to bear to Gentiles the decision demanding, not circumcision, but obedience to some Jewish customs, a decision in harmony with the positions of James and Peter. According to 15:40 he became a companion of Paul in his journeys (confirmed by I Thess 1:1 and II Cor 1:19). *Mark* of I Peter 5:13 is presumably the John Mark of Acts 12:12, whose mother had a house in Jerusalem, and who became a companion of Paul (Acts 12:25—see pp. 191–94 below for detail). If shortly later John Mark broke off from Paul (13:13; 15:37–39—perhaps because he found Paul too alienated from the Law and the observance of Jewish customs), there is a tradition that Mark rejoined Paul before Paul's death (II Tim 4:11—meant to refer to a meeting at Rome?). Is it accidental that these two figures are echoes of the more conservative Jerusalem position *and* of Paul? Do they not fit the hypothesis that the Paul of Romans, a Paul much more moderate in his attitude toward Judaism, was accepted by the Roman church which had itself been founded from Jerusalem by Jewish Christians of a more conservative stance? The association of Sylvanus and Mark under the aegis of Peter in I Peter, then, would not differ in import substantially from the "Peter and Paul" combination of *I Clement* and Ignatius (p. 123 above), or from the Petrine patronizing of "our beloved brother Paul" in II Peter 3:15.[282]

Confirmation of this suggestion can be found in the oft-made observation of the presence of Pauline theology in I Peter—a development perfectly intelligible if the Roman community had accepted some of the main lines of Paul's thought with moderate nuances similar to those found in the letter he had addressed to them, and yet continued to regard Peter as the embodiment of its theological

---

tion would surely have guessed PAULOS (an attribution for which we have no manuscript evidence). No literary features or parallel compositions would have encouraged the guess PETROS. Moreover, in the first half of the second century this letter was already assigned to Peter by II Peter and by Papias, independently.

282. A meeting of minds between a moderated Paul and Peter is not inconceivable historically. Acts and Galatians present Peter as in agreement with the major Pauline stance of circumcision and as less antagonistic to Paul than was James on the issue of the food laws (see also Acts 10:15; 11:3,9).

stance.[283] Some of the ideas in I Peter are too general to be related to a specific Pauline epistle, e.g., the Gentiles as children of Sarah and Abraham in 3:6; righteousness (*dikaiosynē*) in I Peter 3:14; "in Christ" in 3:16; 5:10,14. But most scholars have recognized that the clearest and closest Pauline similarities of I Peter are to Romans.[284] I Peter 1:21 writes of Christian confidence in God who raised Jesus from the dead, while Rom 4:24 writes of the justification of those who believe in Him who raised Jesus from the dead.[285] I Peter 3:21–22 refers to the resurrection of Jesus Christ "who has gone into heaven and is at the right hand of God"; and a similar liturgical refrain is found in Rom 8:34: "Christ Jesus . . . who was raised from the dead, who is at the right hand of God." The theme of ceasing from sin and living in righteousness in I Pet 2:24 is quite similar to the formula in Rom 6:11: "dead to sin and alive to God in Christ Jesus." The conflation of "foundation stone" and "stumbling stone" texts from Isa 28:16 and 8:14–15 is found both in I Peter 2:6–8 and Rom 9:33. None of these similarities presupposes that the author of I Peter had Paul's Romans before him, but they do suggest that the theology and expressions of Paul's letter had worked their way into the life of the Roman church from whose tradition the author of I Peter shaped his message to northern Asia Minor.[286]

Particular strains of thought. Three motifs in Romans and I Peter are of importance in discerning the trajectory of Roman Christianity at the end of the first century—motifs to be found also in Hebrews and *I Clement,* as we shall see below. These significant strains of thought are: first, a frequent use of Jewish cultic language; second, an insistence on obedience to civil authority; and third, an increasing articulation of church structure.

The *first* of these involves the use of Jewish cultic language. A case can be made that there is more cultic language in Romans than

---

283. Best, *I Peter* 61, speaks of a type of biographical build-up of the image of Peter at Rome.

284. Parallels to Ephesians have also been urged; see Chapter X, section B, below, esp. footnote 394.

285. Best, *I Peter* 32, wisely cautions that Rom 4:24 may reflect a primitive confession, lest one assume too quickly that the author of I Peter knew the actual text of Romans (as held by Sanday and Headlam).

286. Thus Best, *I Peter* 34; Goppelt, *Petrusbrief* 50.

in any other undisputed Pauline epistle. (According to the theory advanced in the last chapter, that may have been because he was writing to a community particularly attached to the Jewish heritage, including the liturgical heritage.) In 3:25 he writes of Christ as an expiatory sacrifice (*hilastērion*) by his blood, a unique expression for Paul. In 12:1 he urges Christians to "present your bodies as a living sacrifice [*thysia*] holy and pleasing to God, which is spiritual [*logikos*] worship." In 15:16 he speaks of himself as a minister for Christ "in the *priestly* service of the gospel of God so that the offering of the Gentiles may be acceptable." I Peter, too, makes remarkable usage of cultic language in describing Christ and the Christian. As I noted above, I Peter 1:18–19 refers to the ransoming value of "the precious blood of Christ like that of a lamb without blemish." The titulary of ancient Israel is given to the body of Christians (including Gentile converts) in 2:9: "a chosen race, a royal *priesthood,* a holy nation, God's own people" (a list that confirms strongly my thesis above of the Jewish tone of I Peter's fundamental concepts). The priesthood in that list is explained in I Peter 2:5 (as in Romans above) in terms of offering "spiritual sacrifices [*thysia*] acceptable to God through Jesus Christ,"[287] and 2:12 connects such good conduct with the eventual enlightenment of the Gentiles.[288] Evidently the language of cult, used symbolically by Paul in addressing the Romans before the end of the Jerusalem Temple and its sacrifices, remained viable in Roman thought even after that fall. Indeed, the Christian community could be seen as "living stones built into a spiritual house" (I Peter 2:5; compare II Cor 6:16).

A *second* peculiar strain of thought in Romans and I Peter concerns Roman civil government.[289] The apostle makes his most eloquent appeal for obedience to governing authorities in Rom 13:1–

---

287. "Spiritual" in 2:5 is *pneumatikos,* not the *logikos* of Rom 12:1; but the latter term appears in I Peter 2:2, "spiritual milk."

288. In comparing Rom 12:1 and I Peter 2:2,5,12 one must consider the similarities not only in direct content (spiritual sacrifices for the Gentiles) but also in contextual expressions. Both Rom 12:2 and I Peter 1:14 warn, "Do not be conformed" (to the world, and to former passions, respectively). Rom 12:9–10,16 and I Peter 1:22 stress love of brother or one another.

289. The similarity of the two works on this point has been carefully studied by Goldstein, "Paränesen."

7,[290] an appeal perhaps necessitated because of Roman Christian resentment over Claudius' expulsion some years before. "Let every person be subject to the governing authorities," he instructs, insisting that all authority is from God. "He who resists the authorities resists what God has appointed, and those who resist will incur judgment; for rulers are not a terror to good conduct, but to bad." Paul goes on to state: "One must be subject not only to avoid God's wrath but also for the sake of conscience." He concludes on the note "Give honor to the one due honor." We find a similar message in I Peter 2:13–17, a message purportedly from the Peter who, along with many other Christians, was put to death by the emperor Nero: "Be subject for the Lord's sake to every human institution, whether it be to the emperor as supreme, or to governors as sent by him to punish wrongdoers and to praise those who do right." Peter thinks that such good behavior will silence ignorant foolish people. That observation is very appropriate if the imperial actions at Rome against Christians by Claudius and by Nero had aroused the suspicion that Christians were disloyal. Acts 28:22 records an opinion about Christians vocalized in Rome: "This sect is everywhere spoken against." Peter's ringing conclusion to his remarks should have settled that issue, "Honor the emperor."[291] Respect for imperial authority will be an ongoing issue in the history of the early Roman church as we shall see below (pp. 171–73).

A *third* strain of thought connecting Romans and I Peter is more subtle but still worth mentioning in the light of subsequent developments. In Rom 12:6–8 Paul clearly supposes that there are different assignments of function at Rome. In the one body of Christ there are different charismatic gifts of which he enumerates seven: prophecy, service, teaching, exhortation, contributing, presiding (*proistamenos*), and acts of mercy. The Pastoral Letters (I–II Timo-

---

290. Even if there may be a concept of spiritual powers (angels) behind the human authorities, the latter are certainly involved; for it is to civil government that one pays taxes (Rom 13:7).

291. If one thinks it implausible that the author would promote the emperor after a period of imperial persecution, the example of Josephus is important. Although he had fought against the Romans in the Jewish revolt of the 60s and although the Flavian emperors had conquered Jerusalem and destroyed the Temple, Josephus went to Rome under Flavian patronage, took their name, and wrote works designed to heal the rift between the Jews and the Romans.

thy, Titus), written after Paul's lifetime, show that in some of the Pauline churches of the 80s a more carefully articulated structure was developing: presbyters (elders) and deacons. Similarly in the Petrine church of Rome a structure of presbyters (elders) and younger men (deacons?) is taken for granted (I Peter 5:1–5)[292]—another good reason for thinking that the 80s is a more appropriate period than the 60s for the composition of I Peter. Within a few years after Paul's death in Rome, a disciple wearing his mantle was writing letters that turned the great apostolic missionary into a pastor, one of whose concerns was the structuring of existing communities so that they could survive. So also within a few years after Peter's death, a disciple wearing the mantle of Peter was writing a letter turning the great apostolic missionary fisherman into a shepherd, the pastoral image par excellence. Both authors instruct the recipients about their presbyters and deacons. The Pauline Pastorals and this Petrine pastoral are also similar in the great attention given to households. Elliott may well be right that this emphasis in I Peter on house/home was meant to offset the alienated isolation from society felt by the Christians of northern Asia Minor. In addition, however, for Rome with its house churches (Rom 16) as well as for the churches of the Pauline Pastorals, the stability and order assigned by the respective authors for the households pertains to *church* structure.[293]

B. The Epistle to the Hebrews

It has become fashionable to compare this work to its own description of Melchizedek, "without father or mother or genealogy" (7:3), because there is so much doubt about who wrote it to whom and when. In antiquity Origen summed up the authorship problem pungently: "Who wrote this epistle only God knows" (Eusebius,

---

292. For proof that the "youngers" of I Peter 5:5 may be deacons and not simply an age bracket, see J. H. Elliott, "Ministry and Church Order in the NT," CBQ 32 (1970) 367–91; however, this is a minority opinion. It is noteworthy that both the Pastorals and I Peter assign episcopal or overseeing functions to the presbyters and caution them not to be acquisitive of money; yet in neither has there emerged the structure of the single-bishop supervising the whole community.

293. Elliott, *Home* 264–65, surveys the literature on the importance of house organization in Rome and its relation to the idea of "church."

Hist. 6.25.14). Even the literary form is a mystery since "it begins like a treatise, proceeds like a sermon, and closes like an epistle."[294] Let us look at issues relevant to the possibility of using Hebrews to reconstruct the history of the Roman community.

DATE AND DESTINATION

Title. Acts 6:1 uses the designation "Hebrews" to refer to one type of Jews (who believed in Jesus) as distinct from another type of Jews (who believed in Jesus). It describes *a Hebrew-speaking group loyal to the Jerusalem Temple and its cult* as distinct from "Hellenists," a group speaking (only?) Greek, acculturated to the Hellenistic world and liberated from cultic loyalties.[295] (The "Hebrews" include James, Peter, and even "the apostles," as can be deduced from Acts 8:1ff., indicating who remained in Jerusalem when the Hellenists were scattered.) A similar meaning for the other NT uses of "Hebrew" (by Paul in Philip 3:5; II Cor 11:22) is not impossible, for the contexts stress Jewish loyalty and observance. Commonly, however, the term refers to Jews in general as distinct from other peoples, e.g., the Roman synagogue "of the Hebrews."[296] Working with the general meaning, most scholars assume that the title of this NT epistle, "To the Hebrews," which was *not* supplied by the author, came from an analysis of the contents, i.e., it was deduced that the author was writing to the Jews (who believed in Jesus but whose faith was wavering).[297]

This assumption is complicated by several factors, however. Some modern scholars argue that Hebrews was addressed to Gentile Christians[298]—a warning that an analysis of contents does not produce obvious results about "Hebrews." (Such a disagreement underlines the point already made in the Introduction above that "Jewish

---

294. H. E. Dana, cited by Glaze, *Salvation* 9.

295. The different attitudes may be deduced from Stephen's (Hellenist) speech in Acts 7:48–50; see pp. 7–8 above.

296. Leon, *Jews* 147–49.

297. For the suggestion that it was directed to converted Essenes, see footnote 325 below.

298. Spicq, *Hébreux* 1.223, lists Loisy, Holtzmann, Schürer, Harnack, McGiffert, and Goguel among others. Glaze, *Salvation* 15–16, mentions Röth, Scott, and Moffatt.

Christians" and "Gentile Christians" are not helpful designations unless we know what type of Jewish/Gentile Christianity was involved.) Moreover, the title "To the Hebrews," found in the oldest manuscript we possess (P46), was already in use by the year 200 in such diverse areas as Egypt (Pantaenus) and North Africa (Tertullian); and no other rival title has ever appeared in terms of destination. If the title arose as a scholarly deduction from the contents, when and how did this take place to account for such early unanimity? A counter-suggestion is that the title came from a tradition based on knowledge of the actual circumstances of composition and direction, i.e., that the letter was meant to correct Hebrew Christian views. Is it accidental that the theology of the epistle is very similar to that of Stephen, the *Hellenist* leader,[299] concerning the inadequacy of the Jewish place of cult—a view counterposed to the Hebrew Christian position in Acts? Plausibly the NT writing closest to Hebrews in the theme of replacing Jewish cult is the Fourth Gospel[300] where the incarnate Word is the Tabernacle of God among us (John 1:14: "and *tented* among us"), where Jesus' body is the Temple (2:21), and where Jesus replaces the motifs of the Sabbath, Passover, Tabernacles, and Dedication (Hanukkah),[301] so that they are "feasts of the Jews" but not of Christians. John has been called "The Gospel of the Hellenists,"[302] and a very serious case can be made that the Hellenists of Acts, the author of John, and the author of Hebrews should all be classified as variant species of Group Four of Jewish/Gentile Christians described in the Introduction (p. 7 above). The suggestion is tempting (but unprovable), then, that the title "To the Hebrews," given to the work not too long after it was composed, is

---

299. Spicq, *Hébreux* 1.202–3, lists similarities, including: predilection for the same OT characters as heroes and saints; condemnation of the desert generation of Israelites; typological use of the OT; giving of the Law through angels; construction of the Tabernacle along the lines of a heavenly model; the citation of Scripture as "God said" or "Moses said"; and the idea of "repose/rest." R. W. Thurston, "Midrash and 'Magnet' Words in the New Testament," *Evangelical Quarterly* 51 (1979) 22–39, argues for a literary connection between Acts 6–7 and Hebrews, reflecting a common midrash on Isa 66:1–2 and II Sam 7. Yet see footnote 11 above.

300. A most enduring contribution of Spicq's discussion of the background of Hebrews is his meticulous comparison of that epistle to John (*Hébreux* 1.92–138).

301. R. E. Brown, *Gospel* 1.202–4.

302. This was the title of B. W. Bacon's volume on John (New York: Holt, 1933).

accurate and precise, for the epistle was sent by a Hellenist theologian to dissuade a body of Hebrew Christians from their attachment to Jewish cult.[303] But *even without dependence on the title,* the realities of that observation stand as a plausible diagnosis of the epistle.[304]

Author and Locale. The view that Paul wrote Hebrews, already recognized as problematic in antiquity even by some of the church fathers who accepted it, is now almost universally abandoned. The differences of thought and expression are insurmountable,[305] and even the similarities (advanced by moderates as proof for a strong Pauline influence) have lost much of their persuasiveness since often they involve common NT elements[306] (rather than peculiarly Pauline) and since the discussion must be confined to the undisputed Pauline letters (rather than, for instance, speaking about similarities to Ephesians as proof of involvement with Paul). Among the other proposals for authorship, ancient and modern, Apollos of Acts 18:24ff; I Cor 1:12; 3:6; 4:6 remains the figure who fits most of the characteristics exhibited by the author of Hebrews (thus Luther, Zahn, Spicq, Héring).[307] Yet no discussion of the epistle can depend substantially on a theory of the author's identity, except for the recognition that he was a second-generation Christian (2:3) and not a well-known, first-rank apostle.

The Christian community of almost every city in the ancient world has, at one time or another, been suggested as the destination of Hebrews, but the greatest attention has been focused on Jerusalem

---

303. In the scene Acts 6:1–6 describes, these were two species of Jewish Christians; but Acts indicates further that both groups made Gentile converts. By the time Hebrews was written, the designations would have covered two species of Jewish/Gentile Christians.

304. Somewhat similarly, Glaze, *Salvation* 22ff., argues that Hebrews was sent to Jewish Christians still affiliated with a Jewish synagogue in Rome and that in the eyes of the author this affiliation with non-Christian Jews had compromised their Christianity.

305. Spicq, *Hébreux* 1.144–55.

306. Usually they are deemed to include the redemptive death of Christ as salvifically central, the importance of faith, a new covenant—elements that in my opinion would be advocated by the groups I have designated in the Introduction as Two, Three, and Four.

307. Tied in with the Apollos theory (since he was from Alexandria) is an emphasis on features of Alexandrian or Philonic literary, hermeneutic, and thought style found in Hebrews. See R. Williamson, *Philo and the Epistle to the Hebrews* (Leiden: Brill, 1970).

and Rome. The epistle contains a dissuasive against the levitical priesthood, animal sacrifices, and the earthly Holy of Holies; and Jerusalem is the only place where such cultic features would have been encountered as available realities. The dissuasive, however, seems to be against a *return* (10:32–39) to such features. In Jerusalem before the late 60s Jewish Christians did worship in the Temple, and after the destruction of the Temple in 70 there was no major sacrificial worship in Jerusalem—thus situations that make the language of "return" seem inapplicable. For that reason it has been suggested that Hebrews was addressed to a special Jerusalem group, e.g., to converted priests (Spicq) who would presumably not have been allowed to offer sacrifice after professing Jesus, or to the Jewish Christians who fled from Jerusalem in the 60s rather than join the revolt against Rome and could no longer go daily to the Temple (Acts 5:42). Hebrews could be seen as an appeal made in the late 60s to either group not to return to a cult that was now replaced by Christ. But that suggestion faces formidable obstacles. Would a second-generation Christian, not of apostolic rank, have hoped that his corrective or dissuasive could be influential in a city where James, the brother of the Lord and faithful adherent of Jewish cult, had such eminence? Why would the author write in elegant *Greek* a dissuasive to Jewish-Christian priests who would have known Hebrew as part of the liturgy, or to Jewish-Christian natives of Judea for whom Hebrew or Aramaic would have been a native language? Would not the foreign language and his constant use of the Greek Bible (rather than the Hebrew) have hurt his argument? Why would he have based the argument to either group on the liturgy of *the Tabernacle* as described in the Pentateuch but absent from the actual scene for almost a millennium? Why would he *never have mentioned the Temple* which had been part of the daily life of the reputed recipients? Paradoxically, the literary and idealized antiquarianism of the cultic debate in Hebrews makes Jerusalem the least likely recipient!

On the other hand, the only concrete indications of destination in Hebrews (13:23–24) suit Rome well as the recipient:

Know that our brother Timothy has been released, and with him I shall see you if he comes soon. Greet all your

leaders [*hēgoumenoi*] and all the saints. Those from Italy
send you greetings.

If we begin with the logical assumption that the recipients know
Timothy and are anxious to see him, it must be admitted that his
name is prominent in so many Pauline letters that we cannot hope
for an exact specification from that reference. While there is nothing
in the NT references to Timothy that would encourage one to associate his name with Jerusalem, in Rom 16:21 Paul made certain that
Timothy was the first whose greetings he shared with Rome. Philemon 1:1 associates him with Paul during an imprisonment, possibly
the imprisonment in Rome in the early 60s. II Timothy is deutero-
Pauline, but the author presumably was drawing on a plausible historical setting for the message that he was attributing to Paul. He
presents Paul as in prison and near death; and if II Timothy was
written after Paul died in Rome, could the author have intended any
other setting than Rome? (The Roman setting of II Timothy is virtually settled by the command in 4:11, "Get Mark and bring him with
you"; for as we saw in I Peter 5:13 there was a tradition that Mark
was with Peter in Rome before Peter died.) Paul twice urges Timothy to come to him soon, before winter (II Tim 4:9,21)—an urging
that would be exceedingly odd in a post-Pauline letter if Timothy
had not gone to Paul before the apostle died. One can argue, then,
that Timothy had been to Rome with Paul in the 60s and would have
been well known to the Roman community, so that Hebrews' news
about Timothy would have made sense to that destination.[308] If one is
tempted by the theory that Apollos was the author, we remember
that Priscilla and Aquila, who had trained him in Christian doctrine
in Ephesus in the mid-50s (Acts 18:24–26), were at Rome by the late

---

308. There is no overwhelming reason to regard Heb 13:22–25 as fictional even
though it is an epistolary touch added to a non-epistolary work. That Timothy is
about to be released from prison does not aid us significantly in guessing from where
Hebrews was sent, even if, presumably, the site of Timothy's imprisonment was the
place of composition or emission. Of course, those who thought that Paul wrote Hebrews saw this as a reference to Timothy's imprisonment with Paul in Rome, and a
reflection of Paul's hope to travel again after he himself had been released. This interpretation could favor Jerusalem as the recipient of Hebrews.

50s (Rom 16:3–5); and they would have known Timothy and have appreciated news of him.[309]

The greetings of Hebrews are extended in 13:24 "to all your leaders [*hēgoumenoi*]," a term used twice before in Heb 13. The first usage (13:7) is to past leaders who spoke to the recipients the word of God and set an example by their death and faith; the second (13:17) is to present leaders who keep watch over the souls of the recipients with the responsibility of giving an account. The first usage, if written to Rome, could be a reference to Peter and Paul martyred there in the 60s. (Obviously, however, it could also fit the death of other Christian leaders in other cities, including that of James in Jerusalem.[310]) The second usage of *hēgoumenoi* could also fit Rome. After the list of charisms that Paul assumes to exist in the church of Rome, he urges in Rom 12:10 that the Romans be "leaders [*prohēgoumenoi:* 'leaders in front'] of one another in honor." *I Clement,* written from Rome, expresses admiration for the obedience of the Corinthians to their *hēgoumenoi* (1:3), and indicates that these officials exist at Rome as well (21:6: "Let us show honor to our leaders [*prohēgoumenoi*]"), an indication confirmed by *Hermas, Vis.* 2.2.6; 3.9.7 in the early second century.

The greeting "to all the saints" in Heb 13:24 has been used as an argument for an address to Jerusalem, since "the saints" is a frequent designation for the Christian inhabitants of the Holy City, especially in relation to Paul's collection of money (Rom 15:25,31; I Cor 16:1; II Cor 8:4 etc.). But Rom 1:7 was addressed "To all God's beloved in Rome who are called to be saints"; and Rom 8:27; 16:2,15 show that "the saints" was a familiar designation for Christians at Rome (as it was for Christians in many places). Indeed, it is interesting to compare three texts: Rom 12:9,13: "Let your love be genuine. . . . Con-

---

309. The connection of Priscilla to Timothy led Harnack to propose her as author.

310. A reference to past martyrdom is not refuted by Heb 12:4, "In your struggle against sin, you have not yet resisted to the point of shedding blood," for that may refer to the present generation of recipients, sometime after the past martyrdoms. It has been argued with some justification that the description in Heb 10:32–34 of hard struggle, imprisonment, and plundering of property fits better the persecution of Christians at Rome under Nero than what happened to Christians in Jerusalem in the 60s.

tribute to the needs of the saints"; Heb 6:10 commending: "the love you showed in God's name in serving the saints";[311] and Ignatius' Introduction to *Romans,* commending the church "in the place of the land of the Romans" as "preeminent in love"—a church that never envied anyone but "taught others" (3:1).

In the concluding lines of Hebrews the most debated but potentially fruitful element for identifying the recipients is: "Those from [*apo*] Italy send you greetings." There is no doubt that in the Greek of this period the prepositional phrase can describe extraction and thus be translated simply "the Italians." Accordingly, only logic and context, not grammar, can tell us whether Italy is the place of expedition or of destination, i.e., whether the author is in Italy sending the greetings of the Italians to Christians elsewhere;[312] or the author is elsewhere sending greetings back to Italy, and to Rome in particular,[313] from Italian Christians living abroad (whence he is writing). The use of a country rather than a city in the phrase may favor the destination view. If the place of expedition were meant, so that, for example, the author was writing *from Rome* to Jerusalem, the claim to send greetings from the Italian (rather than the Roman) Christians would seem less personal to the recipients and more sweeping than the author could vouch for.[314] On the other hand, if the place of destination were meant, so that, for example, the author was writing from Jerusalem *to Rome,* he might wish to pass along greetings not only from the relatively few Roman Christians likely to be in Jerusa-

---

311. Also 13:1, "Let brotherly love continue," where, however, the *agapē* of the other citations is not used.

312. That is how the scribe of Codex Alexandrinus understood the phrase, for he added in 13:25 (after the grace): "Written from Rome." Since the Alexandrian scholars attributed Hebrews to Paul, such an addition reflects the theory that Paul wrote it during his Roman captivity—a theory probably reflected also in the arrangement of the third-century Beatty Papyrus (P⁴⁶) in which Hebrews follows Romans.

313. That the work was addressed to an Italian city other than Rome is implausible: It has to be a city with considerable Jewish Christian heritage and tendency, where Timothy is known, where the gospel was preached by eyewitnesses (2:3), and where the leaders died for the faith (13:7)—no other city in Italy would have matched all or most of those descriptions.

314. The extant NT examples of greetings from the place of expedition are more precise and use another construction; for example, the greeter is "the Co-elect *in* Babylon" in I Peter 5:13 [meaning: the church in Rome]; "those from [*ek*] the house of Caesar" in Philip 4:22; and "the churches *of* Asia" in I Cor 16:19.

lem or Judea but also from the larger pool of Italian Christians since they too would have had something in common with the Roman recipients as fellow countrymen. (Acts 28:13–14 mentions a Christian group at Puteoli [Pozzuoli] on the Bay of Naples; and there were Christians at Pompeii and Herculaneum, and probably at Ostia. Perhaps a few Christians from such places were living abroad. The Italian cohort was stationed at Caesarea according to Acts 10:1.)

Obviously such an argument is tenuous, and the real strength of Italy/Rome as the place of destination (rather than of expedition) comes from an external fact that supports the indication just discussed. As we shall see below, Hebrews was written in the period 65–90; yet it was already known in Rome by the year 96! Within *at most* thirty years of being written, Hebrews was cited by *I Clement,* which was written from the church of Rome to Corinth.[315] Indeed, through the whole second century Rome remains the main witness for an awareness of Hebrews, for it was known in and by such Roman evidence as the *Shepherd of Hermas,* the OT commentaries of Hippolytus (+235), Canon Muratori, and the presbyter(?) Gaius. (Only at the end of the second century does Hebrews surface clearly in the East with the Alexandrian Pantaenus, and in North Africa with Tertullian.[316]) Theoretically, one might object that very early and consistent Roman knowledge of Hebrews does not prove that Rome was the destination since a copy might have been kept at Rome even if it was the place of expedition. However, if Hebrews came from Rome, it would represent Roman views, and just the opposite is true: Both *I Clement* and *Hermas,* although using the wording of Hebrews, move

---

315. *I Clem.* 36:2–5 is parallel to Heb 1:3–13; *I Clem.* 17:1 ‖ Heb 11:37; *I Clem.* 17:5 ‖ Heb 3:5; see Spicq, *Hébreux* 1.177–78. Cockerill, "High Priest," argues strongly against the minority opinion that *I Clement* and Hebrews draw upon a common liturgy rather than the former on the latter. *The New Testament and the Apostolic Fathers* (Oxford: Clarendon, 1905), 137, gives a reasonably certain rating to the dependency of *I Clement* on Hebrews; Hagner, *Use* 194, says, "It seems certain."

316. Some posit knowledge of Hebrews in *Barnabas* thought to be written in Alexandria *ca.* 130 (see Spicq, *Hébreux* 1.169); but the Oxford volume cited in the preceding footnote gives a low degree of probability to such knowledge. P. Prigent (with R. Kraft), *Epître de Barnabé* (SC 172; Paris: Cerf, 1971) would place Barnabas in Syria/Palestine rather than Alexandria and attribute it to Hellenist circles. If the author knew Hebrews, this attribution would strengthen the thesis that Hebrews comes from a Hellenist background.

in an almost opposite thought-direction.[317] That is best explained if Hebrews was a work received by the Roman church but never enthusiastically appropriated. Indeed, such an explanation is almost necessitated by Rome's attitude toward the canonical status of Hebrews. Even though Alexandrian and Eastern knowledge of Hebrews appears nearly a century after Roman knowledge, the epistle was relatively quickly accepted as canonical in the East and attributed to Paul. Rome never suggested it was from Paul; and indeed at the very moment Alexandria was making the Pauline attribution, Canon Muratori and Gaius the Roman presbyter[318] were implicitly or explicitly denying it. As late as 380, Ambrosiaster, a good bellwether of Roman feeling, commented on thirteen letters of Paul but not on Hebrews. This was possible, I suggest, because Rome, which received the letter in the first place, knew that it did not come from Paul, and such a memory left its mark. The author was a second-generation Christian authority (Heb 2:3) and respected as such by the Roman recipients, but he did not have the influence of an apostle. Rome's attitude toward the canonicity and hence toward the authority of Christian writings was determined by accepted apostolic origin[319] (an attitude understandable in a church priding itself in having two apostolic "pillars," Peter and Paul); and so Hebrews was not Scripture by the Roman criterion. Only when the opinion that Paul wrote it won the day (*ca.* 400) was Rome willing to accept it as the fourteenth letter of the apostle.

The ultimate test of the theory that Hebrews was a work addressed to the church of Rome will be whether it makes sense on a Roman scene diagnosed from works more certainly associated with Rome. After a brief discussion of the date of Hebrews, I shall at-

---

317. In the next chapter I shall point out that *I Clement* differs markedly from Hebrews in the estimation of levitical cult. *Hermas* is less rigorous than Hebrews in the question of forgiveness after baptism, even though it wrestles with Heb 4:4–6 (*Vis.* 2.2–4; *Sim.* 9.26.6). When some fifty years later Callistus of Rome extended even farther the practice of forgiveness, it was in part because he did not regard Hebrews as binding Scripture.

318. Gaius' attitude toward Hebrews lends support to joining Hebrews and John as examples of a more radical (Hellenist) Christianity. From Gaius came the last gasp of resistance to the acceptance of the Fourth Gospel in the Roman church; see R. E. Brown, *Community* 149.

319. Spicq, *Hébreux* 1.188–89.

tempt below the task of interpreting Hebrews against a Roman background. But even before that crucial step I would conclude by insisting that the Roman direction of Hebrews makes more sense of the introductory material discussed above than does any other theory.

Date. There is not much enthusiasm among scholars for dating Hebrews before the last third of the first century. Hebrews 13:5 implies a well-established church where monetary problems have developed. In 2:3 it is clear that the author and the recipients share a Christianity of the second generation, "attested to us by those who heard him." Indeed, 13:7 suggests that "those who spoke to you the word of God" died long enough ago so that now their faith is the object of imitation. "Jesus Christ is the same yesterday and today and forever" (13:8) makes sense as a refrain only if "yesterday" was sufficiently past that a theme of continuity and stability needed to be emphasized. In 10:32 the author urges, "Recall the former days when, after you were enlightened, you endured a hard struggle with sufferings." It is true that the descriptions of persecution in Hebrews are too general to enable identification with a specific exile or with bad treatment under Claudius or Nero. Yet the portrayed severity of past inflictions, especially if one finds a hint of martyrdom in 13:7, fits poorly any period before the late 60s.[320] Granting that and realizing that *ca.* A.D. 96 *I Clement* quoted Hebrews, one is reasonably safe in fixing 65–95 as the range within which Hebrews was composed.

Attempts to refine the date further center on the cultic descriptions scattered throughout Hebrews, especially on two peculiarities that have been used to support a date before the Jerusalem Temple was destroyed in August of 70: (1) Present tenses would give the impression that levitical sacrifices are still being offered, e.g., "There are priests who offer gifts according to the Law" (8:4); "The priests

---

320. If Hebrews were written to Rome while Peter and Paul were still alive there, omission of a reference to them (while Timothy is mentioned) would be strange. Edmundson, *Church* 140, dubiously claims that Heb 10:33, "You were made a spectacle by insults and afflictions," refers to the Neronian horrors in the Vatican Gardens described by Tacitus where Christians became flaming torches. Similarly uncertain is Edmundson's argument (*Church* 153) that the *Quo vadis* legend (Peter met Jesus going into Rome to be crucified again) is echoed in Heb 6:6, "They crucify again the Son of God."

go continually into the first Tabernacle, performing their ritual duties, but into the second the high priest goes once a year" (9:6–7); "The Law can never make perfect those who draw near by the same sacrifices that are continually offered year after year—otherwise would they not have ceased to be offered?" (10:1–2). (2) In a work that stresses a new covenant replacing the old as obsolete (8:13), there is no reference to the destruction of the Temple,[321] which would have strengthened the argument. In evaluating these two points, I think the first has no decisive weight. Josephus, in *Against Apion* (2.77), twenty-five years after the destruction of the Temple, writes of the Jewish cult in the present tense: "We offer without stopping sacrifices for them [the emperor and the Roman people]." *I Clement* 40:4–5, similarly a quarter century after the destruction of the Jerusalem Temple, says, "Those who make their offerings at the appointed times are acceptable and blessed ... for to the high priest his proper liturgical ministrations are allotted"—a use of present tenses all the more important because the work illustrates the mentality of the church of Rome! Mishnaic documents from a century or more later describe sacrifices and priestly duties in minute detail, as if the cult were still active. Evidently, present tenses in such works describe an ideal, i.e., the permanent customs of a ritual that is thought to have a timeless value. And it is such a value that Hebrews is attacking as now antiquated. The idea that the author to prove his point would have had to appeal to the destruction of the Jerusalem Temple, if that had already taken place, misunderstands his point. The sacrifices ceased when the Babylonians destroyed the First Jerusalem Temple, but they resumed seven decades later when the Second Temple was built; and many would have expected the same recurrence after the Second Temple was destroyed. Hebrews is saying that there is no more value in such cultic observances, not because the Jerusalem Temple has been destroyed—an argument that would have reduced the issue to the temporary and the temporal—but because Christ has replaced forever their significance. This interpretation of the author's point is related to his writing about the Tabernacle rather than the Temple, a choice that we shall need to discuss below.

---

321. Some would see a reference to the destruction of Jerusalem in Heb 13:14: "We have here no lasting city."

If the author had no need to mention the destruction of the Temple, there is, in my judgment, no compelling reason for dating Hebrews before A.D. 70; and the overall evidence favors the thesis that Hebrews was written to the Roman church in the period 75–90. The ultimate test of the plausibility of that thesis, however, is whether the message of Hebrews makes sense as a corrective of Roman church attitudes in the last third of the century, as those attitudes have been reconstructed in previous chapters.

THE MESSAGE OF HEBREWS TO ROMAN CHRISTIANITY

There is no evidence that Roman Jews either gave significant assistance to the Judean revolt of the 60s against Rome or caused any trouble in Rome itself. But the fall of Jerusalem and the destruction of the Temple must have had an impact on them. They would have witnessed the triumphal parade marking the return of Titus from Jerusalem, with the sacred liturgical vessels from the Temple prominently displayed. (Josephus, *War* 7.5.3–6; #118–57.) The length of the campaign in Judea had embarrassed Rome—the great empire had bogged down militarily in disciplining a minor province—and the imperial organs of propaganda needed to emphasize the absoluteness of the victory. For many years afterwards (through Domitian's reign!) the coins celebrating the Jewish defeat (*Iudaea capta*) were struck, and so in their daily monetary transactions the Jews were reminded of the humiliation. In 80 as Titus came to the end of his life the great arch that bears his name was completed at one end of the Roman Forum where one can still see the graphic portrayal of the loot from Jerusalem and the Temple being brought to Rome. The Jews who had hitherto paid a tax-equivalence for the support of that Temple were now forced to pay a special "Jewish tax" for the support of the Roman temple of Jupiter Capitolinus—a not-too-subtle reminder as to which god and which nation had won.

Despite the Roman panoply, hopes would have been raised among some Roman Jews that ultimately the Temple would be rebuilt in Jerusalem: a Third Temple still longed for by some orthodox Jews today.[322] The Jewish apocalypses of the period (*IV Ezra, II Ba-*

---

322. The possibility that some worship continued in the Temple ruins (K. W. Clark, NTS 6 [1959–60] 269–80) shows the strength of levitical hopes—a key to my argument above.

ruch) imply an analogy to the earlier fall of Jerusalem to Babylon. The fact that the Temple was rebuilt after that fall may have prompted the petition in the oldest form of the prayer, the *Shemoneh Esreh,* composed about this time: "Be merciful, O Lord our God ... to Jerusalem, your city; and to Zion, the dwelling place of your glory; and to your Temple, your habitation." How would this panoply have affected *Christians* in Rome if, as I have argued, whether Jew or Gentile by birth, the dominant Christianity was marked by Jerusalem origins, where their spiritual ancestors had combined loyalty to the Temple with faith in Jesus (Acts 2:46; 5:42; 21:23–26)? Many scholars seem to assume that all Christians rejoiced in the fall of the Jerusalem Temple as a divine judgment and so easily moved into denying the need of a special sacred place on earth. I would contend that such a radical attitude is clearly attested only in a few NT works, namely, those characteristic of the Hellenists (Group Four on p. 7 above). It need not have been characteristic of more conservative Christians who might logically have expected the Jerusalem Temple to be replaced by another earthly sanctuary of a peculiarly Christian character. The idea that there should be a *visible* replacement for the Jewish levitical cult, sacrifices, and priesthood may have seemed especially persuasive at Rome where the visible pagan cult with its Pontifex Maximus and the Temple of Jupiter Capitolinus seemed to be the rival replacement after the Roman victory over Jerusalem. After all, Christians had a statement in their tradition about Jesus' destroying the Jerusalem Temple and building an "other." The variety of NT interpretations about the "other"[323] shows that there was no unanimity in understanding whether the replacement would be visible or of another kind, whether it would be a purified continuation or radically different.

On the basis of Hebrews let me suggest a possible form of conservative Jewish/Gentile Christian thought about a replacement for

---

323. John 2:19–22 understands that Jesus was speaking of his own body but that this insight came to the disciples only afterwards. Mark 14:58 (besides the complication of being on the lips of *false* witnesses) has a form of the saying with the added phrases "made with hands" and "not made with hands," showing that the material Temple would be replaced by some form of spiritual temple (the church?). Matthew 26:61 casts the statement in a modal form that does not guarantee what will happen: "I am able to destroy the Temple of God and build it in three days."

the Jerusalem Temple through a purified visible continuity. There is no doubt that the exodus from Egypt and the period in the desert played a role in shaping early Christian self-understanding, especially that of the Jerusalem church described in Acts. Israel became the covenanted people of God in that desert experience centered around Sinai; now God was renewing His covenant through Christ. His procedure with Israel illumined His procedure with the church. The Pentecost scene in Acts 2:1–12 is fully intelligible only when it is understood against the background of God's giving the covenant on Sinai (which was the salvation-history meaning of the Pentecost feast for many Jews[324]). The common goods of the Jerusalem church and the distribution of them to the needy reflect the desert ideal of Deut 15:4 that there would be no poor in Israel. Even the designation "church" (*ekklēsia*) echoes the Septuagint of Deut 23:3,8 which uses that term for "the assembly of the Lord" in the desert. The parallels between the Jerusalem Christian community and the Dead Sea Scroll (Qumran) community have often been noted. They are understandable because both communities regarded themselves as Israel renewed through the covenant of God, and both modeled themselves on the original Israel at the time of the Sinai covenant.[325]

Now, as part of my contention that the mentality of the church of Rome was derived from the Jerusalem church, I showed above (p. 133) that the presentation of Christian basics in I Peter (reflecting

---

324. See B. Noack, "The Day of Pentecost in Jubilees, Qumran, and Acts," *Annual of the Swedish Theological Institute* 1 (1962) 73–95. The wind and the fire reflect the elements of the storm that surrounded God's appearance on Sinai (Exod 19:16–19). The tongues of fire echo some of the midrashic reflections on Exod 20: 18–19 where God's voice had to reach people at a distance. Philo, *De Decalogo* 42: "A voice sounded with fire coming from heaven, filling all with fire; and the flames changed to articulated voices which were entrusted to hearers."

325. Y. Yadin and C. Spicq suggest that Hebrews was directed to Christian converts from the Qumran Essenes who were in danger of relapsing. (For parallels between Hebrews and the Dead Sea Scrolls, see F. C. Fensham, *Neotestamentica* 5 [1971] 9–21.) Rather, I think, it was directed to a Christianity that had attitudes toward cult partially similar to those of the Qumran Essenes. The latter were estranged from the Temple because it had been rendered imperfect by a change of calendar and the loss of the purest high-priestly pedigree. The Christians were living at a time when the Temple was no more, and their attitude toward it was influenced by the saying of Jesus that he would/could destroy the Temple and build another. The Essenes seem to have carried on cult at their desert monastic site, perhaps seeing this as the renewal of the Tabernacle cult.

Roman church thought) was heavily influenced by the OT antecedents of the exodus, desert wandering, and the promised land. After
the destruction of the Jerusalem Temple might not Christians of
such a church think that the Temple was to be replaced by a return
to the levitical sacrificial cult of the desert—a cult no longer tied
down to a fixed building in Jerusalem and for that reason suitable to
a spiritual Israel in the diaspora; a levitical cult not weighed down by
the corruption of wealth and splendor and so more suitable to a pil-
grim people? Remember that Acts 6:7 tells us that "a great number
of the priests" at Jerusalem accepted faith in Christ, and in the
Christian community of Rome there may have been elements of that
levitical heritage. In other words, I wonder whether the Jewish/Gen-
tile Christianity of Rome might not have been attracted by something intermediary between the Jerusalem Temple and a worship "in
Spirit and truth" (if we may use the phrase of John 4:24 to describe
the radical Hellenist alternative), even as presumably Roman Christianity was attracted by something intermediary between insistence
on circumcision and a complete rejection of the Law. I am not suggesting that the thought of having an actual Tabernacle would have
been involved, but "Tabernacle" as the embodiment of the desert
cult is not a bad term for describing such an intermediate theology in
regard to a visible, purified Christian continuity of the levitical cult
not localized in the Jerusalem Temple.

Hebrews would have been written as a corrective to such hopes
if they existed (and I claim no more than plausibility). Representing
the radical (Hellenist) "left" of the Christian spectrum, Hebrews'
conclusion (13:14), "We have here no lasting city, but we seek the
city which is to come," is almost the same as the promise of John
4:21: "An hour is coming when neither on this mountain nor in Jerusalem will you do the worshiping of the Father." From his book
knowledge of the ancient Israelite cult the author of Hebrews has
fashioned the imagery of Jesus as the high priest whose sacrifice on
the cross and intercession in heaven is more effective than could be
the cult in any earthly sanctuary. The only true Tabernacle is now in
heaven (8:1–2; 9:24); there has been a change in both priesthood and
the Law (7:12); the new covenant renders the former covenant obsolete and makes it ready to vanish (8:13).

If this interpretation has merit, Romans and Hebrews, two letters written to the church of Rome some twenty years apart, are an interesting contrast.[326] Paul wrote to that moderate conservative Christian community in the late 50s to assure them that he was not a (Hellenist) radical and was sympathetic to some of the hereditary privileges possessed by Israel. Hebrews was addressed to the same community when in whole or in part it had been seized by a nostalgia for the Israelite heritage—probably because the destruction of the Jerusalem Temple seemed to pave the way for Christianity to make its own that heritage. The epistle is an unabashed Hellenist tractate, considerably more radical toward the Jewish heritage than was Paul. Spicq (*Hébreux,* 1.234) has argued that Hebrews could not have been written to Rome because Paul praised the faith of the Romans (1:8), while Hebrews says that the recipients who ought to be teachers[327] need to be taught the first principles of God's word (5:12). But Spicq does not recognize that such diverse evaluations of Roman Christianity are affected by the fact that Paul and the author of Hebrews were not in the same vein of Christian thought.[328]

Often it has been thought that Hebrews was dissuading Christians from becoming discouraged, going back to Judaism, and thus apostatizing from faith in Christ; but other scholars have argued that neither apostasy nor decline is the exact danger envisioned.[329] An in-

---

326. There is insufficient evidence to tell us if the author of Hebrews knew Romans. Hebrews 10:30a does not cite Deut 32:35 in the LXX form (as is the author's wont) but in the same way as Rom 12:19 cites it. Hebrews 10:38 cites Hab 2:4 (about the righteous living by faith), even as does Rom 1:17; but Romans and Hebrews do not seem to share the same understanding of faith/fidelity in the Habakkuk passage. The relationships between Romans and Hebrews may come through the stability of the Roman community rather than through literary dependence (see Elliott, *Home* 163).

327. Through I Peter the church of Rome teaches the Gentile Christians of northern Asia Minor. Ignatius, *Rom.* 3:1, praises the church of Rome for having "taught others." Hebrews may be challenging such a reputation and practice.

328. In the Introduction above, I characterized Paul as a (leftist) representative of Group Three, and Hebrews as representative of Group Four. Both are to the "left" of mainstream Roman Christianity which I would classify as Group Two. Let me reiterate that all such classification is too simple, not doing full justice to the subtleties of positions.

329. The term "apostasy" is sometimes used to translate "falling away again" in 6:6, but the Greek has no necessary implication of returning to a previous religion. In any case, figurative hyperbole might be involved. See P. Andriessen, "La communauté des 'Hébreux' etait-elle tombée dans le relâchement?" *Nouvelle Révue Théologique* 96 (1974) 1054–66.

telligent case has been made that the attraction being combatted is an orientation not toward Judaism but toward a more conservative form of Jewish Christianity.[330] Perhaps it would be better to speak of the combatted attraction as a deeper commitment to the values of the Jewish cult,[331] with the concomitant tendency to fit Jesus into an uninterrupted schema of salvation history, subsequent to the angels and Moses as revealers of God's will. Hebrews argues insistently *from the Jewish Scriptures* (evidently appealing to those for whom such Scriptures are primary) that, as God's Son, Jesus breaks the schema for he is above the angels who gave the Law and above Moses. Even though he was fully human, like us in everything except sin (Heb 4:15), Jesus has rendered otiose all sacrifices, the levitical priesthood, and an earthly Holy of Holies. "By a single offering he has perfected for all time those who are sanctified" (10:14). He is a high priest, holy, blameless, unstained, exalted above the heavens, who continues forever (7:24–26). In making his point, the author of Hebrews is not simply opposing a movement "back" in favor of the status quo; he is pushing the recipients away from an existing Jewish adherence which he compares to elementary training (5:11 – 6:1). The first order, consisting of the Jewish cult, has been abolished to bring about a new order of God's will (10:9). If the image of Israel in the desert has set the perimeters of the discussion, Hebrews ends with a ringing cry, "Let us go forth outside the camp" (13:13). If nostalgia has been provoked by the fall of Jerusalem, he states, "We have here no lasting city" (13:14).

The author of Hebrews uses considerable oratorical skill and shows diplomacy. He appeals to the "brothers" whom he addresses to bear with the brief "word of exhortation" that he has written them (13:22). When Paul was arguing against an ultraconservative form of

---

330. Dahms, "Readers." Hebrews does not stress the issue of circumcision, so that, in the language of the Introduction above, the movement feared would *not* have been from Group Two toward Group One (footnote 328 above) but toward the rightist extreme of Group Two.

331. Notice Heb 13:9–10: "Do not be led away by diverse and strange teachings . . . we have a [heavenly] altar from which *those who serve the Tabernacle* have no right to eat." It would be peculiar to describe most non-Christian Jews in such a way since they scarcely served a Tabernacle that had not existed for centuries. "Serve the Tabernacle" may describe an appreciative attitude toward Jewish cult held by a group that no longer was affiliated with the Temple.

Jewish/Gentile Christianity in Galatia, he was angry with and harsh toward the "fools" he was addressing (3:1), denouncing circumcision as of no avail (5:2–5). But after Hebrews has argued forcefully against a foundation of dead works (6:1), the author is carefully gentle in tone: "Even though we speak in this manner, yet in your case, beloved, we feel sure of better things that belong to salvation" (6:9). Often his thought is more radical than that of Paul in seeing the old covenant as abolished and replaced; still he acknowledges that it had value, and he does not align what he is arguing against with sin, a curse, and a restraint (contrast Gal 2:10 – 3:26).[332] His reasoning is in terms of a *more excellent* ministry and a covenant based on *better* promises (8:6). The blood of sacrificial animals did in fact purify temporarily, but how *much more* does the blood of Christ purify (9:13–14). Hebrews devotes a whole chapter to the praise of "the elders" of Israel, but as *believers* in the promise they could not yet see,[333] namely, the "better" which God had reserved for the Christians (11:2,39–40). The diplomacy of the author may be seen also in his acknowledgment of the brotherly love of the church addressed and the request that this love continue (13:1), and in the deference he shows for the "leaders" (13:7,17)—themes that, as we have seen (pp. 145–46 above), were at home on the Roman church scene.

This sensitive approach may explain the fate of Hebrews at Rome. It never won the day,[334] but it was not rejected outright. Rather the Roman church "domesticated" its challenge, as we shall see when we discuss *I Clement;* and the end product was a greater attachment at Rome to the levitical cult than Hebrews advocated. Spicq, *Hébreux* 1.224, has suggested that Hebrews was written to a particular group within a church. (In part, he bases this on Heb 10:25 which criticizes some who neglect to come to the common meeting.) That raises the tempting possibility that the whole Roman

---

332. Spicq, *Hébreux* 1.150, points out that Hebrews uses the contrasts type/antitype and shadow/reality, but not the Pauline contrasts: Law/gospel, letter/spirit, slave/free, sin/grace, and curse/blessing.

333. In praising Moses as a man of faith, Heb 11:23–29 does not mention his receiving the covenant; rather later (12:18–22) there is a contrast between the terrifying experience at Sinai and the festive Zion of the heavenly Jerusalem.

334. See footnote 317 above. We do not know whether the dominant Roman Christianity kept some of the Jewish food laws as did the Christianity at Jerusalem associated with James, but Heb 13:9 shows disdain for such observances.

church was not tilting toward an ultraconservative appreciation of the levitical cult, but only a group. Indeed, the suggestion of Glaze (footnote 304 above) that it was a group still affiliated with a Jewish synagogue is fascinating. Perhaps, then, even though the radical solution proposed by Hebrews could not be accepted at Rome, Hebrews was respected because the more balanced section of the Roman church likewise rejected an ultraconservative nostalgia for the levitical cult.

I Peter, also written after the fall of Jerusalem, shows how cultic realities were dealt with by the moderate conservatives in Rome. The authors of both works can agree on Christians' offering sacrifice to God through Christ ("spiritual sacrifices" in I Peter 2:5; "sacrifice of praise" in Heb 13:15). Yet the author of I Peter does not eliminate all priesthood except Christ's as does Hebrews but speaks of Christians as a holy or royal priesthood (2:5,9). The author does not do away with every sanctuary on earth as does Hebrews but speaks of Christians as being built into a spiritual house (2:5). Elliott, *Home* 99, 129, points out correctly that, although I Peter and Hebrews share the same points of concern, I Peter does not direct attention to a heavenly home but speaks of realities in this world.[335] Thus there is a spiritualized continuation of the levitical realities in I Peter (as there was also in Paul's Romans; see p. 137 above), not the otherworldly replacement advocated by Hebrews. The response of I Peter, then, to those who yearned for a material continuation of the cult would have been less drastically antithetical, a response befitting a church tradition with a strong attachment to the Jewish heritage.

---

335. The similarities between the two works stem from the fact that both were dealing with issues pertinent to the life and tradition of the Roman church; see pp. 145–46 above concerning church leaders, love, and hospitality. Surely, however, in insisting that there is no literary dependence or true parallelism of view, Spicq, *Hébreux* 1.139–44, is correct against von Soden, Selwyn (*First Epistle* 463–66), and T. E. S. Ferris, "A Comparison of St. Peter and Hebrews," *Church Quarterly Review* 111 (1930–31) 123–27.

CHAPTER IX

The Roman Church
at the Beginning of the
Third Christian Generation

(A.D. 96—*I Clement*)

THE previous chapters discussed Romans, I Peter, and Hebrews. We now come to a work written from Rome that shows familiarity with basic ideas in the three previous works and perhaps with the works themselves. Yet *I Clement* is not simply repetitive; it reformulates the Jewish cultic heritage and offers a peculiarly Roman view of church order, giving direction to Christian hierarchical patterns for centuries to come.[336] Written in the 90s, it marks the end of the forty-year period (which began with Romans in the late 50s) that I have chosen for studying the origins of the Roman church in NT times, and so *I Clement* becomes the final test of my diagnosis of the moderate character of Jewish/Gentile Christianity at Rome.

DATE, AUTHOR, SITUATION

As seen above (pp. 123–25), *I Clem.* 5 – 6 lists the trials of Peter and Paul as an early example of how "jealous zeal" among Christians led to persecution and death. Clearly the author is *reminding* his readers of the careers of these two church "pillars," even as in chaps. 42 and 44 he speaks of the apostles as a past generation. Thus he is writing some time after the martyrdoms of the mid-60s. Simi-

---

336. For full detail on *I Clement,* see Fuellenbach, *Ecclesiastical,* a virtual encyclopedia of views with an ample bibliography.

larly the author refers to the church of the Corinthians (founded *ca.* 50) as "ancient" (47:6). Yet the author still speaks of Peter and Paul as having "contended in the days nearest to us" (5:1), and of the multitude of Neronian martyrs as having suffered "among us," so that a date many generations later (into the second century) seems impossible.[337] Generally it is assumed that the opening reference (1:1) "to the sudden and repeated misfortunes and calamities which have befallen us" recalls the persecution of some Christians in the latter years of the Emperor Domitian (81–96),[338] a persecution that seems to be in view also in the Book of Revelation when it calls Rome a prostitute "drunk with the blood of saints and the blood of the martyrs of Jesus" (Rev 17:6). For these reasons, scholars date *I Clement* about A.D. 96 just after the persecution ended.

This is a work of the third Christian "generation," by an author who is surely not an apostle, nor seemingly one of those disciples of the apostles who felt close enough to them to write in their name. We have moved from the sub-apostolic period that produced I Peter and the Pauline Pastorals to the fully post-apostolic period of the third generation where a community or author must stand on its or his own authority, at most claiming to be in apostolic succession.[339] *I Clement* is sent from "the church of God which sojourns in Rome,"[340] but the writer never identifies himself by name. The *Shepherd of Hermas,* written at Rome (in part, *ca.* A.D. 100–120), mentions a Clement (*Vis.* 2.4.3) who had the job of sending to other cities writings pertinent to the church. Dionysius, bishop of Corinth (the

---

337. Ignatius, A.D. 109–17, in commenting that the Romans taught others (*Rom.* 3:1), may be referring to *I Clement*'s teaching Corinth, as well as to I Peter.

338. The calamities mentioned in 1:1 which delayed the letter seem closer in time to Clement than are the deaths of Peter and Paul described by him in chap. 5 (footnote 256 above). Presumably Clement is referring to the selective persecutions which occurred after 93 as Domitian became more intolerant of suspected threats to his authority. See the references in footnote 265 above.

339. My remarks above are general. The pseudonymous use of apostles' names continued for centuries; but in my opinion all the pseudonymous works that the church accepted as canonical Scripture belong to the sub-apostolic period of the last third of the first century, with the exception of II Peter.

340. In footnote 239 above I rejected the contention that Paul did not look upon the Roman community as a church. The idea of "sojourning" (*paroikein*), shared with I Peter, represents a Roman legal status for those who are not truly at home (Elliott, *Home* 24ff.). It may stem from the Jerusalem origins of the Roman church—all outside Palestine are sojourners in a diaspora.

Church that received *I Clement*), writes to Rome *ca.* 170 about the letter "which was earlier sent to us through Clement" (Eusebius, *Hist.* 4.23.11). A decade later Irenaeus (*Adv. haer.* 3.3.3.) writes: "In the time of Clement . . . the church in Rome dispatched a most powerful letter to the Corinthians." This evidence, coming from various sources where a knowledge of the author might have been available, has convinced virtually all that Clement was the actual writer, even if he did this "in the name of the Roman church" (Eusebius, *Hist.* 3.16).

Who was this Clement? *Ca.* A.D. 95 the distinguished nobleman Titus Flavius Clemens (a consul, Vespasian's nephew and cousin of Domitian, and thus father of Domitian's presumptive heirs) was put to death for indolence and/or for atheism.[341] Atheism, we remember, was a charge often leveled at Jews and Christians;[342] and Cassius Dio specifically mentions "Jewish ways" in relation to this execution. Flavia Domitilla (the wife and relative of Clemens, the granddaughter of Vespasian and the niece of Domitian) was banished. In the second century the cemetery of Domitilla became a Christian burial place (catacomb); and Eusebius, *Hist.* 3.18, describes her as a Christian. There is confusion in this tradition (which may involve two women named Domitilla), but it led later to an identification of the writer of *I Clement* with the consul—an identification surely to be rejected. More plausible is the suggestion that there was Judaism and/or Christianity in the household of the consul, and that a freedman who took his name from the household where he had been a slave was the Christian Clement who wrote the letter. Many scholars, including some who hold the freedman thesis, judge that Clement was of Jewish birth, whether raised as a Christian or a Christian convert. He does show good knowledge of the OT, but in the LXX form and without the slightest indication that he knew Hebrew. Unfortunately, much of the discussion of whether Clement was a Jewish

---

341. Suetonius, *Domitian* 15–17; Cassius Dio, *History* 67.14.2; also L. Hertling and E. Kirschbaum, *The Roman Catacombs and Their Martyrs* (Milwaukee: Bruce, 1956) 22–25; and Leon, *Jews* 33–35.

342. E. Mary Smallwood, "Domitian's Attitude toward the Jews and Judaism," *Classical Philology* 51 (1956) 1–13, esp. 7–9, argues that Clemens and Domitilla were "God-fearers," i.e., Gentiles attracted to Judaism, while Barnard, "St. Clement" 13–14, argues against her that they were Christians.

Christian or a Gentile Christian fails to recognize the factors I discussed in the Introduction above, namely, that often Gentiles reflected the Christianity of the Jews who converted them. A thorough knowledge of Jewish traditions, such as scholars have uncovered in *I Clement*,[343] tells us little about the ethnicity of the author; for if I have correctly diagnosed the mainstream of Christianity at Rome as a Jewish/Gentile Christianity very loyal to its Jewish heritage (Group Two), such knowledge may have been characteristic of Roman Christianity well into the second century. (We shall see on p. 203 below that it was still characteristic *ca.* 130–140 when *Hermas* was completed.) A Gentile stemming from such Christianity might well use Jewish traditions throughout and still write the Greek of *I Clement*, which is more elegant than that of I Peter (perhaps written by a Jew), and show the patterns of Hellenistic and Stoic thought found in *I Clement*.[344] Certainly the names of the messengers sent to Corinth with *I Clement* (65:1: Claudius Ephebus, Valerius Vito, Fortunatus) suggest that ethnically Gentiles were a strong presence among the Roman Christians. Seemingly this had been true for a long time, since 63:3 states that these men had been part of the Christian community since their youth.

If Clement was not a noble consul of Rome, what ecclesiastical position enabled him to write to Corinth on behalf of the church of Rome? Irenaeus, *Adv. haer.* 3.3.3, lists Clement as having been allotted the Roman bishopric "in the third place from the apostles," Peter and Paul, after Linus and Anacletus. An older generation of Roman Catholic scholars[345] assumed that the single-bishop practice was already in place in Rome in the 90s or earlier; and they opined that, as fourth pope (third from Peter), Clement was exercising the

---

343. Daniélou, *Theology* 43–45, points to midrashic technique in *I Clement* and a knowledge of the *targumim*. The presence of Jewish tradition in chaps. 1–7 has been massively proved by K. Beyschlag, *Clemens Romanus and der Frühkatholizismus* (Tübingen: Mohr, 1966). Barnard, "Early" 372–78, argues strongly for Jewish background but too simply judges that this identifies the author as Jew—it simply tells us about the background of the church that nourished him.

344. See Hagner, *Use* 7; and especially L. Sanders, *L'Hellénisme de Saint Clément de Rome et le Paulinisme* (Studia Hellenistica 2; Louvain Univ., 1943).

345. Fuellenbach, *Ecclesiastical,* gives a history of Catholic scholarship. Since the 1930s the papal primacy approach to *I Clement* has been abandoned by such Catholic scholars as Cauwelaert, McCue, and Brunner (see Fuellenbach, 116).

primacy of the bishop of Rome in giving directions to the church of Corinth. The failure of Clement to use his own name or speak personally should have called that theory into question from the start, were there not other decisive evidence against it. As the ecumenical book *Peter in the New Testament* (done by Roman Catholics and Protestants together) affirmed, the connection between a Petrine function in the first century and a fully developed Roman papacy required several centuries of development, so that it is anachronistic to think of the early Roman church leaders functioning as later popes (see footnote 275 above). Moreover, the Roman episcopal list shows confusion.[346] Differing from the list in Irenaeus, Tertullian, *De praescriptione haereticorum* 32.1–2 (CC 1.213) treats Clement as the first bishop "ordained by Peter"; and Epiphanius, *Panarion* 27.6 (PG 41.372–73), seems to be harmonizing when he treats Linus and Anacletus as auxiliary bishops during the lifetime of the apostles and in their absence. All of this can be explained if we recognize that the threefold order of single-bishop, with subordinate presbyters and deacons, was not in place at Rome at the end of the first century; rather the twofold order of presbyter-bishops and deacons, attested a decade before in I Peter 5:1–5, was still operative.[347] Indeed, the signal failure of Ignatius (*ca.* 110) to mention the single-bishop in his letter to the Romans (a very prominent theme in his other letters), and the usage of *Hermas,* which speaks of plural presbyters (*Vis.* 2.4.2) and bishops (*Sim.* 9.27.2), make it likely that the single-bishop structure did not come to Rome till *ca.* 140–150.[348] In speaking of

---

346. For the problems of Roman succession lists, see W. Ullmann, JTS 11 (1960) 295–317; M. Bévenot, JTS 17 (1966) 98–107.

347. The general equivalence between *presbyteroi* (presbyters, elders) and *episkopoi* (bishops, overseers) may be deduced from *I Clem.* 42:4; 44:4–5; 54:2. Evidence from the Pauline Pastorals and *Didache* 15 shows that the twofold order was widespread at the end of the first century. As Meier has shown (p. 77 above), to explain Ignatius' insistence on and defense of the threefold order, one must posit that the single-bishop model appeared in Antioch and Asia Minor *ca.* 100. In the period under discussion Rome shows itself slow to accept innovations.

348. Note, however, that both those passages in *Hermas* are sometimes attributed to the earlier section of that document, closer to 110 than to 140; see Chapter X, section E below. No magical one moment for the introduction of the single-bishop is in mind. The line of demarcation was surely fuzzy between the fully acknowledged single-bishop and the *de facto* prominence of one of the presbyter-bishops by force of personality, brains, wealth, etc.

Linus, Anacletus, and Clement as if they were single-bishops of
Rome, then, Irenaeus and later authors would simply have been assuming that a structure known in their own times was functional at
an earlier period.[349] The earliest names in the Roman episcopal list
probably represent the more famous presbyter-bishops of the first
hundred years of Roman Christianity, some of them functioning si-
multaneously. Perhaps Irenaeus was showing an awareness of this
when he addressed Victor the bishop of Rome thus: "Among these
too were *the presbyters* before Soter [eleventh from the apostles in
Irenaeus' Roman list, *ca.* 166] *who presided over the church* of which
you are now the leader" (Eusebius, *Hist.* 5.24.14). Now, in the twofold structure of presbyter-bishops and deacons, I Tim 5:17 indicates
that, while presbyters (plural) were overseers in the church of a given
area, not all presbyters need have served as overseers. At some stage
in the development of church order, a single presbyter may have supervised (or been the bishop of) a house church, while the church of
the city was supervised by the collective group of such house-church
presbyter-bishops.

To return to Clement of Rome, as *Hermas Vis.* 2.4.2–3 suggests,
he may have been one of the presbyter-bishops who had the specified
task of writing letters to other churches in the name of the Roman
presbyter-bishops. (Did *de facto* such a task make him important,
whence the later simplification that he was *the* bishop of Rome?)
Thus *I Clement* may have been sent by the collective Roman presbyterate of overseers and have been composed by the hand of its secretary presbyter-bishop.

That Rome did write to other churches is confirmed not only by
the passage in *Hermas,* but also by Ignatius, *Rom.* 3:1 ("You taught
others"), and by Bishop Dionysius of Corinth (*ca.* 170) who, in citing
all the good that Rome did for "many churches in every city," mentions another letter from Rome to Corinth besides *I Clement* (Euse-

---

349. Similarly anachronistic is the later thesis that Peter served as bishop of
Rome (or sometimes Peter and Paul as bishops!). Curiously enough this is often ar-
dently defended by people who think that thus they are honoring Peter, not recognizing that apostles might regard being designated as local bishops as a failure to
appreciate their unique role. Historically, Peter was an apostle who died at Rome. If
part of his apostolate was exercised in that church, this did not make him a local
church supervisor. Philippians 1:1 shows that Paul distinguished himself from bishops.

bius, *Hist.* 4.23.10–11). Does this mean a primacy for the early Roman church even if that is not invested in a single-bishop? Any Christian community (especially a preeminent community with an apostolic heritage) may have had the right in Christ to correct another community, but in fact Rome seems to have exercised this right more frequently than any other church of the period and seems to have felt that such an exercise was expected. This has led some to speak of a *de facto,* not a *de iure,* primacy; but neither "*de facto*" nor "primacy" may be the word to do justice to the situation.[350] One can never discount the possibility that the church of the capital city of the empire felt some responsibility for Christianity throughout the empire; but the chief source of Rome's care is more likely to have had religious rather than political roots.[351] We have seen above (p. 131) that Peter seems to have embodied the responsibility of moderate Jerusalem Jewish Christianity for the Gentile mission. Rome was the city where he bore his last witness, and I Peter was sent posthumously in his name from Rome to show the care of this type of Christianity for the Gentile areas of northern Asia Minor.[352] When Paul also died at Rome, reconciled to the moderate Jewish/Gentile Christianity that flourished there and acknowledged as an apostle (*I Clem.* 47:1), Rome may have assumed responsibility for the Jewish/Gentile Christianity of the Pauline churches as well, whence the letter of Clement to Corinth.[353] Thus Rome would have been writing to other churches and teaching them because it regarded itself as the heir to the pastoral care of Peter and Paul for the respective Gentile

---

350. Fuellenbach, *Ecclesiastical* 115: "No serious Catholic scholar since Altaner has claimed that the letter is a 'categorical assertion' or an 'explicit claim' of a Roman primacy."

351. Richardson, *Early* 36: "Something of Rome's place as the church of the imperial city, and the church of Peter and Paul (chap. 5), must surely have been in the writer's mind." Yet the imperial status of Rome is never invoked in the early Christian works emanating from Rome.

352. Inevitably, the flight of Jerusalem Christianity from Jerusalem during the revolt against the Romans (still historically probable despite revisionist debunking) and the subsequent failure of Jerusalem Christianity to exercise a major missionary role would have helped Rome to take on the mantle of caring for the Gentiles—the heritage of James had been weakened in Palestine and, if Meier is right, may have passed to Antioch (pp. 46–49 above), even as the heritage of Peter came to Rome.

353. We remember that, forty years before, some Christians who would become Paulinists, like Prisca and Aquila, had gone from Rome to Corinth and back to Rome (Acts 18:2; Rom 16:3). See also footnote 280 above.

missions.[354] Is it significant that in one chapter (*Rom.* 3:1) Ignatius mentions that the Roman church taught others, and in the next chapter (4:3) that Peter and Paul gave orders to the Romans? Thus we would be dealing not so much with primacy of authority but with the continuity of apostolic care—not with a directive by a superior, but with a *nouthetēsis* (*I Clem.* 56:2) or "admonition" required among those who loved each other and "which none should take amiss."[355] Nevertheless, a favorable response to *I Clement's* admonition is expected: "You will give us joy and gladness if you are obedient to the things we have written through the Holy Spirit" (63:2); and emissaries are sent to witness the result (63:3; 65:1).

In any case *I Clem.* 47:1-4 gives a reminder that Paul the Apostle wrote previously, correcting Corinth for internal dissension; and clearly Clement hopes that this second intervention from the city where Paul "gave his testimony before the rulers" (5:7) will bear fruit in correcting internal strife. The hope may have been granted, for Donfried[356] argues that *II Clement,* dating from 98–100, is a discourse given to the Corinthian church by the presbyters who owed their restitution in office to the intervention of *I Clement.*

CONTINUATION OF ROMANS AND I PETER

There is no doubt that the author of *I Clement* knew Paul's Epistle to the Corinthians, but a reasonable case can be made for fa-

---

354. The city of Corinth was very Roman (Barnard, "St. Clement" 17). The relation of the two churches may have been particularly close (preceding footnote); indeed, *ca.* 170 Dionysius of Corinth would refer (inaccurately) to the common foundation of the Roman and Corinthian churches by Peter and Paul (Eusebius, *Hist.* 2.25.8). Telfer, *Office* 80, argues that Corinth adopted the presbyteral system under the influence of Rome. Nevertheless, one cannot explain the intervention of Rome in *I Clement* as if this could happen only because of the special relationship between the two churches. The concept of concern for "the whole brotherhood" in *I Clem.* 2:4 shows Rome's wide-ranging care, as does the opposition between dissent and "the common hope" in 51:1. One need not go to the other extreme, however, of classifying *I Clement* as a catholic epistle (written, as it were, through Corinth to the whole church).

355. It has been noted that there are some 70 hortatory subjunctives in *I Clement*.

356. *The Setting of Second Clement* (NovTSupp 38; Leiden: Brill, 1974). His theory implies that *II Clement* does not tell us about the Roman scene *ca.* A.D. 140, as many have assumed, but about the Corinthian scene much earlier.

miliarity with Romans as well.[357] Frequently compared are these passages:

I Clement	Romans	
Opening	1:7	Grace and peace from God and Jesus Christ
32:2	9:5	Christ according to the flesh is from Israel
33:1	6:1	What shall we do/say, then? Sin?
35:5	1:29–32	List of vices
35:6	1:32	Not only doing things but taking pleasure
37:5	12:4–6	Many members in one body
50:6	4:7–8	Ps 32:1–2 on forgiveness

Similarly a reasonable case can be made that Clement knew I Peter:[358]

I Clement	I Peter	
Opening	1:2	Grace and peace
Opening	1:17; 2:11	Sojourning (*paroikein, paroikia, paroikos*)
7:4	1:19	precious blood of Christ
8:1	1:11	Spirit spoke through prophets
16:10,17	2:21–22	Christ as an example from Isa 53:9
30:2	5:5	Prov 3:34: God resists the proud (not LXX)
49:5	4:8	Prov 10:12: Love covers a multitude of sins (not LXX or MT)
57:1	5:5	"Submit yourselves to the presbyters"
59:2	2:9	Called from darkness into light

But such familiarity, whether or not it constitutes literary dependency, tells us little. Far more important is the way some important themes shared by Romans and I Peter appear in *I Clement*. In order

---

357. Hagner, *Use* 220, thinks the relationship is "unassailable."
358. *Ibid.* 246: "Clement probably made use of I Peter"; also E. Lohse, "Paränese und Kerygma im I. Petrusbrief," ZNW 45 (1954) 68–89, esp. 83–85. He also cites ten examples of unusual words shared by the two works.

to see that, let us delineate the central reason for Rome's writing to Corinth.

The Corinthian Christians have removed from liturgical office some presbyters whose character was blameless (44:6; 47:6). We do not know why they did this. Holtzmann and other scholars have wondered whether the issue was a fixed term of office vs. a lifetime occupancy. Somewhat similar is the suggestion (based on the Corinthian situation forty years before when Paul wrote) that the Corinthians were accustomed to charismatic guidance rather than fixed offices, or even that there was a rebellion of impatient youth against the rule of presbyters (elders). The polemic against "jealous zeal" in *I Clem.* 4 – 6 indicates there may have been a more serious division (or "schism" as the author calls it) whereby Christians of different persuasions were trying to get control of the church offices. In this line of thought, it has been suggested that a more radical group at Corinth was claiming to be the real heir to Paul, while for Clement moderate Roman Christianity was Paul's heir since he was an apostle who had died "among us" (6:1). In any case, *I Clement* argues that the presbyters should not be removed, for church order has a divine aspect and should not be tampered with. Moreover, such internal strife prompted by jealous zeal becomes known to outsiders and thus offers them a dangerous tool for persecuting Christians. The experience of the Roman church of how zeal has led to the deaths of Peter, Paul, and a great multitude (p. 124 above) makes that church very sensitive of the need for a united front against those "who dissent from us" (47:7). Division among Christians is a great enemy; and so, citing the Pauline hymn on love from I Cor 13:4–7, *I Clem.* 49:5 adds, "Love admits no schism; love does not give rise to dissent." In 51:1 there is a challenge to those who led the dissent at Corinth to consider "the common hope." Such people must say to themselves, "If sedition, strife, and schisms have arisen because of me, I shall depart. . . . Let the flock of Christ have peace with the presbyters set over it" (54:1–2). "You, therefore, who laid the foundation of the dissent, submit to the presbyters. . . . Learn to be submissive" (57:1–2).

Above (pp. 136–39), the strains of thought traced through Romans and I Peter were: first, the strong heritage from Judaism, especially in terms of cultic outlook; second, insistence on obedience to civil authority; and third, the articulation of church structure. Let us see, one by one, if these themes appear in *I Clement* and how they reinforce the main argument of my treatment of Roman Christianity.

First, Jewish heritage, especially the cult. It is estimated that about one-quarter of *I Clement* is direct citation from the OT,[359] almost always according to the Greek (LXX) version. What is striking for our purposes is the application of cultic language to the functions of church officers. According to both Romans and I Peter (p. 137 above), Christ's bloody death had sacrificial aspects; but for Christians "spiritual sacrifices" were urged. A Christian like Paul renders priestly service by preaching the gospel, and the Christian people are "a royal priesthood," even as the Christian community is "a spiritual house" replacing the Temple. Such a spiritualization of the cult was less radical than the replacement of priesthood, sacrifice, and place of worship urged on Rome by Hebrews (p. 154 above). In *I Clement,* however, there has been a revival of cultic terminology in a less spiritualized form; this constitutes a movement beyond I Peter but in a direction quite opposite to the one urged by Hebrews. As in Hebrews, so also in *I Clement,* present tenses are used to describe the Jewish cult,[360] but approvingly and not as a dissuasive. The following two paragraphs catch the difference in outlook:

> Heb 10:10–12,18: We are sanctified through the offering of the body of Jesus Christ once for all. On the one hand, every priest daily stands liturgically ministering [*leitourgein*], again and again offering the same sacrifices that can never take away sins. But this man [Jesus Christ] has offered forever one sacrifice for sins. . . . There is no more offering for sins.

> *I Clem.* 40:1–5; 41:2: We ought to do in order [*taxis*] all things that the Master commanded us to perform at fixed times. He set offerings and liturgies [*leitourgia*], so that there should be no random and irregular pattern, but fixed

---

359. Hagner, *Use* 21.

360. These tenses do not indicate a pre-70 date for *I Clement,* before the destruction of the Temple. In A.D. 93 (about the time of *I Clement*) Josephus, *Ant.* 3.9–10; #224–55, described the Jerusalem sacrifices and priestly actions in the present tense.

times and hours. Moreover, He has set by His sovereign will where and by whom He desires these things to be done. Those, therefore, who make their offerings at the appointed times are acceptable and blessed. . . . To the high priest his proper liturgical ministries are allotted. To the priests their proper cultic place has been appointed. To the levites their proper ministries have been assigned. The lay person is bound by the rules laid down for the lay people. . . . Not in every place are the sacrifices offered (perpetual offerings, or free-will offerings, or sin offerings, or trespass offerings), but only at Jerusalem . . . before the sanctuary, at the altar, after inspection by the high priest.

Why does *I Clement* place such admiring emphasis on the divinely assigned order in the Jerusalem cult and in its personnel? Chap. 42 gives a clear answer: because there is a similar divinely designed order in the Christian ministry.[361] God sent Christ who appointed apostles; and they, in turn, with the help of the Holy Spirit, both preached the gospel and appointed tested converts to be bishops and deacons. Indeed, the last development was foretold in the (modified) LXX of Isa 60:17: "I will establish their bishops in righteousness and their deacons in faith." Thus, if Judaism had from God a high priest, priests, and levites, God's arrangement for his Christian people is Christ, the apostles, and bishops and deacons. *I Clement* (63:1; 64) agrees with Hebrews (passim) in identifying Jesus Christ as the high priest,[362] but with the effect of solidifying the Christian equivalent of a levitical structure, not of replacing it. The Pauline

---

361. I am concentrating here on ministry, which is only one of the cultic aspects of *I Clement*. Chapters 59–61 give a long, early-Christian prayer with strong Jewish overtones (Barnard, "Early" 377–78), while 34:6–8 suggests that when Christians gathered together (*synagein*—for a synaxis or eucharist?), they prayed the *sanctus* and anticipated the parousia.

362. See footnote 315 above for *I Clement's* use of Hebrews rather than simply a liturgy known to both. Unpersuasive is the counter-argument that *I Clement* cannot have used Hebrews because the two works betray different reactions to Jewish cult. In fact, one does not know whether the author of *I Clement* would have recognized that his views were sharply different from those of Hebrews—for centuries Christians have (wrongly) read the two works as if they were in perfect harmony. I am not challenging the right of the church to harmonize them, but one must recognize that such harmonization tells us little about the original import.

Pastorals, especially I Timothy and Titus, discourse at length about presbyter-bishops and deacons without any suggestion of levitical imagery or cultic functions. Yet for *I Clem.* 44:4 one of the roles of the episcopate is to offer sacrifices. The main fault of the Corinthians is to have removed presbyters from their liturgical ministry,[363] and thus to have upset a divine pattern revealed when the apostles appointed (presbyter-) bishops and deacons to succeed to the liturgical ministry (42:4; 44:2). About the same time that Clement was writing this admonition to Corinth, *Didache* 14:1–3 was interpreting the eucharist as a fulfillment of the prophecy of Malachi 1:11 about a pure sacrifice being offered among the Gentiles. In some of the churches of Asia Minor presidency at the eucharist was becoming a function of the episcopate-presbyterate (already a fixed pattern for Ignatius *ca.* 110). Thus, while Clement does not identify the presbyters as those who presided at the eucharist (which is never mentioned) or call them priests, his work reflects a tendency at the turn of the first century that will coalesce and develop through the second century until the bishop, presbyters, and deacons are pictured as the Christian high priest, priests, and levites, centered around their role in the eucharist as the Christian sacrifice. The author of Hebrews may not have been *polemicizing* against the beginnings of such a development when he urged Roman Christians against slipping back to levitical priesthood and sacrifices;[364] but one has reason to doubt that he would have been enthusiastic about such a development. If my surmise is correct about the origins of the Roman church in a Jerusalem Christianity loyal to the Temple, that Christianity triumphed vicariously in the direction given by *I Clement* to a more-than-spiritual survival of the levitical ideals.

Second, obedience to civil authority. As part of its campaign to get the Corinthian church to restore to their liturgical ministry the presbyters who have been deposed, *I Clement* goes beyond the levitical order that God has revealed to Israel and appeals to a divine or-

---

363. *I Clem.* 44:6; it is important not to translate *leitourgia* simply as "ministry" (= *diakonia*); for one should preserve the cultic tone.

364. G. Theissen, *Untersuchungen zum Hebräerbrief* (Gütersloh: Gerd Mohn, 1969), thinks he was. In any case, Hebrews was taken into a canon that modified its impact, for it was accepted as Scripture by a church (East and West) that harmonized a Christian levitical priesthood with Hebrews' priesthood according to Melchizedek.

der visible in the created universe. The description of this created order in chap. 20 has often been thought to exhibit Stoic influence, as have *I Clement*'s appeal to moral order. But for our purposes, the sequence to Romans and I Peter is particularly visible in *I Clement*'s appreciation of the order manifested in the Roman system of imperial government. If in 41:1 the *tagma* or "orderly ranking" in levitical cult is held up as a model militating against Christian schism and dissent at Corinth, another model is found in chap. 37 in the *tagma* of an army with its generals, prefects, tribunes, etc. "Let us, then, serve as soldiers, my brothers," *I Clement* appeals, "for each in his own orderly ranking executes the order of the emperor" (37:1,3). Neither Caligula's madness nor Claudius' expulsion of Jewish Christians from Rome had discouraged Paul from advising, "Let every person be subject to the governing authorities" (Rom 13:1). Nero's persecution did not prevent I Peter (2:13) from urging, "Be subject for the Lord's sake to every human institution . . . to the emperor as supreme." So also "the repeated misfortunes and calamities which have befallen [under Domitian]" (*I Clem.* 1:1) have not dissuaded *I Clement*'s prayer to God in 60:4 – 61:1: "Grant us to be obedient to our princes and rulers on earth, for you, Master, have given the power of the kingdom to them." The "visitation of the kingdom of Christ" may be yet to come (50:3), but some of the power of God's kingdom is apparently manifested in the Roman empire. There is not so strong a sense of final eschatology in *I Clement* as there was in Paul or even I Peter.[365] Clement's vision of a well-ordered church, patterned to some extent on the imperial system, implies a church that will have a more-than-passing existence. Since this model of order comes from God, it may be appealed to in urging discipline. God who sets people over others in the civil and natural order (61:2) has set the presbyters over the flock of Christ (54:2). Just as Romans and I Peter urge subjection to civil authorities, so *I Clem.* 57:1 urges, "Be subject to the presbyters."

In itself, obedience to church leaders is not novel on the Christian scene. The oldest Christian work (I Thess 5:12–13), a full half-century before, had counseled, "We ask you, brothers, to recognize

365. Important here is the work of O. Knoch, *Eigenart und Bedeutung der Eschatologie im theologischen Aufriss des ersten Clemensbrief* (Bonn: Hanstein, 1964).

. . . those who are over you in the Lord and to esteem them highly in love." Forty years before, in I Cor 16:15–16, Paul appealed for submission to those who minister to the saints. What is new in *I Clement* is the close parallel made between submission to the presbyters and obedience to the civil leaders or military leaders. One gains from this parallelism reinforcement for the thesis that the Roman church of necessity came quickly to terms with the awesome organization of the empire by duly appreciating the strength of the system.[366] The revulsion shown in Roman law for civil disobedience and schism seems to have constituted an *a fortiori* argument for having no sympathy for schism in the church. Indeed, the fact that the church is a sojourner (opening of *I Clement*) does not make *I Clement* less but more appreciative of the need for internal order—non-sojourners who are at home have an ambiance to support them that is lacking to the church.

Third, aspects of church structure. In discussing Romans and I Peter (p. 139 above), we saw the importance of Roman house churches and the emergence of presbyter-bishops in functional succession to the apostolic care. *I Clement* does not specifically refer to house churches; but the attention paid to house order in 1:3 and in chap. 21 (passages that deal with community leaders, elders and younger) suggests that the house church was still an important part of the Roman scene. "The church of God that sojourns in Rome" (opening of *I Clement*) was presumably a spiritual whole consisting of many individual house churches. A reflection of the importance of "houses" may be seen in the emphasis that *I Clem.* 11:1; 12:1,3 places on "hospitality" (*philoxenia*), a word found in the NT only in Rom 12:13 and Heb 13:2.

As for the structure of presbyter-bishops,[367] there is in *I Clement* little development from I Peter (except for the cultic aspect already discussed). The warning that there should be no self-exaltation over

---

366. Even after the great Roman persecutions of the second and third centuries, Christians did not develop an antipathy for the imperial organization. Indeed, for Origen and Cyprian the church was an organism comparable to the Roman state. See Goppelt, "Church" 18.

367. Beyond the structure of presbyter-bishops discussed above, one should note the term *hēgoumenos,* "leader," in 1:3 (also in 37:2–3 for generals in the spiritual Christian army)—a term that occurs three times in Hebrews 13 as descriptive of the Roman situation (p. 145 above).

Christ's flock (16:1) is close in theme to the warning in I Peter 5:3 to the presbyter-shepherds, "Do not lord it over those who constitute the allotment but be examples to the flock." The noteworthy development in *I Clement* is not in presbyteral structure but in the insistence that the presbyterate came through succession from the apostles by appointment.[368] *I Clement* 44:1–2 reports that the apostles were concerned that there would be strife over the episcopate, and so they provided that when they died "other approved men should succeed to their liturgical ministry."[369] *I Clement* 42:4; 44:3 make it clear that these men were appointed by the apostles. Among the other early Christian works that mention presbyter-bishops, the evidence varies on how the appointment came about. *Didache* 15:1 urges its recipients, "Appoint for yourselves bishops and deacons worthy of the Lord." In Titus 1:5 this apostolic delegate is told himself to appoint presbyters in every city, thus setting in order what was left lacking by Paul. If one must conclude from this clear evidence that *I Clement* paints an oversimplified picture of the apostles' appointment of presbyter-bishops, one need not go to the opposite extreme of regarding it as pure fabrication. Acts 14:23 states that Barnabas and Paul appointed presbyters in every church, and it is unlikely that several independent claims of apostolic appointment would have been made without some basis in fact. I Thessalonians 5:12 describes some people over other people in the Lord a few months after Paul founded the community—is it not likely that Paul himself was responsible for such an arrangement? Goppelt ("Church" 9) suggests that *I Clem* 42:4, which has the apostles appointing their first converts bishops, reflects the fact that the first convert offered his house as a gathering place for the congregation

---

368. The idea of succession (*diadochē*) goes beyond insistence on rank or order (*tagma*) assigned by God—an order of Christ, apostles, bishops and deacons. Succession concerns the origin of the episcopate. A distinction should be made between functional succession (the presbyter-bishops take over the pastoral care of churches founded by the apostles once the apostles die) and succession by apostolic appointment. Furthermore, an appointed sequence in legitimate authority is still not the same as a chain of succession to sacramental power—an idea that will later come into the Christian picture.

369. In speaking of "men," Clement uses *andres,* "males," not *anthrōpoi,* "human beings"; but we have no way of knowing whether the phraseology was deliberate in order to exclude women.

and eventually supervised (*episkopein*) the congregation that met there, as in the case of Stephanus (I Cor 16:15–16). Finally, we must remember Clement has to persuade the Corinthians who received his letter; surely, they would have recognized and rejected a pure fabrication about the origins of the presbyterate. The solution that seems most plausible is that *I Clement* has generalized an apostolic practice that was occasional but not consistent or universal.[370]

What practical importance did *I Clement's* thesis of succession by appointment have for the situation at Corinth and for the self-understanding of the Roman church? In resisting the deposition of the presbyters by the Corinthians, the author has appealed to two authoritative models: the Jerusalem levitical priesthood and the imperial political and military organization. The high priesthood was hereditary, and in its two successful periods the *imperium* was inherited (family descent from Augustus to Nero, and from Vespasian to Domitian). Chaos had come in the year 69 with the deposition of three emperors, and it is precisely such chaos that the Corinthians were now inaugurating in the church. Thus, functionally, apostolic appointment may have served in Clement's mind as the Christian equivalent to levitical and imperial inheritance, providing a divine guarantee for an orderly system of governance.[371]

Apostolic succession, however, probably served an even more important purpose for the Roman church since it justified the Roman presbyterate in admonishing Corinth with *apostolic* force. A warning appears in *I Clem.* 59:1, "If some have been disobedient to *what has been said by God through us,* let them know that they will entangle themselves in transgression and no little danger." Obedience is urged by *I Clem.* 63:2 "to what *we have written through the Holy Spirit."* Some scholars characterize this as a style influenced by

---

370. For Roman Catholic proponents of this view, see Fuellenbach, *Ecclesiastical* 87–93, 98–100.

371. R. M. Grant, "Early Episcopal Succession," in *Studia Patristica* II (Oxford Congress Papers of 1967; TU 108; Berlin: Akademie, 1972) 179–84, points out that succession of bishops in Jerusalem may have been hereditary among the relatives of Jesus. Goppelt, "Church" 20, calls attention to the succession in rabbinic teaching and authority described in *Pirqe Aboth* 1:1 (a Jewish work from the period not too long after Clement): Moses, Joshua, elders, prophets, men of the Great Synagogue, Hillel, Shammai. A practice of clear rabbinic appointment (ordination) was coming into Judaism at this time.

imperial Rome. More likely the assurance that divine communication comes through the spoken or written word of the Roman church is to be related to the style of Jerusalem apostolic leadership. Acts 15:28 contains a passage from a directive letter written by the apostles and presbyters of the Jerusalem church to areas under their influence: "It has seemed good to the Holy Spirit and to us."[372] I have contended several times in this book that the Roman church, evangelized from Jerusalem and fortified by the martyrdom of Peter, the leading Jerusalem missionary, may have seen itself as the successor of the Jerusalem apostolic church in supplying direction to the missionary churches like Corinth—this would explain a letter written in the Jerusalem authoritative style.[373] If one objects that Corinth was a church of the Pauline mission, not the Jerusalem mission, we remember not only that *I Clem.* 5:2–5 joined Paul to Peter as the "pillars" and "good apostles," but also that Paul in I Cor 15:5–11 joined himself to Cephas (Peter), the Twelve, James, and all the apostles as part of an authoritative "we" addressing the Corinthians: "Whether I or they, so we proclaimed and so you believed." Clement's notion of the presbyters as the appointed successors of such apostles enables the presbyterate in general (and surely the Roman presbyterate in particular) to ask obedience to what "we" have said or written, as having divine sanction.

EVALUATION

I Clement has been a storm center of recent scholarship.[374] *Those who disapprove* have seen in this work the death knell of a truly Christian understanding of church leadership, for the guidance by Spirit-filled charismatics that dominated in the NT period has ceded to a fixed succession in office, erroneously (or even deceitfully) presented as coming from the apostles and sanctioned by God. In the

---

372. Whether or not this letter is historical, this is how Luke (and surely others) thought Jerusalem spoke. Although Hagner, *Use* 263, judges probable Clement's knowledge of Acts, that knowledge is not necessary for this proposal.

373. See footnote 277 above.

374. Documentation for what follows above may be found in Fuellenbach, *Ecclesiastical*, with convenient summaries of the history of Protestant and Roman Catholic views on 64–71 and 109–17.

extreme form of this thesis defended by R. Sohm, *I Clement* marks the great fall of the church away from the internal and the non-structural to a visible institution. (This thesis has left those inclined to humor with the ecclesial dilemma phrased as "Sohm or Rome.") In a less extreme form of the thesis *I Clement* is blamed for hastening an arteriosclerosis that had already begun in the NT period by supplying a (fictional) divine and historical authentication for a structure that had its real origin in the social necessity of institutionalization. For Harnack, *I Clement* was a blow to "pneumatic democracy."[375] *Some admirers* of I Clement have regarded it as authoritative justification for the "apostolic blueprint" approach to the episcopate whereby, in the mind both of Jesus and of his apostles, governance of the church by bishops and presbyters was divinely specified. (The concept of *de jure divino* is now recognized as more complex, however, since God is seen to work by moving human beings rather than by direct intervention.) With more subtlety, some admire "Clement" as a realist who saw the working of the Spirit in a dangerous situation and determined the way the church should go in order to survive. On both sides many scholars oversimplify the historical situation, agreeing only that for better or worse *I Clement* had remarkable success in shaping future church thought.

The discussion is *not* facilitated by the fact that the underlying motif is often a conflicting view of church organization today. The battle over the unimpassioned pages of *I Clement* is often a surrogate for a battle between the impassioned descendants of the Reformers and of Trent; and since I am a Roman Catholic, I rather doubt I shall be judged objective about the issue. It does seem to me that some who criticize Clement for imposing the divine on a development that had clear human sociological factors do not always turn their critical eye on the descriptions of charismatic functions in the churches of the 50s. Are there not also human sociological factors in the charism of "administrations" (pl. of *kybernēsis,* "governance"), mentioned in I Cor 12:28, in the sense that the people who claimed

---

375. Since Harnack, *I Clement* has often been blamed for the introduction of "early catholicism" into the Christian picture. It is better to avoid this unclear term and the (negative) value-judgment frequently attached to it. Goppelt, *Apostolic* 142 and 202, uses that term, accusing Clement of turning "offices which had emerged of their own accord" (a highly dubious supposition) "into a *jure divino* ordinance" (198).

this gift of God were often reflecting a natural ability (and thus the charism is something that may be said to come from God only in a more general sense)? If some complain that *I Clement*'s sense of divine order destroys the freedom of the gospel, is one sure that those who claim divinely-given charisms in the strict sense are likely to be more tolerant toward disagreement? Can one document the existence of a "pneumatic democracy" in early NT times? In other words, granted that there are several forms of church leadership implied in the pages of the NT and that *I Clement* has helped to solidify one of them, by what criterion do scholars decide *a priori* that one is more Christian than the other, since Jesus himself does not seem to have dealt with the structure of a community that was to carry on his work? If in faith Christians attribute, at least partially, the development of church governance to the work of the Holy Spirit, by what criterion does one judge that an order that is more constitutive and absolutized is less of the Holy Spirit than a charismatic and functional order? If one opts for an *a posteriori* criterion, namely, that church governance is to be judged as Christian by the extent to which it facilitates gospel ideals (or at least does not block them), must not one face the paradox that Paul is *criticizing* the charismatic functioning of the community in I Cor 12 – 14 precisely because sometimes a desire for charisms constitutes a violation of the gospel command to love, whereas Clement is *promoting* a divinely ordered presbyterate in apostolic succession in order to prevent the Corinthians from violating this same command? If one compares the letters written to the Corinthians forty years apart by Paul and by Clement (without worrying about future developments), would one decide that charismatic church governance really forwarded the gospel more than an orderly presbyterate? In fact, however, one may suspect that much of the dislike of *I Clement* stems not from that letter's reaction to the situation it was facing, but to subsequent church developments and attitudes that it was used to justify. Such dislike might more perceptively be dealt with by recognizing that the problem is not of the direction given by *I Clement* but of the constant need for a reforming vigilance in keeping any church structure responsible to the gospel (since it is sure to have a mixture of the human and the divine, unless one thinks that a sociological diagnosis excludes intervention by the Holy Spirit). In other words, if the real objection to *I Clement* is that it is the camel's nose under the flap of the tent, is the wise solution that the camel would be better off without a nose, or the tent without a flap?

The too-long preceding paragraph is clearly a digression, unavoidable because of the passions detectable in scholarly discussion of *I Clement*. More germane to an evaluation made within the goals of this book is *I Clement*'s contribution to the trajectory of Roman Christianity.[376] Indeed, the perilous situation at Corinth may have caused the Roman church to solidify its direction. One must be cautious to trace this trajectory against the background of history. Already Christians had been executed in Rome in the time of Nero and had been persecuted in some sections of the empire in the time of Domitian. How was such a "foreign superstition," regarded as antisocial and atheistic, to survive? Elliott[377] has interpreted I Peter in terms of Christian survival amidst social disintegration—the issue of survival at the time of *I Clement* was even more acute. The greatest enemy in the author's judgment was internal disorder: a jealous zeal of Christians against fellow Christians. *I Clement* would counteract this danger with an appeal to order rooted in two prominent themes of Roman Christianity: a strong Jewish heritage and a respect for imperial authority.

From the Jewish heritage, *I Clement* has drawn the symbolism of the levitical priesthood and adapted it to lend great support to the ecclesiastical structure that had developed in many churches by the end of the first century, i.e., a structure of presbyter-bishops and deacons. This structure is seen to render not only a social service to the community but a sacred service to God, not only a *diakonia* but also a *leitourgia*. This *leitourgia* means for Clement that the Christian ministers have to be respected as part of an order that God has approved and are not to be removed at whim. Such a clearly articulated structure may have developed out of social necessity; but *I Clement*

---

376. Admirably nuanced is the judgment of Richardson, *Early* 39: "Clement's letter reflects the movement away from the Pauline faith to a type of Christianity in which ethical interests and concern for law and order predominate. This does not, however, exclude both acquaintance with and some grasp of the Pauline gospel. . . . Rather, we must say that Roman Christianity is giving evidence of its background in Hellenistic Judaism, and adapting itself to the imperial capital."

377. *Home* 217.

makes certain that the ministry will not become the victim of a sur-
vival-of-the-fittest attitude toward the structure. The sense of the sacred with which *I Clement* describes the divine order (*tagma*) of
God, Christ, apostles, and bishops and deacons challenges Christians
to unshakable allegiance to their presbyter-bishops in difficult times
and so will enable the church to face two hundred years of Roman
persecution.

But *I Clement*'s insight has an origin and implications that go
beyond the Jewish heritage. The author's admiration for military discipline betrays, however inchoately, the understanding that the Roman empire would never be Christianized unless Christianity could
understand and take advantage of the strength of its adversary.
Rome was reasonably tolerant of private cults provided that they
were not immoral and did not challenge the demand for outward
conformity to the religious and social order.[378] Christianity was not
going to be another Oriental mystery religion with pious devotees; it
was going to be a society with exclusive claims that were antithetical
to those of the empire—a recognition that every absolute state has
arrived at ever since! It has been shrewdly observed, "Christians
were constantly amazed to find themselves cast as enemies of the Roman order, but in retrospect we must admit that it was the Romans
who had the realistic insight."[379] Earlier Christian works pertinent to
the Roman church had demanded obedience to the Roman government; *I Clement* goes further in inculcating similar obedience to
church authorities. Christianity would succeed because its communities were well structured and because its institutions effectively held
on to converts. It would shape an organization as tight as (or tighter
than) that of the empire and would offer better motivation for adherence.[380] Thus *I Clement* is offering a formula not only for surviving
persecution but also for overcoming the persecutor. The ultimate victory of Clement's insight would not be when Constantine ceased to

---

378. Guterman, *Religious* 25–31: the cult of unapproved gods was not allowed
publicly nor even privately if altars were erected.

379. Gager, *Kingdom* 27–28. Hinson, *Evangelization* 27, quotes W. R. Halliday:
"A state within a state." See Dix, *Jew* 69–70: Christianity was dangerous as a *collegi-
um*.

380. Hinson, *Evangelization,* is superb on this.

persecute Christianity; it would be when a half-century later Christianity became the official religion of the empire.

With all its novelty, I would insist that *I Clement* is continuing a trajectory that had antecedents in earlier Christian attitudes toward the evangelization of Rome. The Acts of the Apostles dramatically but perceptively simplified Christian history by concentrating the flow of events around Peter and Paul and by beginning the church's story in Jerusalem and ending it in Rome. In this schema Acts embodies a judgment that Christian destiny lay with Rome and with the Gentile world that it governed. Acts has translated into practical political terms the belief that Christianity bore good news for all. Thus, it is not an exaggeration to claim that instinctively early Christianity "had a drive toward Rome."[381] A Paul who disliked going to churches founded by others passionately desired to get to Rome (Rom 1:10,15; 15:22). Why Rome? Athens was the museum of classical antiquity, serving as the great repository of cultural heritage; but Paul gives no evidence of longing to get to Athens. (Indeed, his only visit there, as recorded by Acts 17:15–34, seems to be marked by incompatibility.) Alexandria was the library of classical learning, but seemingly Paul never went there. (Indeed, the NT gives us no information about the spread of Christianity to Alexandria.) Does not the attention to Rome rather than to Athens or Alexandria betray an early understanding that the power to change the world lay in the political capital, and not in the museum or the library? Much has been made of Christianity as a religion centered on an incarnation of the divine in history. Yet some modern Christians seem reluctant to recognize that their earliest ancestors may have been quite practical and unromantic in translating incarnation to mean that the gospel should use political structures as its vehicle. If there was a Christian "drive toward Rome," in part it was because centered in that city was the machinery that ruled the known world and through which that world could be claimed for Christ.

The subsequent history of the Roman church would reflect Clement's choice for clear order over ambiguity and over a freedom

---

381. The phrase and the comparison to Athens and Alexandria are from Schelke, "Römische" 393–94.

that allows church divisions. Of course, in imitating imperial order and authority for evangelistic purposes, the church of Rome was exposing itself to a great danger. Consciously or unconsciously, it had set out on a path to master the empire and opened itself to the peril that internally the values of the Roman system might master the church, so that the church might render too much to Caesar and forget that it had one Lord. In that connection we note that in the judgment of Johannine Christianity, somewhat prejudiced against any shepherd but Christ, Peter was allotted a pastoral role[382] because he met the criterion of the good shepherd by the way he laid down his life. Paradoxically that means that Nero rendered the Roman church a service when he martyred its great apostle in the Circus near Vatical Hill. Equally paradoxically, Constantine did not necessarily render that same church a service when he opened the way for its bishop later to become *pontifex maximus* of Roman religion. The Caesar who sought to kill Christianity may have been less dangerous than the Caesar who sought to use it as an ally.

When one recognizes both the dangers and the grandeur of the trajectory followed in Roman Christianity, it is consoling to realize that our Christian ancestors may have supplied the Roman church with standards useful for self-admonition. In the late 50s Paul wrote the first praise of the Roman church, "Your faith is proclaimed in all the world" (Rom 1:8). Fifty years later in the opening of another letter to the Romans, Ignatius praised the Roman church as "preeminent in love." Praised for its faith and love from the beginning, the Roman church may well be destined to be evaluated on those two points.

The Pauline appreciation of the faith of Rome proved remarkably prescient in regard to the second century[383] when those later recognized as heretics, such as Valentinus, Marcion, and Tatian, fell afoul of the Roman presbyters.[384] This peculiar sensibility for the

---

382. John 21:15-19: a pastoral role, to be sure, based on the love of Christ and one which left the sheep belonging to Christ.

383. W. Bauer, *Orthodoxy and Heresy in Earliest Christianity* (Philadelphia: Fortress, 1971; Germ. orig. 1934) saw in *I Clement* the first sign of Rome's dominant influence in the formation of Christian orthodoxy.

384. Hegesippus, an opponent of heretics, came to Rome sometime before 170; and, as Grant, *Augustus* 152, comments, "In speaking of the Roman church, however,

contents of Christian faith may explain why as a support against heresy Irenaeus cited Rome first: "In this order and by this succession [of the Roman bishops] the ecclesiastical tradition from the apostles and the preaching of the truth have come down to us" (*Adv. haer.* 3.3.2–3). In the christological and trinitarian controversies of the third and fourth centuries, various bishops of the great Christian centers (Antioch, Alexandria, Constantinople) were deposed for heresy or excommunicated, but Rome had an enviable record for cautious orthodoxy. Even in a divided Western Christianity many who disagree with Rome's theology would grant that it has preserved a zeal for orthodox faith.

A sharper debate might be joined over whether Rome has remained equally preeminent in love. Indeed, to some affected by Roman zeal for orthodox faith, a lack of love is apparent; others would speak of a love that has to chastise. Be all that as it may, in our century through the actions of one Roman bishop, John XXIII, many outside the allegiance to the Roman church felt for a moment a touch of love;[385] and it changed their whole way of looking at Rome. Perhaps, then, one may learn a lesson from the history of the beginnings of the church of Rome. If "the church which sojourns at Rome" is to preach to other churches and admonish them, this admonition will be more effective when the zeal for a "faith proclaimed in all the world" is embodied in a church "preeminent in love."[386]

Hegesippus says nothing about heresy. Evidently, he regards Rome as the prime example of the way in which true orthodoxy is preserved in local successions of bishops."

385. I recognize fully the difficulty of analyzing what logically or historically made this so. If the image of John XXIII created by the press was larger than life, that image became a factor in history.

386. Lightfoot, *Apostolic Fathers* I 1.384, comments on the mildness of Clement in praying for the emperors after being persecuted by them: "Who would have grudged the Church of Rome her primacy, if she had always spoken thus?"

CHAPTER X

Possible Supplements to
Our Knowledge of
Early Roman Christianity

IN the preceding chapters I have used four documents written over a forty-year span (A.D. 58–96) in order to reconstruct the dominant Christianity at Rome in NT times. It was a Christianity that had its origins in the Jerusalem mission, that was associated with the stance of the Jerusalem apostles (especially of Peter) in regard to Judaism, and that preserved a fidelity to Jewish origins, heritage, and traditions even when the ethnic membership of the Christian community at Rome became increasingly Gentile—in short, an instance of what I identified in the Introduction as the moderate Jewish/Gentile Christianity of Group Two. I have detected on the fringe in Rome extreme advocates of circumcision (Group One) who were opposed to Peter and even to a modified Paul, and may have contributed to their death in the Neronian persecution. I have also detected either the presence or the fear of a more radical Jewish/Gentile Christianity (Group Four) that had virtually abandoned the Jewish heritage—a Christianity advocated by Hebrews but from which Paul dissociates himself through his positive statements in Romans about the Jewish heritage. But I insist that these last two Groups were truly on the fringe in Rome.

Many other writings besides the four I considered have been associated by scholars with early Roman Christianity. Some are NT writings seen as addressed to or sent from Rome; others are extra-NT writings of the period up to A.D. 150. Precisely because I am conscious of the hypothetical character of the analysis given above, I judge it useful to apply the test of other suggested evidence, excluding only what I regard as fantastic or implausible.[387] Therefore, in this chapter I shall consider some possible supplements (or challenges) to my picture of the Roman church through a very brief analysis of Philippians, Ephesians, Mark, Ignatius to the Romans, the *Shepherd of Hermas,* the Legends of Peter and Simon Magus, and II Peter.[388] I insist that what I give here are programmatic jottings about the possible utility of these works for my main investigation, so that this chapter amounts to an appendix inviting other scholars with greater expertise in these works to participate in the discussion.

A. Paul to the Philippians

This writing was sent to Philippi from Paul in prison (1:13,17,19). The two leading contenders for the place of imprisonment are Ephesus (*ca.* 56–57) and Rome (*ca.* 61–63).[389] Although no imprisonment at Ephesus is recorded in Acts, such a hardship is not unlikely, granted Paul's references in the late 50s to what he suffered at Ephesus or in Asia (I Cor 15:32; II Cor 1:8–10). Most scholars today accept the Ephesus hypothesis, for the proximity of that city to Philippi makes possible the three or four comings and goings between Philippi and Paul in prison implied in the letter. Also Philippians seems to them closer in theme to the letters of the late 50s (Galatians, I–II Corinthians, Romans) than it does to Colossians and Ephesians, thought to belong to Rome and the early 60s. Such arguments are rendered less forceful, however, if one accepts the critical hypothesis that Colossians and Ephesians are post-Pauline and post-

387. No less a scholar than Streeter (*Primitive* 196–200) would have the epistle of James addressed to Rome. By way of exclusion, I indicated in footnote 356 above that *II Clement* probably does not reflect the Roman scene.

388. This list brings us to about A.D. 150. One might wish to continue by studying Justin (who taught at Rome *ca.* 150–165), the Quartodeciman crisis over the Easter feast (*ca.* 190), and the liturgical traditions underlying the early-third century work of Hippolytus (especially *The Apostolic Constitutions*), a priest of Rome and the first anti-pope. The gnostic library of Nag Hammadi might also yield information about the image of Rome, sometimes through a hostile view of Peter as the symbol of the church catholic.

389. The hypothesis of the writing of Philippians during Paul's imprisonment in Caesarea of Palestine *ca.* 58–60 (Acts 23:33 – 27:1) had popularity (Lohmeyer, Paulus, Pfleiderer, Spitta) but seems abandoned in recent times.

70, so that we know for comparison nothing of what Paul wrote from Rome in the early 60s. Moreover, the problem is complicated by the contention of many scholars that Philippians itself is composite, consisting of several letters, not all of which were composed at one time. The Roman hypothesis, which had almost universal acceptance before the eighteenth century and still has respectable advocates (F. W. Beare, Cerfaux, Dodd, Harrison, Guthrie, J. Schmid, Cullmann), has in its favor a reliably recorded imprisonment of Paul at Rome (Acts 28:16,30) and the statement of Marcion *ca.* 150 that Paul wrote Philippians from prison in Rome.[390]

If Philippians *were* written from Rome, what light would it throw on Roman Christianity in the early 60s? I have suggested that Paul's letter to the Romans made a good impression on the church, and that Acts 28:15 is correct in tone in showing Paul being welcomed by delegations as he approaches Rome. I have also suggested that it was the circumcision-insistent Jewish/Gentile Christians (Group One) at Rome who were guilty of "jealous zeal" against Paul (*I Clem.* 5:2–5) and contributed to his martyrdom by the Romans under Nero. Philippians 1:14–15 could confirm both these suggestions. Many of the Christians in the area were strengthened by his imprisonment, but there were others in that area who "preached Christ from envy." The strong polemic in chap. 3 against Jewish Christian missionaries who insisted on circumcision of their Gentile converts suggests the identity of the envious preachers. The Roman hypothesis makes intelligible the reference in 1:13 to the praetorian guard[391] and in 4:22 to Christians of the Emperor's (Caesar's) household (although those references could be explained in the Ephesus hypothesis); for Acts 28:16 mentions that Paul was guarded at Rome, and Rom 16:11 mentions Christians belonging to Narcissus, possibly the figure who was a close advisor of the Emperor Claudius. (Some would identify the Clement who is with Paul in Philip 4:3 as the man who wrote *I Clement* for the Roman church in A.D. 96; but that is a pure guess, for "Clement" is a common name.) In 1:1 Paul

---

390. Also Hagner, *Use* 226–28, cites parallels between *I Clem.* 47:2 and Philip 4:15 ("in the beginning of the gospel"), and between *I Clem.* 21:1 and Philip 1:27 ("conducting oneself worthily"), as evidence for (hesitantly) affirming probable knowledge of Philippians by Clement of Rome.

391. See Lightfoot, *Philippians* 99–104.

greets the bishops and deacons of the Philippian church; if these two functions existed as well in the place from which he was writing, that could fit in with the Roman hypothesis, for the twofold structure is attested in the 80s and the 90s in I Peter and *I Clement.*

That the tone of Philippians is close to Romans and the other Pauline Epistles of the late 50s offers no difficulty to the Roman hypothesis, for it would have been written only three or four years after Romans.[392] In Rom 1:15 Paul wrote, "I am eager to preach the gospel to you also who are in Rome"; in Philip 1:12–13 he would be reporting what actually happened when he arrived in Rome as a prisoner: "I want you to know that what has happened to me has really served to advance the gospel, so that my bondage in Christ has become known through the whole praetorium." Those at Rome encouraged by Paul's sufferings for Christ in prison now preach Christ "out of love knowing that I am put here for the defense of the gospel" (Philip 1:15–16). In Rom 12:1 Paul had urged the Romans to "present your bodies as a living sacrifice [*thysia*] holy and pleasing to God, which is spiritual worship," and in 15:16 Paul spoke of himself as a minister (*leitourgos*) of God in the priestly service of the gospel. In Philip 2:17 Paul speaks of himself in prison (at Rome?) as "being poured out as a sacrifice [*thysia*] and service [*leitourgia*] of your faith."[393] I maintained that in Romans Paul was more moderate about Judaism and OT salvation history than he was in Galatians. It is difficult to decide whether the condemnation of circumcision-insistent extremism in Philip 3 is closer to Galatians or to Romans, for both letters attack insistence on circumcision. Yet Philip 3:4–7 on Jewish status seems to echo Rom 11:1. Moreover, in Rom 16:18 Paul warns that those who sow dissension in Rome "do not serve the Lord Jesus Christ but their own belly," while the enemies of Christ in Philip 3:18–19 are those "whose God is their belly." Overall, then,

---

392. *Ibid.* 41–46; Lightfoot thinks Paul wrote Philippians, Colossians, and Ephesians from imprisonment in Rome in 61–63, but would date Philippians early in that period to separate it from the others and bring it closer in time to Romans. He lists parallels.

393. Cullman, *Peter* 105, argues that such an attitude fits the end of Paul's life in the 60s better than a hypothetical imprisonment in Ephesus in the 50s. The accessibility to Paul in prison implied in Philippians resembles the ease of the Roman imprisonment described in Acts 28:30–31 but not the situation in Ephesus where Paul was "unbearably crushed to the point of despairing of life itself" (II Cor 1:8).

if Philippians were written from Rome in the early 60s, it could fit without difficulty into the picture of Roman Christianity and Paul's experiences in Rome that I have reconstructed in previous chapters.

B. The Epistle to the Ephesians

Colossians (4:3,18) and Ephesians (3:1; 4:1; 6:20) also present themselves as being written by Paul in prison. Whereas the authenticity of the prison setting of Philippians is widely accepted, many scholars think Colossians is post-Pauline. Even more scholars think Ephesians is post-Pauline and written in dependence upon Colossians but by another hand. For the purposes of this book I shall work with the post-Pauline hypothesis.

What imprisonment is thought of as a fictional setting in the two letters? When the letters were thought to be genuine, it was generally assumed that the Roman imprisonment of Paul in A.D. 61–63 was meant. (An argument that Philippians was *not* written from Rome in the 60s was its dissimilarity from Colossians and Ephesians which were so written.) In the hypothesis of a fictional setting, the case for Rome (the city where Paul died) may be even stronger, since the author would scarcely choose a lesser known imprisonment. But even if Rome was in the mind of the author, one must be extremely cautious in deciding what that tells us about the actual situation in Roman Christianity in the 80s (the generally suggested date in the post-Pauline hypothesis). Did he know the Roman church situation or was he using his imagination?

In approaching the material with these cautions, I wish to confine myself to Ephesians for several reasons. Hagner (*Use* 226, 230) applies the judgment "very probable" to Clement's knowledge of Ephesians, but not even "probable" to Clement's knowledge of Colossians. Mitton has made an impressive case for the knowledge of Ephesians (not of Colossians) by the author of I Peter.[394] Although the author of Ephesians draws upon many of the Pauline Epistles, a

---

394. C. L. Mitton, "The Relationship between I Peter and Ephesians," JTS 1 (1950) 67–73. Others, like Selwyn and Boismard, would argue for the dependence of the two works on a common tradition (that of the Roman church?).

close relationship to Romans has been emphasized by many commentators. Thus, there are external reasons for connecting Ephesians rather than Colossians with Rome. Moreover, while the author of Ephesians draws heavily on Colossians, he seems to avoid one crucial section of Colossians, namely 2:16–23, which describes the Jewish gnosticizing heresy that called forth Colossians. In other words, the Ephesians author does not seem to think that the local circumstances of Colossians will be useful to his readers, and no particular heresy or set of adversaries seems to be envisioned by him. Thus, it would seem that Colossians and Ephesians differ as to either the point of origin, or of destination, or both, so that if one relates Ephesians to Rome in one of those roles,[395] it would be wiser to leave Colossians out of the discussion.

We saw that, despite the attempt of Hebrews to persuade the Roman community that Christ had replaced the levitical cult, the tendency in I Peter and *I Clement* was to preserve that cult in some spiritualized form in the church. If I Peter 2:5 spoke of living stones being built into a spiritual house, Eph 2:18–22 speaks of Christians as forming a household of God growing into a holy temple in the Lord. If Paul in Romans 11:17–24 thought of the Gentiles as a wild olive shoot grafted on the tree of Israel, Eph 2:12–16 speaks of the Gentiles as a group that was once alienated from the commonwealth of Israel but is now brought near through the blood of Christ, so that the dividing wall is broken down and the two are one. In other words, Ephesians seems to describe the dreams of Paul in Romans 11 as fulfilled. We remember that the Roman church of the 80s and 90s had reconciled the images of Peter and Paul, so that the two, who were once divided in their understanding of the implications of Christ for Jew and Gentile, were now pillars in the same church (*I Clem.* 5). Consequently, Roman Christianity might be seen idealistically as the meeting place of once divided Christians. In Rome the dominantly Gentile converts would have joined a community that was very loyal to its Jewish heritage, so that Paul's mission coincided

---

395 The address in 1:1 to the saints "who are in Ephesus" is of dubious originality, and so it is not impossible that the author was addressing Christians in the locale where the work was composed. On the other hand, he might be addressing all Christians.

with that of Peter. I have argued that in terms of the Gentile mission Rome may have looked on itself as the successor of the Jerusalem church. In an influential article H. Chadwick[396] has argued that the author of Ephesians insisted on the essential continuity between the original church of Jerusalem, composed of Jewish Christians, and the predominantly Gentile church of Paul's mission. Rome would fit perfectly as the setting of such an outlook. The Paul of Ephesians, while referring to himself as an apostle (1:1), seems to think of "the apostles" upon whom the church (universal) is founded as another group (even if not exclusive of himself)—a view harmonious with that of Rome where "the good apostles" were listed in the order Peter and Paul (p. 123 above).

Thus, in some aspects Ephesians could fit well the Roman Christianity of the 80s (even as Philippians could fit the situation of the early 60s). Yet the case for relating Ephesians to Rome as the place of origin remains very tenuous. True, if Ephesians was composed to sum up the career and thought of Paul,[397] it could appropriately have stemmed from the church that regarded itself as his heir since he died in its midst. Nevertheless, before Ephesians can become a major witness to Roman Christianity, one would have to analyze how much of its contents reflects the local scene and how much is borrowed from Colossians and thus from another milieu. In my reconstruction of the Roman church from 58 to 96, I found no signs of an incipiently gnostic strain of thought. Ephesians, with its almost mystic view of salvation and its timeless universalism, has been found by some to be tinged by gnosticism. If there is any truth in that hypothesis, it would suggest that the relation of the letter to Rome (if there is one) might at most be partial, for Ephesians may have made an amalgam of many post-Pauline church situations and problems.

*   *   *

---

396. "Die Absicht des Epheserbriefes," ZNW 51 (1960) 145–53.

397. In the Goodspeed-Knox hypothesis, adopted and modified by C. L. Mitton, *Ephesians* (New Century Bible; London: Oliphants, 1976) 7–10, Ephesians is related to the collection of the Pauline epistles. Rome could well have served as the collecting place. II Peter, if it was from Rome, is the first NT work to show knowledge of such a collection (3:16).

It will be noted that Ephesians is the only post-Pauline work that I have discussed in relation to Roman Christianity. Personally I find myself unable to decide whether II Thessalonians is really post-Pauline; and even if it is, little would relate it to the Roman scene, unless the Antichrist figure of chap. 2 is Nero or Domitian. In the setting imagined by the post-Pauline Pastoral Epistles, Paul had not yet been imprisoned when he wrote I Timothy and Titus, but by the time of II Timothy (1:8) he had been imprisoned. Since in the latter he asks for Mark to come to him (4:11) and since he is on the point of death (4:6–8), Rome may well have been in mind as the place of imprisonment. (In the 80s, the possible date of II Timothy, it was known that Paul died at Rome; and I Peter 5:13 portrays Mark at Rome [Babylon] near the time of Peter's death.) Certainly "Pudens and Linus" in 4:21 are names familiar in Roman tradition; yet Prisca and Aquila are with the recipient, not with the sender (4:19). In any case, little can be constructed from II Timothy in particular, or from the Pastorals in general, about the situation of the church from which it or they were sent. The Pastorals' interest in the firm establishment of the system of presbyter-bishops and deacons might be compared to *I Clement*'s defense of the presbyters at Corinth. Yet one does not have in the Pastorals the levitical or cultic emphasis of the latter work. Hagner (*Use* 230–36) finds inadequate evidence that *I Clement* drew upon II Timothy, although he finds some probability for familiarity with and use of the other two Pastorals (a rather optimistic judgment[398]). Those who accept the Pastorals as post-Pauline need to do more work diagnosing the probable place of origin before those epistles can become useful for a study of the Roman church.

C. The Gospel According to Mark

Let us begin by listing what is said in the NT about men named Mark: (a) "John who was also called Mark" is mentioned in Acts. His mother Mary had a house in Jerusalem where many Christians

---

398. The work cited in footnote 315 above (pp. 137–38) attributes low probability to Clement's knowledge of Titus, uncertainty to a knowledge of I Timothy, and no evidence to a knowledge of II Timothy.

gathered to pray and to which Peter went in the early 40s when he escaped from prison (12:12). Barnabas and Saul brought John Mark from Jerusalem to Antioch (12:25) and then from Antioch to Cyprus on the "first missionary journey" (mid 40s); however, he left them at Perga of Pamphylia and returned to Jerusalem (13:13). When Barnabas and Saul were ready to set out from Antioch on the "second missionary journey" *ca.* 49, Barnabas wanted to take John Mark again; but Paul refused because of John Mark's previous withdrawal in Pamphylia. This led to a sharp separation of ways between the two apostles, with Barnabas taking John Mark to Cyprus, while Paul went to Asia Minor (15:36–41). (b) In the genuine letters of Paul, someone named Mark is with him (late 50s or early 60s) and sends greetings in the letter from an imprisoned Paul to Philemon (v. 24). In the (probably) post-Pauline Colossians (4:10), the Philemon notice is expanded to include greetings from Mark "the cousin of Barnabas, about whom you received directions—if he comes to you, receive him." In the post-Pauline II Tim 4:11, Paul in prison and near death writes, "Get Mark and bring him with you, for he is very useful in serving me." (c) In the (probably) post-Petrine I Peter (5:13) the Roman church ("the co-elect in Babylon") sends greetings to the Gentile Christians in Asia Minor "and so does my son Mark."

Are the three references to one man? The *first issue* is whether (b) and (c) refer to the same Mark. We have seen above (pp. 188, 191) that in the post-Pauline development of the apostle's image his imprisonment in II Timothy was plausibly intended to be at Rome, as was also the imprisonment of Colossians/Ephesians (derived from Philemon).[399] The thesis of two Marks at Rome in the 60s, one associated with Paul, the other with Peter, seems far less likely than positing the same man. The *second issue* is whether the Roman Mark (b,c) is also the John Mark of Jerusalem (a) who in the 40s was associated with Paul (even if unhappily) and with Peter (through John Mark's mother's house). *A priori* the double apostolic association given both to Mark and to John Mark makes identity likely. *A posteriori*

---

399. It is generally thought that the authors of Colossians and Ephesians used as a setting the Roman imprisonment of A.D. 61–63, while the author of the Pastorals was envisaging a second, later Roman imprisonment during which Paul died. In Colossians Mark is with Paul; in II Timothy Paul asks for him to come.

in the 80s the two were implicitly identified by the author of Colossians who related Mark to Barnabas, even as Acts closely associated John Mark with Barnabas.[400] Overall, then, the evidence favors thinking of one man[401] even if we must suppose that, having separated from Paul in the period 45–50, Mark was again working with Paul in the early 60s. One gets the impression that *ca.* 50 Mark may have stood theologically closer to Peter than to Paul in the dispute at Antioch, just as did Barnabas (Gal 2:13), and that is why after that dispute Barnabas and Mark separated from Paul.[402] Mark could have changed his attitude toward Paul later; and/or the Paul of Romans and of the 60s may have become more moderate and moved closer to Peter's position, lessening the distance between himself and Mark.

Thus far we have surveyed the evidence of the NT; let us turn to tradition. According to what Papias, the early-second-century bishop of Hierapolis, heard from a disciple of the disciples of Jesus (if we may presume that is what he means by the "presbyter/elder"), someone named Mark, who had not been a disciple of Jesus or heard him, became the interpreter of Peter[403] and so wrote down what was said and done by Jesus. This Marcan account, while not in order[404] and representing a memory of Peter's oral adaptations to listeners, was not erroneous or false (Eusebius, *Hist.* 3.39.15). It is not clear from Papias whether Mark wrote while Peter was still alive. The implication may be to the contrary because of the reference to remembering and lack of order—if Peter was still alive, the account should have been more exact. By the last third of the second century the Anti-

---

400. The Pseudo-Clementine *Recognitions* 1.7 and the *Acts of Peter* (Vercelli) 4 associate Barnabas with Rome.

401. After warning that "Mark (Marcus) was the commonest Latin name in the Roman Empire and that the early Church must have contained innumerable Marks," D. E. Nineham, *Saint Mark* (London: Penguin, 1963) 39–41, regards the identity of Mark and John Mark as precarious but does not exclude it.

402. Marcion, the Pauline enthusiast, did not include Mark's gospel in his canon; but Marcion, who was rejected at Rome, may have thought of Mark as associated with that city. Many scholars insist on a strong Pauline influence on Mark, but see pp. 198–99 below.

403. This description is somewhat ambiguous. Chronologically, the next reference to Mark's work comes from Justin (*ca.* 160) who speaks of the "memoirs [*apomnēmoneumata*] of Peter" (*Dialogue* 106).

404. Luke 1:1,3 contrasts the Lucan orderly account with earlier narratives. Does Papias think of Mark as one of these earlier and implicitly less orderly accounts?

Marcionite Prologue[405] prefixed to Mark, and Irenaeus (*Adv. haer.* 3.1.1.) indicate that Mark wrote after the death of Peter and Paul; but Clement of Alexandria, and (later) Epiphanius and Jerome would have Mark writing while Peter was alive. Indeed, Clement (Eusebius, *Hist.* 2.15.2) claims that Peter authorized Mark's work to be read in the churches.

By way of relating the Papias tradition to NT information, one may ask whether the Mark of whom Papias writes is the John Mark of Acts and the Mark of the Pauline and Petrine tradition (who were probably one man). Origen (Eusebius, *Hist.* 6.25.5) identifies the evangelist with the Mark of I Peter, and Jerome in his commentary on v. 24 of Philemon (PL 26.618A) states his opinion that the Mark mentioned there is the author of the gospel. Earlier, Papias knew I Peter (Eusebius, *Hist.* 3.39.17); and so, when he described Mark as the interpreter of Peter, he was almost certainly thinking of the Mark whom Peter, writing from Rome (Babylon: I Peter 5:13), called "my son." If we put together all the connections we have seen, it seems likely that *by the early second century a tradition was in circulation that Mark,* presumably John Mark of Jerusalem, who had traveled with Paul in the 40s and who had been a companion of Peter and Paul at Rome in the 60s, *wrote a gospel at Rome*[406] *under the influence of Peter* just before or shortly after Peter's death (which took place no later than 67).

How reliable is such a tradition? Three factors are involved, Mark, Peter, and Rome;[407] and a question must be asked about each, even if the first two are less important for the purposes of this book.

---

405. See R. G. Heard, "The Old Gospel Prologues," JTS 6 (1955) 1–16, esp. 4–6. This Prologue, which some date considerably later, posits the writing of the gospel in Italy by Mark the *colobodactylus* ("stump-fingered"). Is this adjective, applied to Mark also by Hippolytus of Rome (*Philosophumena* [*Refutation of All Heresies*] 7.18 or 7.30.1; GCS 26.215), a local Roman tradition? Does it signify physical deformity or literary clumsiness?

406. Rome is implied by Papias; Italy is specified by the Anti-Marcionite Prologue. Even though later Mark was associated with Alexandria, Clement of Alexandria specified that Mark wrote at Rome the acts of Jesus which later became the gospel we know, and a spiritual gospel after he came to Alexandria. (See M. Smith, *Clement of Alexandria and the Secret Gospel of Mark* [Cambridge, Mass.: Harvard, 1973].) Mistakenly, almost 200 years later, Chrysostom states that the gospel of Mark was written in Egypt (*Homilies on Matthew* 1.3; PG 57.17).

407. This is clearly pointed out by Moreau, "Rome" 38–39.

First, did (John) Mark actually write the gospel? The modesty of the claim stands in its favor; for the posited author is not a famous apostle,[408] not a disciple who had a uniformly praiseworthy career, not an eyewitness of Jesus (despite John Mark's home in Jerusalem).[409] One is hard pressed to explain an unchallenged tradition of authorship attached to such an unlikely subject as Mark if there were not some truth in it. On the other hand, some would argue that the evangelist does not seem to know the geography of Palestine and so cannot be the John Mark of Acts.[410]

Second, did Mark get his tradition from Peter? Here the probability of invention increases. If Mark was not an eyewitness, whence did he get his knowledge about Jesus? According to the NT Peter had been at John Mark's home; and in Rome Mark was the companion of Peter, indeed his "son." Even without solid information would not one be tempted to *guess* that Mark got the information from Peter? (Indeed the tradition of Mark's relation to Peter develops from writing out memories of Peter, to gaining Peter's subsequent approval, to Peter's encouragement and virtual dictation.) Granted that caution, internal testing becomes important. Even scholars who think the evangelist did have some contact with an eyewitness[411] admit that much of the gospel tradition is best explained as derivative from earlier sources that were once or several times removed from oral, eyewitness presentation. As for vivid Marcan scenes that are (debatably) attributed to direct contact between the evangelist and

---

408. Streeter, *Gospels* 562: "The burden of the proof is on those who would assert the traditional authorship of Matthew and John and on those who would deny it in the case of Mark and Luke." In relation to my third question above (written at Rome?), Streeter gave impetus to attributing each gospel to a great Christian center, a position later defended by T. W. Manson (on p. 52 of the *Studies* cited in footnote 219 above).

409. One can see pure imagination in the claim of Epiphanius (*Panarion* 51.6; PG 41.900a) that Mark was one of the 70 disciples sent out by Jesus (Luke 10:1).

410. E. Schweizer, *The Good News according to Mark* (Richmond: Knox, 1970) 24. Such an argument also militates against Galilee as the place of composition (footnote 413 below).

411. Taylor, *Mark* 78–82, may be consulted as an informed conservative attempt to protect the Petrine tradition. For a more extravagant thesis that makes Peter the real author of the gospel, see J. Chapman, *Matthew, Mark and Luke* (London: Longman, Green, 1937) 83–93. The contrast that runs through John 21 raises the possibility that the insistence in 21:21 that the Beloved Disciple "wrote *these things*" is in contrast to a tradition that Peter stood behind a written gospel.

an eyewitness, Peter is absent from most; and so there is no internal reason to make him the agent of such presentations. True, Taylor and others, however, would argue that Mark was dependent on Peter for "picturesque" stories in which Peter does feature, e.g., the transfiguration, Gethsemane, and the denials. Today most critical scholars, however, would see these as highly theological scenes, not much closer to eyewitness reporting than other "less vivid" Marcan accounts. Moreover, the Marcan picture of Peter is the least favorable of all the gospels, and there are major Petrine scenes found in Matthew that are absent from Mark.[412] Thus, there would be little internal reason to justify Papias' picture of a Mark who writes as an interpreter of Peter, or to support Justin's designation of Mark as the "memoirs" of Peter.

Third, was the Marcan gospel written at Rome? Granted the information in Acts about John Mark at Jerusalem and Antioch, and the later tradition about Mark's going to Alexandria, it is noteworthy that tradition does not attribute Mark to one of those cities. The lack of a serious traditional contender[413] favors the historicity of the second-century tradition naming Rome. Nevertheless, since both Pauline and Petrine epistolary evidence associates Mark with Rome, it is not impossible that, if Mark was thought to be the evangelist, the association of his gospel with Rome represents an early guess. Once again internal testing becomes important. The gospel explains Aramaic expressions (3:17; 5:41; 7:11, etc.) and elementary Jewish customs (7:3–5), so that Palestine as place of composition may be plausibly excluded. There are more Latinisms in the Greek of Mark[414] than in any other gospel, and that statistic suggests an environment where Latin was frequently spoken. In particular, it has been argued that the bronze *kodrantēs* coin of Mark 12:42, "two *lepta* which constitute one *quadrans*," was not in circulation in the eastern section of the empire,[415] so that Mark would be offering a coinage

---

412. Matthew 14:28–31; 16:17–19; 17:24–27; see R. E. Brown, *Peter* 78–105.
413. Some modern scholars suggest Galilee (Lohmeyer, Marxsen, Kelber), but that finds no antecedent in the tradition.
414. Taylor, *Mark* 45; Lane, *Mark* 24–25. P. L. Couchaud went so far as to suggest that the gospel was originally written in Latin!
415. W. M. Ramsay, *Expository Times* 10 (1898–99) 232, 336. On the one hand, A.E.J. Rawlinson, *The Gospel According to St. Mark* (Westminster Commentaries; 3rd

equivalent for western readers. Mark 15:21 identifies Simon of Cyrene as "the father of Alexander and Rufus," presumably because
these two sons are known to Mark and his readers; and attention has
been called to the only other Rufus in the NT who lives at Rome
(Rom 16:13),[416] but the identification is adventurous. Even more adventurous is the attempt to find in 9:49, "Every one will be salted
with fire," a reference to the persecution of Christians by Nero at
Rome after the fire.[417] Most scholars think that independently the authors of Matthew and Luke knew and used Mark within two decades
of its being written (and even John is close at times to Mark), and so
one suspects that the place of composition was one that had contacts
with other, widely separated Christian communities. Overall, then,
the internal evidence is not unfavorable to the tradition that Rome
was the place of provenance for Mark.[418]

Let me summarize the answers given to the three questions that
probed the reliability of the second-century tradition that Mark
wrote a gospel at Rome under the influence of Peter. The role of Peter as the source for the gospel is the most dubious element; but
Mark as the author and Rome as the site cannot be quickly dismissed
as implausible.

* * *

Because of that judgment it is appropriate to consider, briefly at
least, how the Marcan gospel might be related to the documents I
have associated with Rome and to the Christian situation analyzed

---

ed.; London: Methuen, 1931) xxxi, finds Mark written in "the kind of Greek which
might be *spoken* by the lower classes at Rome." On the other hand, H. J. Cadbury,
The Making of Luke-Acts (New York: Macmillan, 1927) 88–89, argues that Mark's
Latinisms are widely distributed in the Greek and Semitic of the time and do not lo-
calize Mark in Italy.

416. An Alexander is mentioned in I Tim 1:20 and II Tim 4:14 who could be
placed in Rome, but he is an enemy of Paul.

417. Lane, *Mark* 24.

418. Bacon, *Mark* 46, is too certain: "That this earliest of extant Greek Gospels
should attain its short-lived supremacy under the simple 'According to Mark' is expli-
cable under the theory of Roman provenance, but hardly otherwise." Positive, too, is a
foe of Marcan priority, namely, W. R. Farmer, "Modern Developments of Griesbach's Hypothesis," NTS 23 (1976–77) 275–95, who asserts (288): Mark "no doubt
fits a Roman provenance."

there. While *I Clement* shows knowledge of material about Jesus found in the Synoptic Gospels, it is very difficult to be certain that the author knew a specific gospel. Those who allow the possibility are more inclined to posit a knowledge of Matthew (and Luke) than of Mark.[419] (A. Fridrichsen[420] has suggested that the "envy" [*phthonos*] mentioned in *I Clem.* 5 as the cause of the martyrs' deaths at Rome may echo Mark 15:10 where the high priests deliver up Jesus to Pilate out of envy; but this connection is tenuous.) Indeed, the absence of any attention to Mark in Roman documents of the early post-NT period constitutes a problem for the thesis that Mark was composed at Rome and especially for deriving Mark from Peter, the great apostle of the Roman church.

Similarly, while the author of I Peter knows Jesus-material found in the gospels, one may suspect that he drew his knowledge from a pre-written-gospel level of the tradition; and so there is no reason to think he used Mark.[421] Some instances of parallels between the two works are offered by Best (*Peter* 52–54), but it is difficult to be sure that the themes involved are specific enough to be attributed to the peculiar theology of the Roman church. For example, I Peter 1:18 and Mark 10:45 attribute to Jesus' death the aspect of ransom; and I Peter 4:13 and Mark 13 relate the themes of persecution and parousia.

As for a relation between Mark and Paul's letter to the Romans, the failure to believe in Jesus is explained in Rom 11:8 through reference to Isa 6:9 about the eyes not being able to see, and the ears to hear. The failure of the people to understand Jesus' parables is explained in Mark 4:12 by the same Isaian passage: "So that they may see but not perceive, may hear but not understand." Obviously, however, that is a common Christian theme (Acts 28:27; John 12:40), even as is the suggested parallelism between Rom 13:9–10 and Mark 10:19; 12:29–30 in terms of listing the commandments of the decalogue and summing them up in the commandment of love. In Rom 14:9 Christ is "the Lord of the dead and of the living," while in Mark 12:27 God "is not God of the dead but of the living." More impres-

---

419. Telfer, *Office* 52; Hagner, *Use* 171–78.
420. See Cullmann, *Peter* 108.
421. E. Best, "I Peter and the Gospel Tradition," NTS 16 (1969–70) 95–113, esp. 99–102.

sive for possible relation to Roman theology is a comparison between the gospel formula (presumably known to the Roman church) in Rom 1:3–4 which places divine sonship over Davidic descent, and Jesus' question in Mark 12:35–37 which points in the same direction. Bacon, who calls attention to parallels, speaks of the "anti-Jewish radicalism of Mark" (*Mark* 75) in terms of certain passages where Mark seems to be more severe than Paul. Romans 14:20 states in relation to the food laws: "Everything is indeed clean, but it is wrong for anyone to make others fall by what he eats," while Mark 7:19 makes no such pastoral amelioration: "Thus he declared all foods clean." Romans 11:25–26 admits that a "hardening" (*pōrōsis*) has come upon part of Israel; but that is "until the full number of the Gentiles come in, and so all will be saved." Without qualification in Mark 3:5 Jesus is angered at the *pōrōsis* he encounters in the synagogue. Mark 7:3 speaks of "the Pharisees and all the Jews" with a third-person tone that suggests his audience is not Jewish;[422] indeed the first one to confess the Son of God is a Roman centurion (Mark 15:39). According to Mark 7 the traditions of the Pharisees are of men and not of God; indeed at times they are contrary to God's will. This seems more radical than the Paul of Romans.[423]

Overall, then, a comparison of Mark with the documents commonly related to the Roman church (Romans, I Peter, *I Clement*) is not decisive, partly because one does not know whether Mark was written to confirm a community in its outlook or to correct that community and help it to change its mind. If the latter, Mark might well be in conflict with some of those Roman documents.

Bearing in mind that difficulty, let us now turn to comparing Mark to Roman Christianity. To study all the evidence in Mark would require a book in itself. Consequently I propose simply to list observations about Mark that, were the gospel written at Rome, might challenge negatively or support positively my reconstruction of the dominant Christianity at Rome, namely, as derived from Jerusalem, with strong Jewish origins and continued loyalties to the Jew-

---

422. One is tempted to wonder whether an author who writes thus can have been Jewish, but I Thess 2:14–15 (if genuinely Pauline) portrays Paul as similarly distancing himself from the Jews.

423. Note, however, that Kümmel, *Introduction* 93, has Mark defending Jesus against the charge that he has abandoned the Jewish Law.

ish cultic heritage. These observations are culled from modern scholarship and reflect the enormous range of disagreement that characterizes contemporary discussion of Mark.[424] Furthermore, they are affected by our inability to distinguish with much surety between Mark's redaction or editing and the tradition that came down to him—a surety that, were it possible, might isolate more clearly the situation of the evangelist and his community.

NEGATIVE CHALLENGES: (1) Even if by the last third of the first century Gentiles were an ethnic majority in Roman Christianity, could they have been so ignorant of basic Jewish purity customs as Mark 7 presupposes, if their Christianity continued to have strong Jewish attachments? One may respond that loyalty at Rome to the Jewish heritage was selective, concentrating on cult and not on Pharisee cleansing rituals; but one must admit that Mark seems to envisage a Gentile audience that knows little at all of Judaism. (2) According to the more moderate interpretations of Mark, during the ministry of Jesus Peter is portrayed as one who is well-meaning but who fails to understand the Son of God. In the more radical interpretations (T. J. Weeden; W. H. Kelber) Mark attacks Peter and the Twelve as the proponents of a false christology which stresses Jesus as a divine man confirmed by miracles. Mark's hostility is aroused because such teachers have led Jewish Christianity to false hopes in a parousia—hopes connected with the Jewish revolt against Rome. The latter view (often rebutted) can be reconciled with a localization of Mark at Rome only if the Gospel is seen as a corrective of a Roman idealization of Peter.

POSITIVE SUPPORT: (1) Scholars of the most diverse schools of interpretation[425] have detected in Mark (especially but not exclusively in Mark 13) an emphasis on persecution as inevitable and even as a present or imminent reality. Some would identify specific references to the events of the Jewish War against Rome, the flight of the

---

424. See the almost despairing note struck by C. F. Evans in *The Cambridge History of the Bible* (3 vols.; Cambridge Univ. 1960–63) 1.270–71.

425. E.g., R. H. Lightfoot, S. E. Johnson, Rawlinson, Weeden; see B.M.F. van Iersel, "The Gospel according to St. Mark—Written for a Persecuted Community?" *Nederlands Theologisch Tijdschrift* 34 (1980) 15–36.

Jerusalem Christians to Pella, the persecution under Nero, and the destruction of the Temple—in short, the events of A.D. 65–70. Obviously the Christian community at Rome, if it had strong Jewish roots, would have been affected by developments both in Jerusalem and Rome. The anti-Jewish elements in Mark and the antipathy toward the high priest have been seen as an apologetic addressed to the fellow citizens of the Christians at Rome, telling them that the same Jewish forces involved in the revolt against Rome were hostile to Jesus, so that Roman anger should be directed against the Jews, not the Christians.[426] (2) Even more commonly scholars have detected in Mark an emphasis on the necessity of the suffering and crucifixion of Jesus, so that Jesus cannot be understood without that optic. Thus Mark is interpreted as a statement that only by suffering can the Christians of Mark's time attain real faith in Jesus. By almost a *tour de force* Mark is turning the suffering undergone at Rome into a positive catechesis about a way of life in which the redemption has its effect. (3) In the same line of thought the somewhat negative picture of Peter during the ministry can be understood. To some, the death of Peter at Rome may have seemed a defeat: the great apostle who had been delivered so many times from death at the hands of Jewish opponents had fallen before the Roman emperor. But Mark teaches that even the first of the Twelve could not fully understand Jesus without taking up the cross. Otherwise, Peter might be seen as one whose faith depended on the miraculous success of Jesus (and on his own miraculous career). The death of Peter (and the death of Paul), through the eyes of Mark, could be seen as the acme and not the nadir of the apostolic career.[427]

The evidence is obviously inconclusive in the sense that the attribution of Mark to Rome, while presenting some difficulties, could probably be reconciled with the situation I have envisaged for Christianity there. Yet such attribution would add only slightly to knowledge derivable from other documents.

---

426. See S.G.F. Brandon, "The Date of the Markan Gospel," NTS 7 (1960–61) 126–41.

427. Such an approach is diametrically opposite to that of Kelber and Weeden.

D. Ignatius to the Romans

While being taken under guard from Antioch where he had been bishop to Rome where he would be martyred under Trajan (98–117), Ignatius wrote a series of letters. They reflect his experience at Antioch,[428] and with one exception they tell us about internal doctrinal struggles and divisions in the recipient churches. Romans is that exception—was there no heresy at Rome? Either because Ignatius was not informed in detail about Rome or because his only interest was to prevent the Romans in their kindness from cheating him of martyrdom, Ignatius' letter casts little light on Rome and thus on the topic of this book. A few facts may be listed, most of which have already been cited in preceding chapters as fitting into my construction of Roman Christianity:

■ Ignatius' greeting "to the church that presides in the chief place of the country of the Romans" is more fulsome and laudatory than that to any other church. The church of Rome is "worthy of honor, worthy of felicitation, worthy of praise, worthy of success, worthy of holiness." Since Ignatius agrees with *I Clement*'s greeting which speaks of "the church of God that sojourns in Rome," both works militate against the thesis that the community in Rome did not constitute a church (because it was not founded by apostles or because it was split up in synagogues).

■ In particular, it is a church "preeminent in love" (see also 2:2; 3:2), a church that has never been jealous, indeed a church that has taught others (3:1).

■ It is a church that has received directions from the apostles Peter and Paul (4:3)—a fact that may explain Ignatius' respect.

■ No single-bishop is mentioned at Rome, probably because the church still had the twofold structure of presbyter-bishops and deacons.

---

428. L. W. Barnard, "The Background of St. Ignatius of Antioch," in his *Studies* 19–30. See also Chapter IV above.

E. The Shepherd of Hermas

This long and puzzling work of Christian prophecy, sometimes evaluated as idiosyncratic mediocrity, other times as profound theology, deserves much more attention than allotted here. Although no single complete Greek text has survived (perhaps because its christology was suspect as Arian), Irenaeus (*Adv. haer.* 4.20.2) spoke of it as Scripture; Origen (*In Rom.* 16:14[10:31]; PG 14.1252B) called it "divinely inspired"; and Eusebius (*Hist.* 3.3.6) reported that it was read publicly in churches. There is no doubt that it was written at Rome (*Vis.* 1.1.1.; 2.1.1; 4.1.2); and the suggestion that Clement would send it abroad (*Vis.* 2.4.3) may mean that Hermas' revelations had church status in Rome. There is little agreement as to composition,[429] but one respectable view divides the work chronologically in two parts. *Visions* 1 – 4 (where Clement is mentioned), and perhaps *Similitude* 9, may have been written in the early second century. The Shepherd makes his appearance in *Vision* 5, and the rest of the work may have been written about 135–145.[430] *Hermas* gives evidence of Hellenistic traditions and concepts, but scholars are divided on whether these are mere clothing or more deeply appropriated. Virtually all agree that, while the author does not speak of the Jews or their customs, or even quote the OT, he has been deeply influenced by Jewish traditions.[431] For some this means he was a convert Jew; for others, that he belonged to a select Jewish congregation at Rome; indeed even special Essene influence has been suggested.[432] However,

---

429. See Barnard, "Shepherd," for various views.

430. The Muratorian Fragment reports that Hermas wrote while his brother Pius was bishop of Rome (140–155)—perhaps another sign of church status. Certainly there are no signs in the work of the Montanist crisis, so it belongs in the first half of the second century.

431. See Daniélou, *Theology*, esp. refs. on 432; Barnard, "Early" 378–84; also Barnard, "Hermas, the Church and Judaism," in *Studies* 151–63. J. Reiling, *Hermas and Christian Prophecy* (NovTSupp 37; Leiden: Brill, 1973) 26, states, "The blending of genuine Jewish Christian elements with these unmistakable hellenistic elements constitutes the milieu of Hermas."

432. J.-P. Audet, RB 60 (1953) 41–82, has compared *Hermas* to the Qumran *Manual of Discipline* (1QS); he suggests that Hermas was the son of a Jew who belonged to the Qumran community and that Hermas was brought to Rome as slave (*Vis.* 1.1.1) after the war of 70. The idea of Essene influence at Rome has been taken

Barnard ("Shepherd" 34–35) may be closer to the mark: "Thus *I Clement*, like *Hermas*, is a Christian work which leans heavily on late-Jewish and early Jewish-Christian tradition and apologetics, and this raises the question as to the composition of the Roman Church in the late first and early second centuries. There would appear to be grounds for thinking that the influence of the Jewish-Christian element in the Church remained strong into the second century." I would rephrase slightly, for I think of Rome as containing a dominant Jewish/Gentile Christianity that had strong loyalties to Jerusalem and the Jewish tradition. The author of *Hermas* may have been ethnically a pure Gentile, but he would be representative of that continuing strain of Christianity. The indication that there was still a church structure of presbyter-bishops and deacons[433] indicates how conservative the Roman church was. One wonders if the striking ecclesiological symbolism[434] in *Hermas* portraying the church as an old woman who was created before all things and for whom the world was established (*Vis.* 2.4.1; see *II Clem.* 14.1) is not a reflection of Lady Wisdom created before the world began (Sir 1:4) who came to dwell in Israel (24:8–12), so that the church becomes the continuation of Israel.

In any case, there is no real difficulty fitting *Hermas* into the trajectory of Roman Christianity that I have diagnosed in this book. For example, just as *I Clement* showed Roman instincts by modifying Hebrews' rejection of levitical priesthood and cult, so *Hermas* (*Vis.* 2.2.4) claims a divine vision as basis for teaching that sins committed after baptism can be forgiven, a doctrine that modifies the position of Heb 6:4–6 which declares forgiveness after "enlightenment" impossible. Rome did not like extreme positions.

---

up by E. G. Hinson (in an article in the papers of the Seventh International Oxford Patristic Congress), who points to a military interest in *I Clem.* 37, and to information on the Essenes in Hippolytus, writing later at Rome.

433. See p. 163 above. All the references to presbyters and bishops are in the sections that some would judge chronologically early. However, if the men sitting on the bench in *Man.* 11.1 are presbyters, then the structure of presbyter-bishops lasted into the 140s. Telfer, *Office* 61, however, thinks it unquestionable that by the time Hermas was finished there was a single-bishop at Rome.

434. See L. Pernveden, *The Concept of the Church in the Shepherd of Hermas* (Studia Theologica Lundensia; Lund: Gleerup, 1966).

F. Legends of Peter and Simon Magus at Rome

Acts 8:9–24 tells the story of a magician named Simon, from a city in Samaria, who was hailed as "The power of God which is called great." Believing in Jesus, he was baptized by Philip; but later he came to envy the gift of the Spirit which the apostles Peter and John could confer. His offer of money for this sacred power (whence "simony") was angrily rejected by Peter who judged that Simon was in the bonds of iniquity. The story ends with Simon, in fear of divine punishment, asking Peter's prayers. Simon was not the only "magus" to be encountered by gospel preachers; and he comes off more sympathetically than Elymas bar Jesus, the magus and false prophet who tangled with Paul at Paphos in Cyprus (Acts 13:6–11). Nevertheless, Simon became the subject of a legend that embodies symbolically second-century church conflicts.

About 155, Justin, a native of Nablus in Samaria, who came to Rome before 150 and was martyred there about 165, addressed his *First Apology* to the emperor Antoninus Pius (138–161). In chap. 26 he reports that Simon, a magus from Gitto in Samaria, did diabolic magic in Rome during the reign of Claudius (41–54), so that he was considered a god. Indeed, a statue was erected to him on an island in the Tiber between the two bridges with the Latin inscription: *Simoni deo sancto,* "To Simon the holy god." A woman named Helena, a former prostitute, went with him, hailed as "the first idea generated by him" as god. Meander, also a Samaritan, was Simon's disciple. Now the Simon of this account is never identified as the Simon Magus of Acts 8 and is never said to be a Christian, but then Justin does not cite Acts in his writings. It is extremely unlikely that there were in Christian writings two Simons who were magicians from Samaria, who functioned in the 30s and 40s, and who were hailed as god. It is fairly clear that the statue of which Justin speaks is to be related to the marble inscription found on the island of the Tiber in 1574 dedicated to Sabine god Semo Sancus: *Semoni Sanco Deo Fidio Sacrum.* Some have thought that misreading the inscription caused Justin to compose the Simon legend. It is much more likely that the Simon legend was known to him either from Samaria or from Rome, and that he wrongly associated the statue with the legend.

Some twenty-five years later Irenaeus, *Adv. haer.* 1.23, presents us with a more developed form of the Simon legend. Very clearly now it is Simon Magus of Acts 8 who was honored by a statue in the reign of Claudius Caesar. He contended against the apostles; his faith in Jesus was a sham; and he was glorified as a god. He presented himself as the Father of all; and his Phoenician slave companion, Helena, whom he saved by descending to deliver her from earthly contamination, was the first conception of his mind. His thought is presented as full-fledged gnosticism (only hinted at in Justin); and he becomes the father of all gnostic heresies, with Menander as his successor. True, Irenaeus does not say Simon Magus came to Rome, but the reference to the statue seems to imply that.

Shortly later the apocryphal *Acts of Peter* (180–225?), perhaps composed in Asia Minor or Syria, tells us that Peter, summoned by divine vision, came to Rome to refute Simon Magus (more a diabolic magician that a gnostic) who was hailed as a god.[435] (In the *Acts of Paul,* that apostle is also involved in the confrontation at Rome.) About the same time (222) Hippolytus, writing in Rome (*Philosophumena* or *Refutation of All Heresies* 6.1–15), devoted a great deal of attention to Simon Magus as a gnostic and the progenitor of Valentinus. Peter resisted him in Rome, and Simon Magus perished there when he was buried alive but failed to rise on the third day (*Philos.* 6.15).

By the fourth century there was in existence a large body of literature attributed (falsely) to Clement of Rome. In particular, the term *Pseudo-Clementines* is often used to refer to the Clementine *Homilies* and *Recognitions* and some letters addressed to James. Scholars have detected sources behind the *Pseudo-Clementines* reaching back into the second century, some of them surely Jewish Christian in origin,[436] i.e., composed by Jewish believers in Christ

---

435. This was all accepted as factual by Eusebius, *Hist.* 2.14–15, who states that Simon Magus sought to avoid the apostles by coming to Rome where he was honored as a god by the erection of a statue. Close after him *in the same reign of Claudius,* Peter was brought by Providence to fight against Simon, appearing in Rome "like a noble captain of God clad in divine armor." (The combination of the statue made under Claudius and Peter as the adversary of Simon helps to explain the tradition that Peter came to Rome in the 40s. See pp. 102–3 above.)

436. See F. S. Jones, "The Pseudo-Clementines: A History of Research," *The Second Century* 2 (1982) 1–33, 63–96.

who saw Christian faith as the only difference between themselves and non-Christian Jews (*Recog.* 1.43.2; 1.50.5–6). Prominent in some of the earliest sources of this literature is James, the brother of the Lord, who ordained him bishop of Jerusalem (1.43.3). In a letter supposed to have been sent by Peter to James, the latter is addressed as "lord and bishop"; and another letter from Clement to James has an address to "the bishop of bishops who rules Jerusalem, the holy church of the Hebrews, and the churches everywhere." In the underlying story James is highly successful in Jerusalem in the early days, winning over the Jerusalem Jews to belief, so that even the high priest is ready to be baptized (*Recog.* 1.69.8). But then Saul makes his appearance, physically attacking James and undoing the work of conversion, with the result that 5,000 persecuted Christians flee from Jerusalem to Jericho (1.70–71). The flight almost certainly reflects the tradition that the Christians fled to Pella after James' death in the 60s rather than joining the Jewish revolt against Rome. The superimposition of this on the persecution of Christians by Saul before his conversion in the 30s makes scholars suspect that the real target in the second-century *Pseudo-Clementine* sources is the Christian Paul, who in the judgment of later Jewish Christians caused their failure to convert large numbers of Jews by his radical stance toward the Law. The very next chapter (1.72) in the *Recognitions* has Peter going to Caesarea to confront Simon, a Samaritan magician, thus beginning a very long series of arguments between Simon and Peter. (Once again scholars detect behind the figure of Simon an anti-Pauline bias, and an echo of the dispute between Paul and Peter at Antioch [Gal 2:11].) The disputes take place at Caesarea, although Clement of Rome is the narrator, and from the start Peter has travel plans to go "even to the city of Rome" (*Recog.* 1.12–13). Ultimately Simon flees Caesarea to go to Rome where he will be publicly honored as a god; and after three months Peter leaves Caesarea to follow him (3.63–74). Thus, even if Simon and Peter do not actually struggle in Rome, that tradition is known and has been shifted to Palestine, probably because the *Pseudo-Clementines* were written in the Palestine-Syria area.[437]

This scattered evidence shows that by the second century the

---

437. Ibid. 9: "The modern consensus is that none of the PsCl arose in Rome."

legend was widespread that in the early days of Christianity a diabolic, evil thinker, Simon Magus, had been bested by Peter, first in Palestine (Samaria) and then in Rome.[438] The nature of Simon's evil
doctrine depends on the viewpoint of the storyteller, e.g., gnosticism
(Justin [incipiently], Irenaeus, Hippolytus), or Hellenistic, anti-Jewish Christianity (reconstructed from *Pseudo-Clementines*). In these
legends one is encountering the trajectory of Peter's image extended
beyond his lifetime in and through the Roman reaction to second-
century movements judged heretical, e.g., when Rome resisted both
Valentinus the gnostic and Marcion the arch-Paulinist in the 140s.
The next work to be considered shows us a similar trajectory *within*
the NT.

G. II Peter

This work was written after I Peter by another author and probably at a considerable interval of time. Indeed, most critical scholars
date it in the second century on the basis of content and thought.[439]
Very Greek in style and thought, II Peter has the characteristics of a
valedictory or last discourse by Peter, comparable to Paul's pseudepigraphical valedictory in II Tim 3–4.[440] There is no internal indication of the place of origin; but the reference to a previous letter by
Peter (3:1) raises the possibility that II Peter is to be related either to
Asia Minor which received I Peter, or to Rome whence I Peter was

---

438. It is interesting that, despite the *Pseudo-Clementine* respect for James and
for Jerusalem as supreme, it is Peter who resists Simon outside Jerusalem. What was
the relation of second-century Jewish Christians toward Jerusalem? Eusebius, *Hist.*
4.5.3–4, lists fifteen Jewish bishops down to the time of Hadrian (130), and then (5.12)
fifteen Gentile bishops—a symbolic remembrance that during the Second Jewish Revolt, Jerusalem became entirely a Gentile church (see von Campenhausen, *Jerusalem*
25–28). However, B. Bagatti, *The Church from the Circumcision* (Jerusalem: Francis-
can, 1971) 10–14, argues that a rival Jewish Christian community remained in Jerusalem for centuries, and that the Cenacle (neglected by Gentile Christian pilgrims) was
in their hands. Jerome, *In Eziechelem* 4.16.161 (PL 25.139B), mentions Christian divisions in Jerusalem in his day.

439. Reicke, *Epistles* 144–45, dates it in the early 90s because it speaks respect-
fully of government and magistrates (2:10) and so must precede Domitian's persecution. Similar respect, however, is shown by *I Clement* after the persecution; see
footnotes 366 and 386 above.

440. See Fornberg, *Early* 10–11.

sent.[441] The indication that this previous letter of Peter was sent to the addressees of II Peter (3:1: "This is the second epistle that I write to you") has no precision because 3:15–16 speaks of letters of Paul known to the addressees ("wrote to you")—there is no one geographical region addressed in common by I Peter and the Pauline epistles (plural).

But one may ask what we learn about the setting of the author from the implications of the letter. Peter is the most important authority for the author. If Peter's authority needs to be defended, it is because the tradition he and others have transmitted, especially about the parousia, is being pitted against false prophecy and false teachers (1:16 – 2:3). The epistles of Paul are known to the author and seemingly treated as Scripture (3:16–17).[442] They are being distorted (not necessarily by the false prophets), but that is because the difficult thoughts of "our beloved brother Paul" are misunderstood. (Note there is no suggestion that Paul is wrong.) Nevertheless, the bulk of II Peter is not based on either I Peter or Paul, the acknowledged authorities, but upon the unacknowledged Epistle of Jude, "the brother of James" (Jude 1). On the basis both of content and of the reference to James, Jude is thought to stem from a Christianity with deep roots in Judaism. We have seen that in early and mid-second century the Jewish Christians responsible for the *Pseudo-Clementines,* who claimed James as a guide, respected Peter but hated Paul. On the other hand, at the same time Marcion was totally rejecting the Jewish heritage and claiming Paul as the apostle par excellence. In the second century the Roman church, which in my hypothesis derived its Christianity from Jerusalem, was still drawing on Jewish traditions and yet exalting Peter and Paul in that order. Thus, the strange combination of authorities behind II Peter would

---

441. That II Peter 3:1 refers to I Peter and not to another lost Petrine work seems likely because of the similarities between II Peter 1:1–2 and I Peter 1:1–2. Curiously, Fornberg, *Early* 130–47, opts for Asia Minor without discussing Rome, even though II Peter does not touch issues that Fornberg admits are germane to Asia Minor (emperor cult, hostility between Jew and Gentile).

442. The treatment of *Christian* writings as Scripture has often been used to assign a late date (mid-second century). But John (18:9) treats the fulfillment of Jesus' words on the same level as the fulfillment of the OT prophets' words; and *II Clem.* 2:4 (which may stem from the end of the first century—see footnote 356 above) treats a saying of Jesus as Scripture.

have been at home in Rome.[443] Indeed, one wonders whether the false teachers and the wicked distorters of Paul (distinct groups?) attacked in II Peter might not echo Rome's struggle with Valentinus and his gnostic followers and with Marcion about A.D. 140. (Yet that must remain no more than a guess for the descriptions in II Peter are general, and the date of the work is very uncertain.) The great respect for prophecy, so that in II Peter 3:2 "the holy prophets" are listed alongside the apostles as guides, plus the insistence that prophecy must not be a matter of private interpretation, may represent a church where a prophet like Hermas is the brother of a bishop and has his visions sent out by Clement, a presbyter-bishop.

In any case, as the final NT contribution to the Petrine trajectory, II Peter portrays Peter as a figure who embraces Paul (properly understood) and yet implicitly draws on the brother of James as an authority. The key to Peter's ecclesiastical utility in his lifetime may have been his ability to hold the Christian middle together, being acknowledged as an apostle by Paul, yet not alienating James' more conservative backers. If II Peter came from Rome, a key to the ecclesiastical role of that church in the mid-second century may have been its use of the image of Peter to keep alive a middle position, when extremists were using "James" and "Paul" as alienating symbols for their claim to represent the pure Christian position.

---

443. F. Danker, "2 Peter 1: A Solemn Decree," CBQ 40 (1978) 64–82, finds parallels to an imperial decree in 1:3–11, as if an emperor were addressing civic assemblies throughout his realm. Danker points out that II Peter does not contain frequent citations from the OT in the manner of *I Clement*, but that may result from virtually copying Jude.

CONCLUSION

IN Meier's treatment[444] of Antioch, he has described a first generation marked by struggle among various types of Jewish Christians
and their Gentile converts. In the 40s at Antioch there were face-to-
face disputes among the Hellenists and Paul on one side of the spectrum, and Peter and men from James on the other side. The issue at
stake was what the gospel meant in relation to the Jewish heritage.
Well into the second generation there continued at Antioch strains of
Christianity produced by these early struggles, so that the church
there after 70 would have contained conservative and liberal Jewish
Christians, and (spiritually closer to the latter) an ever increasing
majority of Gentile Christians. By introducing new insights and at
the same time combining "old" traditions from the various strains,
Matthew, the evangelist of Antioch, sought to hold this mixed Christianity together, establishing a clear church identity. His view of salvation history and of the Law was more conservative than Paul's; but
his attitude toward the Gentiles more liberal than that associated
with James. The figure of Peter served Matthew as a bridge, embodying the church's teaching and enabling it to insist on a centrist position. Seemingly such authority was still being exercised through
prophets and teachers, and Matthew shows great caution lest the
leadership of the institution become dominating and monopolistic.
Nevertheless, within two decades of Matthew, and thus by the time
of the next generation, a firm authoritative structure of single-bishop,

---

444. This conclusion is composed jointly by R. E. Brown and J. P. Meier.

presbyters, and deacons had made its appearance at Antioch. Indeed, Ignatius, the bishop of Antioch, became a propagandist for this structure as an answer to the continued theological battles between the Christian "left" and "right" (even more extreme now). From their openness to the Gentile world, Christians who were more liberal had taken on the coloration of gnosticism, pressing a high christology to the point of a docetism that evaporated Jesus' humanity. Opposite to them on the more conservative extreme of the spectrum there remained Judaizers, even if they were relatively few in number. Staking out a middle position, Ignatius seems to have had only marginal communion with the extremes, even though a full-blown schism may not yet have existed. The notion of the church catholic proposed by Ignatius had Pauline roots but a wider heritage.

In Brown's treatment of Rome, he has suggested that the strongest strain of Christianity at Rome came from Jerusalem in the 40s and represented an attitude similar to that of James and Peter toward Judaism. The Gentiles converted by this mission would thus have been more loyal to the Jewish heritage than were Gentiles converted in the Pauline mission. When Paul wrote to Rome in the late 50s to gain support for his collection on behalf of Jerusalem and with the ultimate hope of visiting Rome, his stance toward Judaism was more moderate than it had been at an earlier period—a change stemming partly from experience, partly from a desire to be received. This more moderate Paul was received in Rome; but chiefly his martyrdom there (after he was denounced by extremely conservative Jewish Christian zealots?) was what won him a place of honor next to Peter in the Roman list of heroes ("pillars"). Peter's image remained dominant; and in the name of Peter (I Peter) or of Peter and Paul (in that order: *I Clement*) the Roman church took over the older Jerusalem mission to the Gentiles, attempting to instruct other churches. These instructions presumed the continued value and imagery of the Jewish cultic heritage; for even Hebrews, eloquently stressing the replacement of the cult by Christ, could not persuade Rome. At the end of the century *I Clement* joined the levitical heritage to another heritage that was characteristic of works associated with Rome, i.e., an appreciation of the Roman imperial order and authority. Although Antioch had already attached cultic and teaching authority to the single-bishop (with presbyters and deacons under him), Rome retained longer the structure of plural presbyter-bishops (with deacons under them). Nevertheless, there was no less authority in the Roman church, since the ideology of the levitical and imperial order was associated with church structure. Conse-quently, if Ignatius of Antioch influenced the church catholic in its ultimate adoption of the threefold order of bishop, presbyters, and deacons, Rome's appreciation of fixed order based on apostolic suc-cession, as seen in *I Clement,* gave that structure much of its sacral and sociological import.

As we two authors finish our related studies of the great Chris-tian centers of Antioch and Rome, in both of which Peter and Paul preached, while men from James had influence, we are conscious of the need for further work in two directions. *First,* we insisted in the Preface on the tentative character of much of what we propose. We are painfully conscious of weak links in the chain of evidence, partic-ularly in the second generation. Meier, positing within two decades at Antioch a move from the prophets/teachers of Matthew to the bishop/presbyters/deacons of Ignatius, is leaping over a wide chasm. Brown's diagnosis of Hebrews as an unsuccessful corrective ad-dressed to Rome and his use of its attack as a mirror reflecting the Roman situation is audacious—a plausible guess relative to a NT work about which one can do no more than guess. If other scholars are willing to study our thesis, they may help us to strengthen these weak links. Nevertheless, in our judgment, our main case does not depend on such points; and so disagreement with individual sugges-tions need not mean a negative judgment on the whole enterprise. In-deed, we issue an invitation to those who are tempted to pass a completely negative judgment: Give us, then, a better reconstruction that makes more sense of the disparate material discussed. All bibli-cal scholarship involves reconstruction; and we reiterate that, if we cannot win acceptance for our own solution, we shall be happy if we have provoked someone to offer a better solution.

Second, other Christian centers and their mixtures of Christian-ity need to be studied. For instance, through the Pastorals, Colos-sians and Ephesians, and Acts, strains of Pauline Christianity and their divergence can be traced after Paul's life. Studies of Johannine

Christianity have already been made.[445] If Ephesus (rather than Syria) was the center of the Johannine Community, perhaps it was there that two strong heritages, the Pauline and Johannine (as well as other strains of Christianity), coexisted in tension. Asia Minor was far more adventuresome than Rome in developing new Christian hypotheses in the second century. Does the second-century life of the two churches reflect their different life in the first century, with Ephesus as an area where no one Christianity dominated, and Rome as an area with a dominant (more conservative) Christianity?

Perhaps some will discuss this book without feeling any compulsion to offer a contribution on either of the two points mentioned above. They may judge that the various NT works can be left in isolation and there is no need for efforts at an overall picture. With that judgment we disagree strongly. Peter, Paul, and James dealt with each other, keeping *koinōnia* or communion, seemingly even when they disputed. A work written afterwards in the name and tradition of one sometimes mentions the other (II Peter mentions Paul), or implicitly refers to the thought of the other (James rejects a Pauline slogan on faith and works), or deals with the same cast of characters (both Ignatius and *I Clement* mention Peter and Paul; both Pauline writings and I Peter mention Mark). In other words, the Christianity of the works we have discussed was interrelated, and an adequate interpretation of these works requires an effort to discover the interrelationship.

To be honest, however, our interest in the interrelationship of early Christian churches and their varieties of Christianity is not purely academic. Antioch may have disappeared as a church, but Rome continues; and as we saw above (p. 183) the advice of Paul and Ignatius to the first church of Rome remains good advice for the current church of Rome. On a wider level, the theological debates and political struggles, the shifts in Christian existence and reinterpretations of Christian life, the internal divisions and external persecutions that marked the NT churches during the first three generations—all these provide abundant lessons and paradigms for Christian churches and individual believers in our own day. Indeed,

---

445. See the reconstructions summarized in Brown, *Community* 171–82.

the problem of a moderate center between left and right wings that threaten to pull the church apart is one of the most enduring pictures in every Christian church and denomination. By the 80s and 90s of the first century both Antioch (Matthew) and Rome (*I Clement*) were appealing to the image of Peter as a symbol for the center. James and Paul left a heritage in different degrees in the two churches, but seemingly in their lifetime they had been too absolute to serve these communities as the ideal reconciling image. During his career Peter was castigated by Paul face to face while being pulled in the opposite direction by men from James (Gal 2:11–12). By a twist of history, his stance which involved being pummeled from both sides[446] was used after his lifetime to justify a middle position between those who used James and Paul as figureheads for an ever-hardening extremism.

As we write this last paragraph, we feel a certain uneasiness. We may reap opposition from our judgment that Peter functioned figuratively for the central mainstream in the history of Antioch and Rome. We are both Roman Catholics, and we can see the possibility that some will detect in our work a covert, sophisticated apologetics for papal primacy. But then with gallows humor we have reflected that, if such might be our fate among the few who are ever ready to detect papist plots, some extremists among our own coreligionists will be ready to detect an antipapist plot. After all we have discussed the two traditional sees of Peter and we found him neither wearing the tiara nor serving as a bishop at either city. If that disturbs Roman Catholics who mistakenly think that the subsequent role of the papacy depends on Peter having been the first bishop of Rome (foot-

---

446. Cullmann remarks in *Peter* 53: "Mediators always have a particularly difficult position, and Peter ... probably had to mediate between the Hellenists and the Judaizers from the very beginning of the Primitive Church." So too an ecumenical study (R. E. Brown, *Peter* 162): "Peter's theological stance probably was intermediary between that of James and that of Paul. ..." Dunn, *Unity* 385, maintains "Peter was probably in fact and effect the bridge-man who did more than any other to hold together the diversity of first-century Christianity. James and Paul ... were too much identified with their respective 'brands' of Christianity. ... But Peter, as shown particularly by the Antioch episode in Gal. 2, had both a care to hold firm to his Jewish heritage which Paul lacked, and an openness to the demands of developing Christianity which James lacked."

note 349 above), perhaps we can offer them consolation by affirming that Peter was more than a bishop at Antioch and Rome. Peter was an apostle. Indeed despite Paul's confining him to the apostolate for those from the circumcision (Gal 2:7–8), he seems to have had a remarkably enduring success in building the church of the Gentiles.

LIST OF ABBREVIATIONS

Besides the standard abbreviations used for the books of the Bible, this volume has employed the following abbreviations for versions, periodicals, series, etc.

AB	Anchor Bible
BA	Biblical Archaeologist
CBQ	Catholic Biblical Quarterly
CBQMS	Catholic Biblical Quarterly Monograph Series
CC	Corpus Christianorum
CSEL	Corpus Scriptorum Ecclesiasticorum Latinorum (Vienna)
ETL	Ephemerides Theologicae Lovanienses
GCS	Die Griechischen Christlichen Schriftsteller (Berlin)
HTR	Harvard Theological Review
ICC	International Critical Commentary
IDB	Interpreter's Dictionary of the Bible
JBC	The Jerome Biblical Commentary
JBL	Journal of Biblical Literature
JTS	Journal of Theological Studies
LXX	The Septuagint (Greek) Translation of the OT
NovT	Novum Testamentum
NovTSupp	Novum Testamentum, Supplements
NT	New Testament
NTS	New Testament Studies
OT	Old Testament
PG	Patrologia Graeca-Latina (Migne)
PL	Patrologia Latina (Migne)
RB	Revue Biblique
SBL	Society of Biblical Literature
SC	Sources Chrétiennes
TDNT	Theological Dictionary of the New Testament
TS	Theological Studies
TU	Texte und Untersuchungen
ZKT	Zeitschrift für Katholische Theologie
ZNW	Zeitschrift für die neutestamentliche Wissenschaft

BIBLIOGRAPHY

Albertz, M., *Die Botschaft des Neuen Testamentes.* I/1 *Die Entstehung der Botschaft. Die Entstehung des Evangeliums.* (Zurich: Evangelischer Verlag, 1947).

Altaner, B., *Patrology* (New York: Herder and Herder, 1960).

Applebaum, S., "The Organization of Jewish Communities in the Diaspora," in *The Jewish People in the First Century* (eds. S. Safrai and S. Stern; Philadelphia: Fortress, 1974) 464–503.

Audet, J.-P., *La Didachè* (Paris: Gabalda, 1958).

Bacon, B. W., *Is Mark a Roman Gospel?* (Cambridge: Harvard, 1919).

——*Studies in Matthew* (New York: Holt, 1930).

Barnard, L. W., *Studies in the Apostolic Fathers and Their Background* (Oxford: Blackwell, 1966).

——"The Early Roman Church, Judaism, and Jewish Christianity," *Anglican Theological Review* 49 (1967) 371–84 (on *I Clement* and *Hermas*).

——"St. Clement of Rome and the Persecution of Domitian," in his *Studies* 5-18.

——"The Shepherd of Hermas in Recent Study," *Heythrop Journal* 9 (1968) 29–36.

Barnes, A. S., *Christianity at Rome in the Apostolic Age* (London: Methuen, 1938).

Barth, G., "Auseinandersetzungen um die Kirchenzucht im Umkreis des Matthäusevangeliums," ZNW 69 (1978) 158–77.

——"Matthew's Understanding of the Law," *Tradition and Interpretation in Matthew* (Philadelphia: Westminster, 1963) 58–164.

218

Bartsch, H.-W., *Gnostisches Gut und Gemeindetradition bei Ignatius von Antiochien* (Gütersloh: Bertelsmann, 1940).

Baumstark, A., "Die Zitate des Mt.-Evangeliums aus dem Zwoelfprophetenbuch," *Biblica* 37 (1956) 296–313.

Beaujeu, J., "L'incendie de Rome en 64 et les Chrétiens," *Latomus* 19 (1960) 65–80, 291–311.

Beker, J. C., *Paul the Apostle* (Philadelphia: Fortress 1980) esp. 59–99 on Romans and Rome.

Benko, S., and J. J. O'Rourke, *The Catacombs and the Colosseum* (Valley Forge, Pa.: Judson, 1971).

Berger, K., "Almosen für Israel: zum historischen Kontext der paulinischen Kollekte," NTS 23 (1977) 180–204.

Best, E., *I Peter* (New Century Bible; Greenwater, SC: Attic, 1971) esp. 13–66.

Betz, H., *Galatians* (Philadelphia: Fortress, 1979).

Beyer, H. and P. Althaus, "Der Brief an die Galater," *Die kleineren Briefe des Apostels Paulus* (Göttingen: Vandenhoeck & Ruprecht, 1970).

Bietenhard, H., "Die syrische Dekapolis von Pompeius bis Traian," in *Aufstieg und Niedergang der römischen Welt* 2.8 (Berlin: de Gruyter, 1977) esp. 220–61.

Blair, E., *Jesus in the Gospel of Matthew* (New York: Abingdon, 1960).

Bommes, K., *Weizen Gottes* (Cologne-Bonn: Hanstein, 1976).

Bonnard, P., *L'évangile selon saint Matthieu* (2nd ed.; Neuchatel: Delachaux et Niestlé, 1970).

Bornkamm, G., "The Authority to 'Bind' and 'Loose' in the Church in Matthew's Gospel," in *Jesus and Man's Hope* 1 (eds. D. Hadidian *et al.;* Pittsburgh Theological Seminary, 1970) 37–50.

———*Paul* (New York: Harper and Row, 1971).

Brandon, S., *The Fall of Jerusalem and the Christian Church* (2nd ed.; London: SPCK, 1957).

Broer, I., *Freiheit vom Gesetz und Radikalisierung des Gesetzes* (Stuttgart: KBW, 1980).

Brown, R. E., *The Birth of the Messiah* (Garden City, N.Y.: Doubleday, 1977).

———*The Community of the Beloved Disciple* (New York: Paulist, 1979).

———"*Episkopē* and *Episkopos:* the New Testament Evidence," TS 41 (1980) 322–38.

———*The Gospel According to John* (2 vols.; AB 29, 29A; Garden City, N.Y.: Doubleday, 1966, 1970).

———"Not Jewish Christianity and Gentile Christianity, but Types of Jewish/Gentile Christianity," CBQ 45 (1983) 74–79.

————*et al.* (eds.) *Peter in the New Testament* (New York: Paulist, 1973).

Bruce, F. F., *Peter, Stephen, James, and John: Studies in Non-Pauline Christianity* (Grand Rapids: Eerdmans, 1979).

Burgess, J., *A History of the Exegesis of Matthew 16:17–19 from 1781 to 1965* (Ann Arbor, Mich.: Edwards Brothers, 1976).

Burton, E., *The Epistle to the Galatians* (Edinburgh: Clark, 1921).

Camelot, P. Th., *Ignace d'Antioche. Polycarpe de Smyrne. Lettres.* (Paris: Cerf, 1951).

Campbell, W. S., "The Romans Debate," *Journal for the Study of the New Testament* 10 (1981) 2–18.

Carlston, C. E., "The Things that Defile (Mark vii.14) and the Law in Matthew and Mark," NTS 15 (1968–69) 75–96.

Catchpole, D., "Paul, James and the Apostolic Decree," NTS 23 (1977) 428–44.

Cockerill, G. L., "Heb 1:1–14, *I Clem.* 36:1–6 and the High Priest Title," JBL 97 (1978) 437–40.

Conzelmann, H., *History of Primitive Christianity* (Nashville: Abingdon, 1973).

————"Present and Future in the Synoptic Tradition," *Journal for Theology and the Church* 5 (1968) 26–44.

Cope, O. L., *Matthew. A Scribe Trained for the Kingdom of Heaven* (Washington: CBQMS, 1976).

Corwin, V., *St. Ignatius and Christianity in Antioch* (New Haven: Yale Univ. Press, 1960).

Cullmann, O., "Les causes de la mort de Pierre et de Paul d'après le témoignage de Clément Romain," *Revue d'Histoire et de Philosophie Religieuses* 10 (1930) 294–300.

————*Peter: Disciple, Apostle, Martyr* (2nd ed.; London: SCM, 1962).

Dahms, J. V., "The First Readers of Hebrews," *Journal of the Evangelical Theological Society* 20 (1977) 365–75.

Dautzenberg, G., *Urchristliche Prophetie* (Stuttgart: Kohlhammer, 1975).

Davies, W. D., *The Setting of the Sermon on the Mount* (Cambridge Univ. Press, 1966).

Dibelius, M., "The Apostolic Council," *Studies in the Acts of the Apostles* (London: SCM, 1973) 93–101.

————"The Conversion of Cornelius," *Studies* 109–22.

————"Rom und die Christen im ersten Jahrhundert," in *Botschaft und Geschichte* (2 vols.; Tübingen: Mohr, 1956; orig. 1941) 2. 177–228.

Dietzfelbinger, C., "Die Antithesen der Bergpredigt im Verständnis des Matthäus," ZNW 70 (1979) 1–15.

Dix, G., *Jew and Greek: A Study in the Primitive Church* (Westminster: Dacre, 1953) esp. 68–75.

Donfried, K. P. (ed.), *The Romans Debate* (Minneapolis: Augsburg, 1977).

Downey, G., "Antioch," IDB 1.145–48.

———*A History of Antioch in Syria from Seleucus to the Arab Conquest* (Princeton Univ. Press, 1961).

Drane, J. W., "Why Did Paul Write Romans?" in *Pauline Studies* (ed. D. A. Hagner and M. J. Harris; F. F. Bruce Festschrift; Grand Rapids: Eerdmans, 1980) 208–27.

Drijvers, H., "Hatra, Palmyra und Edessa," in *Aufstieg und Niedergang der römischen Welt* 2.8 (Berlin: de Gruyter, 1977) 799–906.

Dumbrell, W., "The Logic of the Role of the Law in Matthew v. 1–20," NovT 23 (1981) 1–21.

Dunn, J., *Unity and Diversity in the New Testament* (Philadelphia: Westminster, 1977).

Edmundson, G. *The Church in Rome in the First Century* (Bampton Lectures; London/NYC: Longmans, Green, 1913).

Edwards, R., *A Theology of Q* (Philadelphia: Fortress, 1976).

Elliott, J. H., *A Home for the Homeless* (Philadelphia: Fortress, 1981) on I Peter.

Farmer, W., "The Post-Sectarian Character of Matthew and Its Post-War Setting in Antioch of Syria," *Perspectives in Religious Studies* 3 (1976) 235–47.

———*The Synoptic Problem* (New York: Macmillan, 1964).

Fischer, K., "Redaktionsgeschichtliche Bemerkungen zur Passionsgeschichte des Matthäus," in *Theologische Versuche* 2 (eds. J. Rogge and G. Schille; Berlin: Evangelischer Verlagsanstalt, 1970) 109–28.

Fitzmyer, J. A., *The Gospel according to Luke I-IX* (AB 28; Garden City, NY: Doubleday, 1981).

———"The Languages of Palestine in the First Century A.D." *A Wandering Aramean* (Missoula, Mont.: Scholars Press, 1979) 29–56.

———"A Life of Paul," in *Jerome Biblical Commentary* (eds. R. E. Brown et al.; Englewood Cliffs, NJ: Prentice Hall, 1968) 2.215–22.

———"The Phases of the Aramaic Language," *A Wandering Aramean* (Missoula, Mont.: Scholars Press, 1979) 57–84.

————Review of Robinson's *Redating the New Testament* in *Interpretation* 32 (1978) 309–13.

————"The Use of Explicit Old Testament Quotations in Qumran Literature and in the New Testament," NTS 7 (1960–61) 297–333.

Foerster, G., "The Early History of Caesarea," *The Joint Expedition to Caesarea Maritima. Vol. 1. Studies in the History of Caesarea Maritima* (Missoula, Mont.: Scholars Press, 1975) 9–22.

Fornberg, T., *An Early Church in a Pluralistic Society: A Study of 2 Peter* (Coniectanea Biblica, NT Series 9; Lund: Gleerup, 1977).

Frankemölle, H., "Amtskritik im Matthäus-Evangelium?," *Biblica* 54 (1973) 247–62.

————*Jahwebund und Kirche Christi* (Munster: Aschendorff, 1974).

Frey, J.-B., "L'ancien Judaïsme, spécialment à Rome, d'après les inscriptions juives," *Corpus Inscriptionum Iudaicarum* (Vatican Press, 1936) 1.1iii–cxliv.

————"Les communautés juives à Rome aux premiers temps de l'Église," *Recherches de Science Religieuse* 20 (1930) 267–97.

Freyne, S., *Galilee from Alexander the Great to Hadrian* (Wilmington: Glazier, 1980).

Fuchs, H., "Tacitus über die Christen," *Vigiliae Christianae* 4 (1950) 65–93.

Fuellenbach, J., *Ecclesiastical Office and the Primacy of Rome: An Evaluation of Recent Theological Discussion of First Clement* (Washington, D.C.: Catholic University of America Press, 1980).

Funk, F., *Patres Apostolici* 1 (Tübingen: Laupp, 1901).

Funk, R., "The Enigma of the Famine Visit," JBL 75 (1956) 130–36.

Gärtner, B., "The Habakkuk Commentary (DSH) and the Gospel of Matthew," *Studia Theologica* 8 (1954) 1–24.

Gager, J. G., *Kingdom and Community: The Social World of Early Christianity* (Englewood Cliffs, NJ: Prentice Hall, 1975).

Gamble, H., Jr., *The Textual History of the Letter to the Romans* (Studies and Documents 42; Grand Rapids: Eerdmans, 1977).

Garland, D., *The Intention of Matthew 23* (Leiden: Brill, 1979).

Gasque, W., *A History of the Criticism of the Acts of the Apostles* (Tübingen: Mohr, 1975).

Giet, S., *L'énigme de la Didachè* (Paris: Ophrys, 1970).

Glaze, R. E., Jr., *No Easy Salvation* (Zachary, La.: Insight, 1966) esp. 13–29, "The Occasion and Purpose of Hebrews."

Glover, R., "The Didache's Quotations from the Synoptic Gospels," NTS 5 (1958) 12–29.

Gnilka, J., *Das Evangelium nach Markus. 1 Teil* (Zurich: Benziger, 1978).

——"Die Kirche des Matthäus und die Gemeinde von Qumran," *Biblische Zeitschrift* 7 (1963) 43–63.

Goldstein, H., "Die politischen Paränesen in I Petr 2 und Rom 13," *Bibel und Leben* 14 (1973) 88–104.

Goppelt, L., *Apostolic and Post-Apostolic Times* (London: Black, 1970).

——"Church Government and the Office of the Bishop in the First Three Centuries," in *Episcopacy in the Lutheran Church?* (eds. I. Asheim and V. R. Gold; Philadelphia: Fortress, 1980) 1–29.

——*Der erste Petrusbrief* (MeyerK XII¹, 8th ed.; Göttingen: Vandenhoeck & Ruprecht, 1978).

Goulder, M., *Midrash and Lection in Matthew* (London: SPCK, 1974).

Grant, R. M., *Augustus to Constantine: The Thrust of the Christian Movement into the Roman World* (New York: Harper & Row, 1970).

——Review of Robinson's *Redating the New Testament,* JBL 97 (1978) 294–96.

Green, F., *The Gospel according to Saint Matthew* (Oxford: Clarendon, 1949).

Grundmann, W., *Das Evangelium nach Matthäus* (3rd ed.; Berlin: Evangelischer Verlagsanstalt, 1972).

Gundry, R., *The Use of the Old Testament in St. Matthew's Gospel* (Leiden: Brill, 1975).

Guterman, S. L., *Religious Toleration and Persecution in Ancient Rome* (Westport, Conn.: Greenwood, 1971; reprint of 1951 London ed.)

Haenchen, E., *The Acts of the Apostles* (Philadelphia: Westminster, 1971).

——"Matthäus 23," *Gott und Mensch* (Tübingen: Mohr, 1965) 29–54.

——"Petrus-Probleme," *Gott und Mensch* (Tübingen: Mohr, 1965) 55–67.

Hagner, D. A., *The Use of the Old and New Testaments in Clement of Rome* (NovTSupp 34; Leiden: Brill, 1973).

Harder, G., "Der konkrete Anlass des Römerbriefes," *Theologia Viatorum* 6 (1954–58) 13–24.

Hare, D., *The Theme of Jewish Persecution of Christians in the Gospel according to St. Matthew* (Cambridge Univ. Press, 1967).

Hare, D., and D. Harrington, "Make Disciples of All the Gentiles (Matt 28:19)," CBQ 37 (1975) 359–69.

Held, H.-J., "Matthew as Interpreter of the Miracle Stories," in *Tradition and Interpretation in Matthew* (Philadelphia: Westminster, 1963) 165–299.

Hengel, M., *Acts and the History of Earliest Christianity* (Philadelphia: Fortress, 1980).

——————*Judaism and Hellenism* (2 vols.; Philadelphia: Fortress, 1974).

Hennecke, E., and W. Schneemelcher (eds.), *New Testament Apocrypha* (2 vols.; Philadelphia: Westminster, 1963 and 1965).

Hill, D., *The Gospel of Matthew* (London: Oliphants, 1972).

——————*New Testament Prophecy* (Atlanta: Knox, 1979).

Hinson, E. G., *The Evangelization of the Roman Empire: Identity and Adaptability* (Macon, Ga.: Mercer, 1981).

Hoffmann, P., *Studien zur Theologie der Logienquelle* (Munster: Aschendorff, 1972).

Hoffmann, P., and V. Eid, *Jesus von Nazareth und eine christliche Moral* (Freiburg: Herder, 1975).

Holmberg B., *Paul and Power* (Philadelphia: Fortress, 1980).

Hort, F. J. A., *Judaistic Christianity* (Cambridge: Macmillan, 1894).

Hubbard, B., *The Matthean Redaction of a Primitive Apostolic Commissioning: An Exegesis of Matthew 28:16-20* (Missoula, Mont.: Scholars Press, 1974).

Hübner, H., *Das Gesetz in der synoptischen Tradition* (Witten: Luther-Verlag, 1973).

Hummel, R., *Die Auseinandersetzung zwischen Kirche und Judentum im Matthäusevangelium* (2nd ed.; Munich: Kaiser, 1966).

Jeremias, J., *The Eucharistic Words of Jesus* (London: SCM, 1966).

——————"Sabbathjahr und neutestamentliche Chronologie," *Abba* (Göttingen: Vandenhoeck & Ruprecht, 1966).

Jervell, J., *Luke and the People of God* (Minneapolis: Augsburg, 1972).

Jewett, R., *A Chronology of Paul's Life* (Philadelphia: Fortress, 1979).

——————"Romans as an Ambassadorial Letter," *Interpretation* 36 (1982) 5-20.

Joly, R., *Le dossier d'Ignace d'Antioche* (Editions de l'Université de Bruxelles, 1979).

Judge, E. A., and G. S. R. Thomas, "The Origin of the Church at Rome," *Reformed Theological Review* 25 (1966) 81-94.

Käsemann, E., "Die Anfänge christlicher Theologie," *Exegetische Versuche und Besinnungen* (Göttingen: Vandenhoeck & Ruprecht, 1964) 2.82-104.

Kennard, J., "The Place of Origin of Matthew's Gospel," *Anglican Theological Review* 31 (1949) 243-46.

Kilpatrick, G., *The Origins of the Gospel according to St. Matthew* (Oxford Univ. Press, 1946).

Kimelman, R., "*Birkat Ha-Minim* and the Lack of Evidence for an Anti-

Christian Jewish Prayer in Late Antiquity," in *Jewish and Christian Self-Definition* (ed. E. Sanders; Philadelphia: Fortress, 1981) 2.226–44.

Kingsbury, J., "The Composition and Christology of Matt 28:16–20," JBL 93 (1974) 573–84.

————*Matthew* (Proclamation Commentary Series; Philadelphia: Fortress, 1977).

————"The Structure of Matthew's Gospel and His Concept of Salvation-History," CBQ 35 (1973) 451–74.

Klein, G., "Paul's Purpose in Writing the Epistle to the Romans," in *The Romans Debate* (ed. K. P. Donfried; Minneapolis: Augsburg, 1977) 32–49.

Kleist, J., *The Epistles of St. Clement of Rome and St. Ignatius of Antioch* (Westminster, Md.: Newman, 1946).

Kloppenborg, J., "Didache 16:6–8 and Special Matthean Tradition," ZNW 70 (1979) 54–67.

Köster, H., *Synoptische Überlieferung bei den apostolischen Vätern* (Berlin: Akademie, 1957).

Kraeling, C., "The Jewish Community at Antioch," JBL 51 (1932) 130–60.

Kraft, R., *The Apostolic Fathers 3. Barnabas and the Didache* (New York: Nelson, 1965).

Krauss, S., "Antioche," *Revue des Etudes Juives* 45 (1902) 27–49.

Kümmel, W. G., *Introduction to the New Testament* (rev. ed.: Nashville: Abingdon, 1975).

Lagrange, M.-J., *Epître aux Galates* (Paris: Gabalda, 1950).

Lake, K., *Landmarks in the History of Early Christianity* (New York: Macmillan, 1922) esp. 75–103 comparing Rome and Ephesus.

Lane, W. L., *The Gospel According to Mark* (New International Critical Commentary cʌ the NT; Grand Rapids: Eerdmans, 1974).

Lange, J., *Das Erscheinen des Auferstandenen im Evangelium nach Mattäus* (Würzburg: Echter, 1973).

La Piana, G., "Foreign Groups in Rome during the First Centuries of the Empire," HTR 20 (1927) 183–403, esp. 341–93.

————"The Roman Church at the End of the Second Century," HTR 18 (1925) 201–77.

Lassus, J., "La ville d'Antioche à l'époque romaine d'après l'archéologie," in *Aufstieg und Niedergang der römischen Welt* 2.8 (Berlin: de Gruyter, 1977) 54–102.

Layton, B., "The Sources, Date, and Transmission of Didache 1.3b–2.1," HTR 61 (1968) 343–83.

Lemaire, A., *Les ministères aux origines de l'église* (Paris: Cerf, 1971).

Leon, H. J., *The Jews of Ancient Rome* (Philadelphia: Jewish Publication Society, 1960).

Lieberman, S., "Response to the Introduction by Professor Alexander Marx," in *The Jewish Expression* (ed. J. Goldin; New Haven: Yale, 1976) 119–33, esp. 128–31 on Roman Jews.

Lightfoot, J. B., *The Apostolic Fathers. Clement, Ignatius, and Polycarp* (2 parts in 5 volumes; London: Macmillan, 1889–1890).

——*The Epistle of St. Paul to the Galatians* (reprint of 1865 ed.; Grand Rapids: Zondervan, 1978).

——*Saint Paul's Epistle to the Philippians* (rev. ed.; London: Macmillan, 1885).

Löning, K., "Paulinismus in der Apostelgeschichte," *Paulus in den neutestamentlichen Spätschriften* (Freiburg: Herder, 1981) 202–34.

Lohmeyer, E., " 'Mir ist gegeben alle Gewalt!'," in *In Memoriam Ernst Lohmeyer* (ed. W. Schmauch; Stuttgart: Evangelischer Verlag, 1951) 22–49.

Lohse, E., "Die Entstehung des Bischofsamtes in der frühen Christenheit," ZNW 71 (1980) 58–73.

——"Paränese und Kerygma im I. Petrusbrief," ZNW 45 (1954) 68–89.

Lüdemann, G., "The Successors of Pre-70 Jerusalem Christianity: A Critical Evaluation of the Pella-Tradition," in *Jewish and Christian Self-Definition*, Vol. 1 (ed. E. Sanders; Philadelphia: Fortress, 1980) 161–73.

——"Zur Geschichte des ältesten Christentums in Rom," ZNW 70 (1979) 86–114.

Lührmann, D., *Die Redaktion der Logienquelle* (Neukirchen-Vluyn: Neukirchener Verlag, 1969).

McConnell, R., *Law & Prophecy in Matthew's Gospel* (Basel: Reinhardt Kommissionsverlag, 1969).

MacMullen, R., *Enemies of the Roman Order* (Cambridge: Harvard Univ., 1966) esp. 128–62.

McNeile, A., *The Gospel according to St. Matthew* (London: Macmillan, 1915).

Maier, P. L., *The Flames of Rome* (Garden City, NY: Doubleday, 1981).

Malina, B., "The Literary Structure and Form of Matt. XXVIII. 16–20," NTS 17 (1970) 87–103.

Martyn, J. L., *The Gospel of John in Christian History* (New York: Paulist, 1979).

Massaux, E., *Influence de l'évangile de saint Matthieu sur la littérature chrétienne avant saint Irénée* (Louvain: Publications universitaires, 1950).

——"L'influence littéraire de l'évangile de saint Matthieu sur la Didachè," ETL 25 (1949) 5–41.

Mattill, A., "The Value of Acts as a Source for the Study of Paul," in *Perspectives on Luke-Acts* (Danville, Va.: Association of Baptist Professors of Religion, 1978) 76–98.

Maurer, C., *Ignatius von Antiochien und das Johannesevangelium* (Zurich: Zwingli, 1949).

Meeks, W., and R. Wilken, *Jews and Christians in Antioch* (Missoula, Mont.: Scholars Press, 1978).

Mees, M., "Die Hohepriester-Theologie des Hebräerbriefes im Vergleich mit dem Ersten Clemensbrief," *Biblische Zeitschrift* 22 (1978) 115–24.

Meier, J., *Law and History in Matthew's Gospel* (Rome: Biblical Institute, 1976).

—————*Matthew* (New Testament Message 3; rev. ed.; Wilmington: Glazier, 1981).

—————"Nations or Gentiles in Matthew 28:19?" CBQ 39 (1977) 94–102.

—————"Salvation-History in Matthew: In Search of a Starting Point," CBQ 37 (1975) 203–15.

—————"Two Disputed Questions in Matt 28:16–20," JBL 96 (1977) 407–24.

—————*The Vision of Matthew: Christ, Church, and Morality in the First Gospel* (New York: Paulist, 1979).

Metzger, B., *The Early Versions of the New Testament* (Oxford: Clarendon, 1977).

—————"The Formulas Introducing Quotations in the New Testament and the Mishnah," JBL 70 (1951) 297–307.

Michaelis, W., "Judaistische Heidenchristen," ZNW 30 (1931) 83–89.

Michel, O., "Der Abschluss des Matthäusevangeliums," *Evangelische Theologie* 10 (1950) 16–26.

Moreau, Jules, "Rome and the New Testament—Another Look," *Biblical Research* 10 (1965) 34–43.

Müller, P.-G., "Der 'Paulinismus' in der Apostelgeschichte" *Paulus in den neutestamentlichen Spätschriften* (Freiburg: Herder, 1981) 157–201.

Müller, U., "Zur Rezeption Gesetzeskritischer Jesusüberlieferung im frühen Christentum," NTS 27 (1981) 158–85.

Murray, R., "Jews, Hebrews, and Christians," NovT 24 (1982) 194–208.

Mussner, F., *Der Galaterbrief* (Freiburg: Herder, 1974).

Neirynck, F., "The Symbol Q (=Quelle)," ETL 54 (1978) 119–25.

Nepper-Christensen, P., *Das Matthäusevangelium. Ein Judenchristliches Evangelium?* (Aarhus: Universitetsforlaget, 1958).

Neusner, J., "The Formation of Rabbinic Judaism: Yabneh (Jamnia) from A.D. 70 to 100," in *Aufstieg und Niedergang der römischen Welt 2.19,2* (Berlin: de Gruyter, 1979) 3–42.

O'Connor, D. W., *Peter in Rome: The Literary, Liturgical, and Archaeological Evidence* (New York: Columbia Univ., 1969).

Orr, J., *Neglected Factors in the Study of the Early Progress of Christianity* (Morgan Lecture at Auburn, NY; New York: Armstrong, 1899).

Paulsen, H., *Studien zur Theologie des Ignatius von Antiochien* (Göttingen: Vandenhoeck & Ruprecht, 1978).

————"Zur Wissenschaft vom Urchristentum und der alten Kirche—ein methodischer Versuch," ZNW 68 (1977) 200–30.

Penna, R., "Les Juifs à Rome au temps de l'apôtre Paul," NTS 28 (1982) 348–64.

Perkins, P., "Gnostic Christologies and the New Testament," CBQ 43 (1981) 590–606.

Perrin, N., *The New Testament: an Introduction* (New York: Harcourt, Brace, Jovanovich, 1974).

Pesch, R., *Das Markusevangelium* (2 vols.; Freiburg: Herder, 1976 and 1977).

Pfeiffer, R., *History of New Testament Times* (New York: Harper and Brothers, 1949).

Piper, J., *'Love your Enemies'* (Cambridge Univ. Press, 1979).

Polag, A., *Die Christologie der Logienquelle* (Neukirchen-Vluyn: Neukirchener Verlag, 1977).

Preisker, H., "Das historische Problem des Römerbriefes," *Wissenschaftliche Zeitschrift der Friedrich-Schiller-Universität Jena* (1952–53) 25–30.

Prümm, K., *Religionsgeschichtliche Handbuch* (Rome: Biblical Institute, 1954).

Quasten, J., *Patrology* 1. (Westminster, Md.: Newman, 1950).

Rathke, H., *Ignatius von Antiochien und die Paulusbriefe* (Berlin: Akademie, 1967).

Reicke, B., *The Epistles of James, Peter, and Jude* (AB 37; Garden City, NY: Doubleday, 1964) esp. XX-XXVIII, 69–75, 143–46.

Rengstorf, K. H., "Die Stadt der Mörder (Mt 22,7)," in *Judentum, Urchristentum, Kirche* (Berlin: Töpelmann, 1960).

————"Paulus und die älteste römische Christenheit," *Studia Evangelica* 2 (TU 87; Berlin: Akademie, 1964) 447–64.

Richard, E., *Acts 6:1–8:4. The Author's Method of Composition* (Missoula, Mont.: Scholars Press, 1978).

Richardson, C. C., *The Christianity of Ignatius, Bishop of Antioch* (New York: thesis of Union Theological Seminary, 1934).

————*Early Christian Fathers* (Westminster: Philadelphia, 1953) esp. 21–30 on *I Clement*.

Rius-Camps, J., *The Four Authentic Letters of Ignatius the Martyr* (Rome: Institutum Orientalium Studiorum, 1979).

Robinson, J. A. T., *Redating the New Testament* (Philadelphia: Westminster, 1976).

Robinson, J. M. (ed.), *The Nag Hammadi Library in English* (New York: Harper and Row, 1977).

Rohde, J., *Rediscovering the Teaching of the Evangelists* (London: SCM, 1968).

Rothfuchs, W., *Die Erfüllungszitate des Matthäus-Evangeliums* (Stuttgart: Kohlhammer, 1969).

Safrai, S., and M. Stern (eds.), *The Jewish People in the First Century* (2 vols.; Philadelphia: Fortress, 1974 and 1976).

Sanders, E. (ed.), *Jewish and Christian Self-Definition* (2 vols.; Philadelphia: Fortress, 1980 and 1981).

Schelkle, K. H., "Römische Kirche im Römerbrief," ZKT 81 (1959) 393–404.

Schlier, H., *Der Brief an die Galater* (Göttingen: Vandenhoeck & Ruprecht, 1965).

————*Religionsgeschichtliche Untersuchungen zu den Ignatiusbriefen* (Giessen: Töpelmann, 1929).

Schmidt, K. L., "*ekklēsia*" TDNT 3.501–536.

Schoedel, W., "Are the Letters of Ignatius of Antioch Authentic?" *Religious Studies Review* 6 (1980) 196–201.

————"Theological Norms and Social Perspectives in Ignatius of Antioch," in *Jewish and Christian Self-Definition* (ed. E. Sanders; Philadelphia: Fortress, 1980) 1.30–56.

Schütz, J., *Paul and the Anatomy of Apostolic Authority* (Cambridge Univ. Press, 1975).

Schulz, S., *Q. Die Spruchquelle der Evangelisten* (Zurich: Theologischer Verlag, 1972).

Schweizer, E., "Die Kirche des Matthäus," *Matthäus und seine Gemeinde* (Stuttgart: KBW, 1974) 138–170.

————*The Good News according to Matthew* (Atlanta: Knox, 1975).

————"Zur Sondertradition der Gleichnisse bei Matthäus," *Matthäus und seine Gemeinde* (Stuttgart: KBW, 1974) 98–105.

Selwyn, E. G., *The First Epistle of St. Peter* (London: Macmillan, 1964).

Senior, D., "The Death of Jesus and the Resurrection of the Holy Ones," CBQ 38 (1976) 312–29.

Sevenster, J., *Do You Know Greek?* (Leiden: Brill, 1968).

Sherwin-White, A. N., *Roman Society and Roman Law in the New Testament* (Oxford Univ., 1963) esp. 108–19.

Silberman, L., "Whence *Siglum* Q? A Conjecture," *JBL* 98 (1979) 287–88.

Smith, D. M., "The Use of the Old Testament in the New," in *The Use of the Old Testament in the New and Other Essays* (ed. J. Efird; Durham: Duke Univ. Press, 1972) 3–65.

Stendahl, K., *The School of St. Matthew* (2nd ed.; Lund: Gleerup, 1968).

Stern, M., "The Jewish Diaspora," in *The Jewish People in the First Century* (S. Safrai and M. Stern, eds.; Philadelphia: Fortress, 1974) 1.117–83.

Stoldt, H.-H., *Geschichte und Kritik der Markus-Hypothese* (Göttingen: Vandenhoeck & Ruprecht, 1977).

Strecker, G., "Die Antithesen der Bergpredigt (Mt 5:21–48 par)," ZNW 69 (1978) 36–72.

———*Der Weg der Gerechtigkeit* (3rd ed.; Göttingen: Vandenhoeck & Ruprecht, 1971).

Streeter, B. H., *The Four Gospels* (8th impression; London: Macmillan, 1953).

———*The Primitive Church* (London: Macmillan, 1929) esp. "The Church of Rome," 181–230.

Stuiber, A., " 'Das ganze Joch des Herrn' (Didache 6,2–3)," *Studia Patristica* 4.2 (ed. F. Cross; Berlin: Akademie-Verlag, 1961) 323–29.

Suhl, A., "Der konkrete Anlass des Römerbriefes," *Kairos* 13 (1971) 119–50.

Telfer, W., *The Office of Bishop* (London: Darton, Longman & Todd, 1962), esp. chap. 3: "The Church of Rome" 43–63.

Theissen, G., *Sociology of Early Palestinian Christianity* (Philadelphia: Fortress, 1978).

———*Studien zur Soziologie des Urchristentums* (Tübingen: Mohr, 1979).

Thiering, B., "*Mebaqqer* and *Episkopos* in the Light of the Temple Scroll," JBL 100 (1981) 59–74.

Thompson, W., "An Historical Perspective in the Gospel of Matthew," JBL 93 (1974) 243–62.

———*Matthew's Advice to a Divided Community* (Rome: Biblical Institute, 1970).

Thompson, W., and E. LaVerdiere, "New Testament Communities in Transition: A Study of Matthew and Luke," TS 37 (1976) 567–97

Tracy, D., *The Analogical Imagination* (New York: Crossroad, 1981).

———*Blessed Rage for Order* (New York: Seabury, 1975).

Trilling, W., "Die Auferstehung Jesu, Anfang der neuen Weltzeit (Mt

28,1–8)," *Christusverkündigung in den synoptischen Evangelien* (Munich: Kösel, 1969) 212–43.

———"Der Tod Jesu, Ende der alten Weltzeit (Mk 15,33–41)," *Christusverkündigung in den synoptischen Evangelien* (Munich: Kösel, 1969) 191–211.

———*Das wahre Israel* (3rd ed.; Munich: Kösel, 1964).

van Segbroeck, F., "Les citations d'accomplissement dans l'évangile selon saint Matthieu d'après trois ouvrages récents," in *L'évangile selon Matthieu: Rédaction et théologie* (ed. M. Didier; Gembloux: Duculot, 1972) 107–30.

van Tilborg, S., *The Jewish Leaders in Matthew* (Leiden: Brill, 1972).

Vassiliadis, P., "The Nature and Extent of the Q-Document," NovT 20 (1978) 49–73.

Viviano, B., "Where Was the Gospel according to Matthew Written?" CBQ 41 (1979) 533–46.

Vögtle, A., "Das christologische und ekklesiologische Anliegen von Mt 28,18–20," in *Studia Evangelica* 2 (ed. F. Cross; Berlin: Akademie, 1964) 266–94.

von Campenhausen, H., *Ecclesiastical Authority and Spiritual Power in the Church of the First Three Centuries* (Stanford Univ. Press, 1969).

von Campenhausen, H., and H. Chadwick, *Jerusalem and Rome* (Facet Historical Series 4; Philadelphia: Fortress, 1966).

Vööbus, A., *Liturgical Traditions in the Didache* (Stockholm: ETSE, 1968).

Vokes, F., *The Riddle of the Didache* (London: SPCK, 1938).

Walker, R., *Die Heilsgeschichte im ersten Evangelium* (Göttingen: Vandenhoeck & Ruprecht, 1967).

Walsh, J. E., *The Bones of St. Peter* (Garden City, NY: Doubleday, 1982).

Walter, N., "Die Bearbeitung der Seligpreisungen durch Matthäus," *Studia Evangelica* 4 (ed. F. Cross; Berlin: Akademie, 1968) 246–58.

Ward, R. B., "The Example of Abraham in Romans 4 and the Purpose of Paul's Letter to the Romans." SBL Abstracts 1981,§340B.

Weijenborg, R., *Les lettres d'Ignace d'Antioche* (Leiden: Brill, 1969).

Wiefel, W., "The Jewish Community in Ancient Rome and the Origins of Roman Christianity" in *The Romans Debate* (ed. K. P. Donfried; Minneapolis: Augsburg, 1977) 100–19.

Wilckens, U., "Zur Entwicklung des paulinischen Gesetzverständnis," NTS 28 (1982) 154–91.

———*Die Missionsreden der Apostelgeschichte* (3rd ed.; Neukirchen-Vluyn: Neukirchener Verlag, 1974).

Worden, R., "Redaction Criticism of Q: a Survey," JBL 94 (1975) 532–46.

Wuellner, W., "Paul's Rhetoric of Argumentation in Romans: An Alternative to the Donfried-Karras Debate over Romans," in *The Romans Debate* (ed. K. P. Donfried; Minneapolis: Augsburg, 1977) 152–74.

Yamauchi, E., *Pre-Christian Gnosticism* (Grand Rapids: Eerdmans, 1973).

Zuckschwerdt, E., "Das Naziräat des Herrenbruders Jakobus nach Hegesipp," ZNW 68 (1977) 276–87.

BIBLIOGRAPHIC INDEX

This is *not* an index of the discussion of various authors and their views. Rather it lists the page where full bibliographical information is supplied for an author's works. Names beginning with prepositions are listed under the preposition, e.g. "von" under "v."

SUBJECT INDEX